Suburban Howls

Tracking the Eastern Coyote in Urban Massachusetts

Jonathan G. Way, PhD With Foreword by Marc Bekoff, PhD

Suburban

Tracking the Eastern Coyote in Urban Massachusetts

Jonathan G. Way, PhD

Published by Eastern Coyote Research

in association with Dog Ear Publishing

COVER AND INSIDE PHOTO CREDITS

Jonathan G. Way, PhD

Suburban Howls: Tracking the Eastern Coyote in Urban Massachusetts / Jonathan G. Way

Includes Index.

ISBN 978-159858-367-0

1. Way, Jonathan G. 2. Coyotes. 3. Wildlife Studies. 4. Massachusetts. 5. Nature. 6. Urban Ecology

First published by Dog Ear Publishing
4010 W. 86th Street, Ste H
Indianapolis, IN 46268
www.dogearpublishing.net

Dedication

To the Eastern Coyote, in the hope that this book and our ongoing research makes your world a better and more tolerant place to inhabit.

Contents

List of Tables

List of Figures

Foreword

Coyotes: Victims of Their Own Success

Our relationship with animate and inanimate nature is a complex, ambiguous, challenging, and frustrating affair. Many people claim to love nature and to love other animals, and then, with little forethought, concern, or regret, go on to abuse them in egregious ways, far too numerous to count. I often say when someone tells me that they love various animals or landscapes and then they partake, either directly or indirectly, in subjecting them to intentional pain and suffering or wanton destruction, that I'm glad that they don't love me!

Coyotes are a prototype example of an animal whose reputation precedes them. However, more likely than not, people don't really know who these magnificent mammals are and the reputation they entertain is a false and misleading one. When one thinks of the word "coyote" it normally evokes a picture of an animal who is a varmint, an unwanted pest. We have been led to believe, largely through mass media and those who get paid to manage and control, that is kill, unwanted predators such as coyotes, that these amazingly adaptable carnivores are little more than an unwanted guest. In my own long-term experience studying coyotes in the Grand Teton National Park outside of Jackson, Wyoming, and in various other settings, my colleagues and I discovered that coyotes were remarkably intelligent, playful, mischievous, cunning, and social animals, often as family-oriented as wolves. However, much of society has not yet caught up with what scientific research has been telling us for many years.

For too long, biologists have struggled to remain unemotional about the animals they study in order to be objective, in order to distance themselves from their "subjects". But this just doesn't work. For when we study other animals, we naturally connect with them and we feel their ups and downs, their joys and sorrow, their victories and defeats. Coyotes, like many other animals, must be viewed as individuals, with personalities and a point of view on the world in which they live. Showing compassion and respect for animals is natural and makes for better science. After all, if a scientist or researcher doesn't show respect for the animals they study and some compassion for what befalls them, how is the general public supposed to fully understand or acquire an appreciation of the animals with whom we are supposed to coexist?

In *Suburban Howls*, Jonathan Way brings the reader a deep sense of appreciation for this misunderstood species. In his well-written book, Jon presents his compelling personal story studying eastern coyotes for ten years in the suburban wilds of Massachusetts, and pulls no punches relating just about everything that a biologist studying a controversial predator experiences. His accounts of tracking coyotes along a Cape Cod golf course for long hours on a snowy evening, tracking an individual coyote for over 25 miles in one night, and hand-raising and bonding with a captive litter of five youngsters will fascinate you. However, the stories of bureaucratic indifference to his project, the radio-collared coyotes blatantly shot by hunters, the coyotes who were poisoned, and the loss of a litter that he hand-raised from 3-week old pups will anger you. You will come to realize that coyotes live difficult lives and so, too, do the researchers studying and trying to protect them.

Jon zealously offers a refreshing paradigm for wildlife management in which the interests of all stakeholders need to be considered. Scientific data about territorial behavior in coyotes and their patterns of dispersal strongly argue against the random killing of coyotes. Yet, to this day, most states do little to prevent a person from recklessly shooting and killing these intelligent predators. But society is becoming increasingly reluctant to accept the wanton and inhumane killing of predators so these practices must change. Jon provides legitimate reasons why we must stop this pointless slaughter and how to go about doing it, and he also points out the value of these animals in the heart of a healthy ecological environment. Coyotes and other carnivores are integral members of numerous webs of nature and are not disposable "things", the absence of which will have no consequences for other members of the ecosystem in which they live.

Suburban Howls is also one of few books to feature a carnivore in an urbanized area. As we lose more and more space almost weekly in the name of human growth and development, it is crucially important to document how species live in human-dominated areas. Jon shows us that it is perfectly natural to have predators living among us in urban areas. In fact, it is only a matter of time before coyotes show up all over North America, because during dispersal it is natural for them to colonize areas where other coyotes do not already live—and that includes cities. Jon writes that instead of worrying about losing our small pets to a coyote, we should be happy to realize that we live within a healthy ecosystem that is able to support a medium-sized predator like the coyote. He even argues that their value as 'rodent exterminators', particularly in city settings where severe rat problems have begun surfacing, has barely been tapped.

Jon nicely shows that we need a compassionate ethic of caring for and sharing our planet. Sensitivity and humility are essential components of our guiding ethic. Expanding our circle of respect and understanding can help bring us all together. We are animals' guardians and we owe them unconditional compassion, respect, support, and love. We may have control and dominion over other animals, but this doesn't mean that we have to exploit and dominate them.

Ethics, compassion, humility, respect, coexistence, and sustainability are among the principles that should guide us when we interact with other animals. In most cases there are more humane alternatives than the methods that we use to intrude into animals' lives and less invasive alternatives when we violate landscapes. When we harm other animals and earth, we harm ourselves. We're really *that* connected. We need to keep a worldwide community-based ethic in our hearts. We can always do better in our interactions with other animal beings and earth. *Always*. We must always work to reduce harm and cruelty. *Always*.

All in all, *Suburban Howls* is written with the energy of a young biologist who is beginning to carve his niche in the scientific world. Those who know Jon know that he is determined to learn as much as he can about eastern coyotes, and predators in general, and to share his knowledge widely with people who might not be able to meet these interesting animals up close and personal. Jon's goal is to revise the misleading stereotypes of these amazing beasts. This book, along with the other valuable scientific data that Jon has collected, is an important step toward upgrading society's view toward more logical wildlife management. *Suburban Howls* also highlights Jon's progression as a field biologist, and nicely promotes his ultimate goal of providing more protection for eastern coyotes, the species that is dearest to his heart.

Marc Bekoff, PhD, University of Colorado, Boulder, CO;

Co-founder with Jane Goodall of Ethologists for the Ethical Treatment of Animals, Fellow of the Animal Behavior Society, and Former Guggenheim Fellow; Author of Minding Animals, The Ten Trusts (with Jane Goodall), Animal Passions and Beastly Virtues: Reflections of Redecorating Nature, and editor of Coyotes: Biology, Behavior, and Management and the Encyclopedia of Animal Behavior

Preface

Many books have been written about wolves, but scarcely any on their smaller cousin, the coyote. While many wolf biologists, notably Dr. L. David Mech, have written books about their subjects, I have not encountered any books written by coyote biologists explaining their research.

Non-scientists have published adventures associated with coyotes, whereas coyote biologists have focused on more technical aspects of coyote ecology. Notable among them is *Coyotes: Biology, Behavior, and Management*, a scientific anthology published in 1978, edited by Dr. Marc Bekoff. This book is a classic of canid literature, summarizing what was known on coyotes at the time. Dr. Stuart Ellins, in *Living with Coyotes*, describes the use of food aversion conditioning experiments to keep coyotes from killing livestock. Weaving anecdotes and personal stories throughout, this book focuses on non-lethal alternatives to allow coyotes to coexist with humans. Hope Ryden's manuscript, *God's Dog*, tracks her adventures with coyotes in Yellowstone National Park. It is a delightful story and a heart-warming plea to protect coyotes, but it has a different focus than this book.

In *Suburban Howls*, I'm attempting to meld the scientific aspect of our research with the adventure of our project. To this end, I offer vignettes that relate to our peer-reviewed research at the beginning of chapters, but I also try to explain to the reader what we have discovered through our studies later in the chapters. This book is, as much as anything, a testament to the hard work of myself and my entire research team, perseverance, support from friends and family, and a little luck here and there. Although seemingly glorified in the pages that follow, any research undertaking, especially on a large carnivore, is not easy, as exemplified by the more than six months it took us to receive our initial research permits so that we could simply begin box-trapping coyotes back in 1998. Wading through red tape is frustrating, to say the least.

Also, this project has consistently had very limited funding, much of it coming from my personal income. While I was completing my Master's of Science degree at the University of Connecticut Storrs (UConn), I worked as a substitute teacher and coached track at my former high school (Barnstable High on Cape Cod, Massachusetts). This was necessary in order to pay the bills consisting mostly of car payments and my traveling expenses (which accelerated dramatically with the spike in gas prices from 2003–2005). Fortunately, rent was minimal because I lived with family.

While I was at UConn, Boston College bought most of the needed project equipment in piecemeal fashion. This helpful arrangement came about because my former high school ecology teacher, Dr. Peter Auger, was also a professor at Boston College, and Dr. Eric Strauss, the Director of the Environmental Studies Program at BC, was also one of Dr. Auger's former students at Barnstable. They provided course budget and other small grant money to procure traps and radio-collars a few at a time in order to make our project viable. Instances such as four $250 radio-collars stolen out of my truck while I was camping in the White Mountains of New Hampshire were devastating to this study.

One might say, "Gee, Dummy, you shouldn't have had the collars in the truck in the first place." As it happened, I headed straight up to New Hampshire (the White Mountains are two hours north of Boston) right after checking traps that were set for that morning. It is sad to have to worry about ones' belongings while on vacation in the middle of nowhere. That is just one reason why I have come to trust *Homo sapiens* less than most 4-footed creatures.

In all fairness, however, I also have had much luck during this project. First, my cousin Marcy's work and living arrangements have been seemingly tailored to follow me wherever my studies have taken me. Although, in reality, that statement should probably be reversed, with me trailing her around. When I was at UConn she lived 45 minutes from campus so I stayed with her near Worcester, Massachusetts while completing course work. Second, when I was accepted to Boston College for a Ph.D. program, she had moved to the north Boston area for a new job and I again stayed with her a few nights a week. I later shared that same apartment at a reduced rate thanks to her kindness.

Being adaptable, like my study subjects are renowned for, has allowed flexibility in my living habits. Before moving in with Marcy, I occasionally stayed with my grandmother in Lynn or with friends in the Boston area on the weekends. Of course, I have always had my parents and my other grandparents, who live less than two miles apart from each other, when I am working down on Cape Cod.

Another stroke of fortune occurred when I discovered that the Stone Zoo was planning a captive coyote exhibit on their grounds. I asked them if they would be interested in a potential collaboration and Zoo New England's director, John Linehan, replied, "Normally we wouldn't have the space for a new species exhibit, but you won't believe this—next year we are building an exhibit called "Sierra Madre" and coyotes are going to be one of the featured animals. Although the Sierra Madre ecosystem is about desert-adapted animals, we could probably get by using coyotes from the Northeast." The rest is history. And unfortunately, the conclusion of this experience proved to have a dramatically negative effect on my life, as you will read in later chapters.

Still, I hope to convey to the reader that dreams are obtainable. Sacrifices come with the territory, but if you want something, do not lose sight of your goal. There may be many times when you want to quit because of a lack of resources or frustrating conditions such as I did after finding one of my collared coyotes dead. This book, while highlighting our sometimes difficult and always time-intensive research on eastern coyotes, is also intended to chronicle our adventures, both the trials and tribulations, and our joys of working with this species of unique wild animal who lives among us.

I am writing this for the lay person, but I include many scientific phrases throughout. To maintain flow, I have refrained from describing all the terms as used, and ask the reader to consult the glossary at the end of the book for the meanings of any words not understood. Throughout the text, I often refer to the "north Boston" study site. While there is a South Boston, no official 'north Boston' exists, but it is a convenient way of referring to the towns and cities on the north side of Boston such as Everett, Revere, Saugus, Malden, and Melrose. Finally, for a complete listing of our animal study subjects who generated all of the anecdotes and data presented in this book, please refer to Appendix 1 at the back of this book.

Acknowledgements

I would foremost like to thank my family and Drs. Peter Auger, Eric Strauss, and I. Morty Ortega; as well as the Hyannis Animal Hospital (specifically, Drs. Larry Venezia and Paul McCartin); Zoo New England for the captive coyote study; and Boston College for helping make these studies possible. Also, the Saugus Animal Hospital (specifically, Dr. Bob Binder), and colleagues David Eatough and Stephen Cifuni (and his family) for the Boston component of our study.

I would particularly like to acknowledge the following people for helping to make this study and the writing of this book possible, realizing that there were other important players who provided assistance along the way. I apologize in advance if I missed anyone.

I would especially like to acknowledge my family for supporting me in every endeavor that I pursued. Their moral support motivated me to take on these challenging projects. My parents, cousin Marcy, and my wonderful grandparents always provided me with a warm meal and a bed to sleep in, no matter what time, or how often, I came home. I'm fairly sure that my now-deceased grandmother in Lynn never quite understood why I showed up to "visit" her at such odd times and then slept most of the day away.

My father's parents on the Cape not only allowed me to live in their finished basement, but to take in five coyote pups there as well. My sister Nicole and her husband Tom were not surprised when I came up with ridiculous statements like, "Hey, I am getting five coyote pups and will be raising them in Gram and Papa's basement." Or, "I am planning to open up this discovery center on coyotes next year. All I need is to come up with $500,000. Are you interested in working with me on this idea?" In reality Nic, being very diligent in matters such as arts and crafts, would no doubt make the center very successful.

My brother Jeff occasionally tracked with me, but usually provided me with mental breaks from research in the form of activities like "playin' ball" (basketball) at a local court. Full-time caregiver and editor-extraordinaire, my mother helped me with everything from brainstorming about funding issues to reviewing drafts of this book. My dad reported to me local coyote sightings on the way to his news stand and also assisted me from time to time with checking traps, including one in his backyard, a mere 100 feet from the house. My Aunt Jill and Uncle David Feder helped with financial aspects of the project while my cousin Scott had a knack for visiting me from New York City whenever a 'major coyote event' occurred. I am deeply grateful to all my family members for their support. If it weren't also for my deep respect and appreciation of the eastern coyotes themselves, I would have dedicated this book to my family instead.

The veterinarians and staff at the Hyannis Animal Hospital on the Cape and the Saugus Animal Hospital up in north Boston really made this project possible. They donated all their time and resources and truly were amazing. I hope that our research and this book help achieve some of their goals of wildlife education for the general public. I will forever be grateful for their support, interest, and enthusiasm for this project. Maybe one year we will find some funding to pay them back.

In addition, the Cape Wildlife Center, part of the Humane Society of the United States, helped in collaring a few of our animals. I greatly appreciate their collaboration, especially veterinarian technician Judy Ellal, and for their interest in preserving elements of the Cape's wildlife, especially sick and disabled ones.

My friends and mentors, Drs. Eric Strauss and Peter Auger at Boston College, both of whom I have known since high school, have given me the encouragement and helped with funding so this project could continue. They are both great teachers and inspired me to continue this project. Boston College and Barnstable High School (my former high school where Dr. Auger also taught) are lucky to have them.

Dr. I. Morty Ortega at UConn Storrs was my initial advisor on the coyote project and I appreciate his support, especially considering the shoestring budget that he experienced at a state-run school. I now consider him a friend and colleague. With his excellent computer skills, Morty assisted with making the map of coyote territories found in the appendices.

The idea for these projects developed when I was an undergraduate at the University of Massachusetts Amherst, under the tutelage of Professor Todd Fuller. My work with Dr. Fuller resulted in my Honors Thesis that included a preliminary assessment of coyote, fox, and white-tailed deer on Cape Cod.

Dave Eatough and Steve Cifuni also deserve a special thanks. Dave is a science teacher at Revere High School and Steve received his undergraduate degree at Boston College. Both are referenced throughout this book. They have literally been through the trenches with me and we have shared some frustrating moments in our urban north Boston study. I was also grateful to have them review a draft of this book. Dave helped spice up the anecdotes in the book by revisiting stories that I had forgotten about and providing many additional details to others. While conducting the day-to-day research in north Boston, they proved to be two of the most dedicated biologists I could have met in my young career and are just about the only ones that will actually listen and understand when I say, "Guys, we really need to get some more 2:00–3:00 AM locations to even out our data set." Keep in mind that more times than not we are using our own gas money to locate a given coyote or to check a trap. Steve's family, mainly his parents Laurel and Steve, but also his sister Rachel and cousin Jill Moore, also let me crash on their couches on many cold nights after often unsuccessful net-launchings. Although I know they thought we were crazy for the odd hours we kept, hopefully this book will begin to explain the method to our madness. At the very least, it was nice to make some new friends (who were human) during this project.

I would also like to thank the Lynch School of Education at Boston College for accepting me as a graduate student and the Biology Department for providing support through teaching assistantships during my doctoral tenure there. The Environmental Studies Program and Urban Ecology Institute (with Charlie Lord) were instrumental in forging and keeping alive the collaboration between Boston College and the area schools that I worked with. Much of the funding for the ecology component of this study (like traps and radio-collars) occurred because of these institutions. Mike Barnett, my dissertation chair, helped me evolve from merely a scientist into a science educator as well.

The following people and institutions were invaluable and will continue to be as these studies continue—I'm sorry I can't name all of you, but there were many people, especially from Barnstable High School (including Pete Auger's son Jeff, my brother Jeff, Matt Joseph, Matt Ryan, Josh Alper, Katie-Jo Glover, Matt Norton, Chris Riley, Roswell Joseph [deceased], and Christel Kalweit), from Boston College (Robert Proietto, Dean-Lorenz Szumylo, and Maria Aucoin first come to mind), and from Revere High School (especially Joe Dreeszen, Alana Popp, Laura Demaso, and Janelle Parachanian) students who assisted me and my colleagues by putting in many late nights (and early mornings) in order to radio-track coyotes. Rob actually lived on the Cape for eight months and assisted with the Cape Cod study. Greg Auger (Pete's older brother) and Amy Schneider also tracked some of our collared coyotes.

Many environmental organizations, notably the Massachusetts Society for the Prevention of Cruelty to Animals (MSPCA; especially Stephanie Hagopian), the Cape Wildlife Center, Massachusetts Audubon at Wellfleet (with Melissa Lowe), the Cape Cod Museum of Natural History (with Dick Wheeler), Sudbury Valley Trustees, and Wild Care, among others, allowed me to use their facilities to present and relay our research findings to the general public. This book really is a product of the questions entertained and discussions had with those organizations and their wonderful audiences. Grant sources like the International Fund for Animal Welfare, MSPCA, Saugus River Watershed, UConn, Boston College and the Barnstable Green Grant Youth Council have helped fund portions of this project. This has allowed me to purchase additional equipment like cameras and more radio-collars. Grants such as these are critical in making this project long-term in nature.

Furthermore, interested citizens have donated $15–100 here and there, which was not insignificant—thank you all! That amount can provide roughly a week's worth of gasoline while tracking coyotes, or help pay for other needed expenses. My gratitude to all who have helped us in this project.

I would also like to give thanks to five supermarkets: Friend's Supermarket, the Osterville A&P, and more recently Star Market in Hyannis, all of which are located on the Cape; Fiore's in Revere, and the Winthrop Meat Market. They, by donating their meat-scraps, saved us thousands of dollars and were critical in allowing us to catch and radio-tag coyotes for these studies.

My gratitude also goes to the many coyote and wolf biologists who, through conversations and their published works and/or peer-review of my research, provided me with a solid base and fundamental knowledge of canid behavior. This list includes Marc Bekoff, Dave Mech, Bob Crabtree and Jennie Sheldon, Doug Smith, John Theberge, Rolf Peterson, Eric Gese, Brent Patterson, Dan Harrison, and Dick Thiel, among others. Fellow coyote biologists, Bob Crabtree and Jennie Sheldon in Yellowstone National Park, have shared their expertise with me on numerous occasions. Seeing their study site a few times, which is one of the most amazing places that I have ever visited, has enabled me to compare western coyotes with the eastern ones that I have been studying. Bob and Jennie, realizing the difficulties of being a graduate student while trying to run a full-time study, have also helped provide funding and even equipment such as a laptop, to my project. My experiences in Yellowstone, also greatly aided by the presence and generosity of wolf naturalist Rick McIntyre, have been once-in-a-lifetime.

My conversations with and reading material from world renowned expert and author/editor Marc Bekoff has also helped me tremendously. His knowledge of canids, an unsurpassed contribution to the field of animal behavior and cognition, and his relentless concern for animal welfare, has made people think twice about man's traditional dominance over other animals. His thoughtful review of an earlier draft of this book helped me greatly.

Two of my childhood friends, brothers Andy and Jimmy Sacchetti, made significant editorial comments to multiple versions of this manuscript, greatly improving its clarity and content. Likewise, Bill Buckley, teaching colleague at Boston College, immensely improved the readability of the manuscript with his numerous and thoughtful comments. John Maguranis, Belmont Animal Control Officer, has been very encouraging and shares my fascination and respect for the creatures we study and protect.

Local Cape Cod coyote naturalist Peter Trull, Massachusetts-based writer Catherine Reid, and Adam Gamble, of On-Cape Publishing, provided me with important publishing advice, making the manuscript stronger. Most importantly, my editor, Marie Thomas, deserves a special thanks as she fine-tuned this book into the professional version that you are reading today. Without her tireless efforts I would not have been close to achieving the full potential of my writing abilities.

Lastly, to Nadia Lima, your companionship was very important and meaningful to me during the course of my research and the writing of this book. Your culture taught me a lot about life. However, your habit of falling asleep while tracking with me left something to be desired!

Permits and protocols were approved and obtained through the University of Connecticut at Storrs, Boston College, Zoo New England, and the Massachusetts Division of Fisheries and Wildlife to handle the animals, and from numerous private, town, and state lands that allowed us to put traps in the field and to track collared coyotes. The Department of Conservation and Recreation, specifically Anthony Guthro, has been particularly useful for our Boston research. I appreciate all of these entities who provided documents and support, especially the towns/cities of Barnstable (including rangers, administrators, and animal control), Melrose, Revere, Everett, Malden, and Saugus, among others, for allowing us to use all or some of their land as if it were our own.

Introduction

The coyote living throughout northeastern North America, known generically as the eastern coyote, is the largest version of the species, weighing 30 to 45 pounds or more and resembles a wild-looking German Shepard with penetrating yellow or brown eyes and erect ears. Its color ranges from blonde to darker brown and black, but is usually tawny brown. Their three to three-and-a-half inch long oval tracks are found throughout the northeast and are relatively easy to differentiate from a dog's, especially if tracks are found away from recent human tracks. A mated pair of coyotes regularly patrols their ten square mile territories together, often with help from their older offspring, as they look for prey. Their howls are often heard before they are observed due to their mostly nocturnal activities.

This book is a portrait of what I have learned in my continuing study of the eastern coyote, an elusive predator who literally lives among us. As the leader of the Eastern Coyote Project in Massachusetts, the work that I have done for the last decade of my life has truly been a labor of love. The notion that a biologist should feel affection for their study subjects is thought by some to be too subjective for sound science, however, many well-respected biologists, notably renowned ethologist Marc Bekoff, argue that researchers need to admit and show their fascination with their target research animals in order to have any real conservation influence to protect them. Throughout this manuscript it will be obvious that I have developed strong feelings for the eastern coyote and I hope that this empathy and sense of advocacy, because of the sound science conducted, does not detract from this book, but rather enhances its aim to help ensure a well-deserved place for this amazing animal throughout its range.

We began conducting this study because there have been few ecological studies of eastern coyotes, and no studies have been conducted in Massachusetts or in any urbanized area of eastern North America. This project began as an honors undergraduate project at the University of Massachusetts at Amherst and continued as a Master's of Science project at the University of Connecticut at Storrs. It was designed to be long-term in nature so it has naturally evolved into a full-fledged ecological investigation of an elusive, yet prevalent carnivore. Before describing our project in detail, it is necessary to present a brief timeline, starting with the beginnings of this project, then providing an outline of our multiple coyote studies from startup to the present.

I have always been fascinated with wildlife, particularly predators. My dream throughout childhood and during college was to travel to some far off place such as Yellowstone National Park or even Africa and study wolves, big cats, or any large "exotic" carnivore. Toward the end of my undergraduate years at the University of Massachusetts at Amherst (1993–1997), however, I became interested in wildlife closer to home. I began background readings and literature reviews on coyotes and soon realized that few studies had been conducted in the northeastern United States and there was no scientific information at all available on eastern coyotes in Massachusetts. In particular, there was nothing known about coyotes who inhabit suburban or urban areas.

I became increasingly intrigued with the possibility of studying coyotes within my home town of Barnstable, Massachusetts, because I hoped to add to knowledge of coyote ecology on Cape Cod. I obtained my Master's of Science degree from the University of Connecticut at Storrs in May 2000 by documenting the ecology of eastern coyotes on suburban Cape Cod—focusing my efforts in and around the town of Barnstable. I regularly involved high school students in the data collection process and, unknowingly at the time, was having them participate in authentic scientific apprenticeship programs. This research, which is ongoing, currently consists of colleagues from the University of Connecticut, Boston College, and Barnstable High School, as well as Dr. Larry Venezia and his staff at the Hyannis Animal Hospital.

After receiving my M.S. degree, I worked as a zookeeper at the Bronx Zoo for seven months. This job gave me valuable experience in learning how to handle and care for wild animals, which enhanced the eventual captive coyote project that I later initiated.

I knew that there was scant funding available to study coyotes (or any other animal for that matter), but while at the zoo during summer and fall 2000, I was informed of the Urban Ecology Institute (UEI) at Boston College. This was a Ph.D. program where I could involve students and teachers in the scientific research process. I was accepted into the Ph.D. program in Science Education at Boston College in January 2001. My plan was to study coyotes in Boston much as I had done on Cape Cod for my Master's research. I would use teachers and their students in the Boston area participating in the UEI as subjects, thus involving them in developing curriculum based on our scientific research. To have them collect scientifically sound data that could eventually be published in scientific journals was the ultimate goal of having students work with us. This idea was perfect because I had always involved students and teachers in the scientific process. Why not "officially" include them using the UEI's model?

In January 2001 I began to work with Dave Eatough, science teacher at

Revere High School, to accomplish two long-standing, joint goals: 1) Curriculum development and science education provided to teachers and their students through this project; 2) Collection of data on coyotes in urban Boston. Likewise, this book is an attempt to bridge the gap between the worlds of science and education, with a focus on scientifically describing coyote ecology in layman's terms.

Additionally, I expanded the Cape Cod Coyote Study to include two new projects: 1) raising a captive litter of five coyotes (born wild on Cape Cod) at the Stone Zoo in Stoneham, Massachusetts; and 2) starting an ecological study of coyotes in urban north Boston—ranging from East Boston, Chelsea, and Everett to the south side of route 128/95 in Saugus and Lynn. After obtaining the required permits, both of these projects officially began in spring 2002.

The information obtained from these studies has been developed into curriculum models for high school classes in eastern Massachusetts for two reasons: 1) so students and their teachers can learn about and become engaged in understanding local wildlife populations; and 2) to give pupils the motivation and empowerment to authentically participate in field-based (captive or wild) studies of coyotes. I completed my Ph.D. requirements related to these projects on 21 June 2005, just after turning 30. For those interested in keeping up with our current events, http://www2.bc.edu/~wayjo/ or http://easterncoyoteresearch.com/ will lead you to the personal web site that I continually journal on for updates with our research progress and results.

At public forums, I have often been asked, "Why are you studying coyotes in just those locations (Cape Cod and north Boston)?" Other people have said, "You should come to my town, there are tons of coyotes there." Selection of study sites is often a function of logistics and goals. Our study team wanted to examine coyote ecology and behavior in urbanized (suburban and urban) areas. Thus, we needed to select these two types of habitats to fulfill our goal of studying coyotes in highly developed urbanized locales.

Logistically, these studies have been successful because they have taken place close to where we, the researchers, live and work. In other words, there are quite a few places, especially for the suburban component of our free-ranging coyote study, which would have worked. I am sure that just about every town in Massachusetts has its own suite of coyotes who, if studied scientifically, could turn into the now well-known coyotes who are highlighted in this book. For those of us doing the on-site tracking, Cape Cod and north Boston were the most convenient and practical locations for our work. In addition, many of our findings can be extrapolated to other environments with similar conditions in the northeast. Some people think it is the coolest thing that we are doing research in their neck of the woods, while others think that I should 'trap them from their property and move them elsewhere'. As you will read in this book, that is neither a feasible, nor an ethical position.

Because of the media coverage that coyotes have received during the past few years, we have made it our mission to learn and teach as much about the eastern coyote as possible. Therefore, to gain reputability, it was important that we collect scientifically sound data in order to accurately document the basic natural history traits displayed by these animals in the eastern part of the state. The following account is our enduring story about a misunderstood species living among us in Massachusetts.

Throughout the narrative portion of this book, I use quotations from both myself and others to describe, to the best of my recollection, conversations that actually took place. This is to give the reader an understanding of what was happening in our minds and the actual situations at the moments described. As such, most quotations may not be verbatim, but are paraphrased to the best of my recollection.

Jon Way

Chapter 1

Capturing Coyotes
in Urban Environments

The First One

"Oh my god! We captured a coyote! I can't believe this," I thought out loud as I looked into a large cage trap from which I was being eyed submissively by a wild canid just two feet away.

It was 4:45 AM on 8 June 1998 and I was nearly in shock that I had actually captured my first coyote of the study. I looked around nervously, glad that no groggy-eyed early morning walker had observed me in my uncontrollable excitement, jumping up and down just out of sight of the trap. It would surely-be an odd sight considering the woodsy setting there in that large conservation area in Marstons Mills, a quiet suburban village in the city of Barnstable, Massachusetts on Cape Cod.

After finding the trapped coyote, my next thought was to run to my car to call Pete Auger, my former high school teacher and collaborator in the coyote project.

"Hey Pete?" I said hesitantly.

"What's up, Jon?" Pete asked, probably realizing that something interesting had happened since I was calling him at 5:00 AM.

"I'm in the West Barnstable Conservation Area and I just captured a coyote. And it's kind of weird because it's not as big as I'd expect an adult coyote to be, yet it looks too big to be a pup." I was somewhat confused with the capture, knowing only that it had to be some type of coyote.

"Okay, well hold tight," Pete replied. "Give me directions and I'll meet you in about an hour at the entrance of the conservation area."

I anxiously waited until Pete and his brother Greg arrived to assist me. Upon a second inspection in a much more relaxed state, I easily realized that our trapped canine was indeed a coyote pup, though quite large for early June. It was very leggy, a dead giveaway of its youth, but it had the look of a mini-adult, despite being only about 10 weeks old. Its ears were fully erect, its coat had all of its guard hairs (i.e., not just the natal down it was born with) in place, and its eyes were the deep brown color of a normal adult coyote.

I waited until 6:15 AM, then contacted Dr. Larry Venezia, the veterinarian working with us on the Cape Cod component of our coyote study.

"Hi Larry, sorry to call you so early," I apologized, "but we captured a coyote pup. It is large, approximately 20 pounds, in spite of it being so early in the year. What are the chances that one of my three traps is situated near a coyote den?"

Larry paused to assess the situation and said "Congratulations, Jon. That's great you captured your first coyote, but, if the animal is too small, do not collar it. Despite its size, it will definitely grow quite a bit more, assuming it is a pup. We could try inserting one of those implants that you have. Meet me at the clinic (Hyannis Animal Hospital) at about 8:00 AM and we will take it from there."

And that marked the start of our coyote study. Since that interesting first capture, I have learned to accurately judge the size and usually even the sex of our captures by sight. The coyote mentioned in the account above was designated as "Pon", and looking back at our data he was 14.7 pounds; especially big for that time of the year. A site near his den had been baited for a couple of months before a trap was deployed there five days before his capture. No doubt the adults of his pack were heavily feeding all of the pups to fatten them up.

Pon's cute puppy face and baby teeth gave him away as a youngster while we handled him, our first sedated coyote. Dr. Venezia implanted him with a finger sized abdominal radio-transmitter from Telonics, an Arizona-based company, and we released him back to his group in the wee hours of 9 June 1998.

In order to study coyote behavior in detail in the wild, or that of any other elusive animal species, researchers must first capture and radio-tag them. There is really no other way of gaining significant amounts of data without radio-marking (via tag, collar, or implant) and tracking their quarry. Snow tracking is seasonal and subject to intermittent periods of time and is often complemented with radio-telemetry. For example, after a snowstorm new tracks are visible, but researchers cannot be quite sure if they are tracking the same or different individuals unless the animals are sighted or identified via radio-collar signals.

Studying an animal's droppings gives insight into the general eating habits of a population, but unless sorted out genetically in the laboratory there is no way to determine individual consumption. Combining radio-telemetry with these approaches allows a large amount of accurate data on such things to be collected. Most importantly, radio-telemetry allows individual animals to be conclusively identified.

Bob Crabtree's crew in Yellowstone is about the only team I've heard of that has identified non-marked animals in a study on coyotes, although their work

Coyote in box-trap

is aided by having collared animals. Collaring some animals helps them find their study packs in an open landscape where coyotes have little fear of people because they have not been hunted for over 70 years.

Some Trapping History

Capturing coyotes was our first and biggest problem with the study because the padded leg-hold (or foot-hold) trap, the typical method used to capture wild canids, became illegal in Massachusetts in 1996, even for research purposes. Before the ban environmental groups sensationalized the issue by showing pets chewing their paws off in large bear traps. Those traps, however, had been out-lawed since 1916 in Massachusetts. Regardless of that issue, it is clear that a mostly non-hunting and non-trapping population in Massachusetts (about 1.5% of the population hunts and about 300 people trap in all of Massachusetts) cringes at the thought of a coyote (or any animal for that matter) being held, even if not injured, in a leg-hold trap and approached by a person who raises a shotgun to its forehead to kill their quarry. That is exactly how most trapped coyotes are killed.

Worse, some fur trappers, when dealing with very submissive coyotes in a trap, club them to death in order to preserve their coats so no bullet hole tarnishes the head region of the pelt. Using this technique, a coyote is pressed to the ground often with one's foot, then repeatedly clubbed over the head. First they lose consciousness, then slowly their life, with each successive blow. I often speculate if the coyotes ever wonder what they have done to deserve such a violent death.

Despite these obvious ethical issues, leg-hold trapping remains the most common way to deal with—or more aptly, kill—problem-causing coyotes in the United States and Canada, even though over 80 countries have banned these capture devices. The killing of problem coyotes will, unfortunately, always be a reality, but the question that needs answering is, which coyotes truly constitute a problem? That is a topic explored later in the book, mainly in Chapters 6, 9 and 10.

A Trapping Solution

Since we could not use leg-hold traps, we tested the feasibility of using cage- or box-traps, which were the only known legal alternative capture devices for coyotes. Many people told me that it would be "impossible" to capture coyotes in cages since canids are far too wary to enter an enclosed device. However, I disagreed with those "experts" (most of whom have actually never tried box-trapping themselves) and took it as a personal challenge to figure out a way to capture coyotes in these large traps.

We decided on a capture technique that involved using supermarket meat scraps and road-killed animals, mainly squirrels, to entice coyotes to approach and enter these ungainly traps. You could only imagine the looks that I have received from passing motorists or hikers as I retrieved a splattered squirrel by the tail from the highway and deposited it in the back of my truck; or when I walked through the woods with a plastic bag filled with meat scraps wearing an equally gross plastic glove coated with blood and other raw meat residue, a result of my frugality in using the same gloves at multiple sites.

Capturing a smart, elusive animal like a coyote is certainly easier said than done, and a very time-consuming process. To begin with, traps are baited at new sites in the field for several months before they are set for capture. This is called a 'conditioning period' and the traps are literally wired open. Other animals, like raccoons and skunks, routinely enter the traps from day one, but coyotes must be acclimated to go inside. The theory is that coyotes will not enter a trap where animals have been previously captured. This is probably because: 1) the captured animals leave a 'scent of fear' that the coyotes detect; or 2) the coyotes see them in the trap and associate the trap with getting ensnared.

Once all bait is being taken on a regular nightly basis, we assume coyotes are feeding there because they are the only animals in our study area that can pick a trap clean in one night. (Black bears exhibit this behavior, but currently do not reside at our research sites, although they do inhabit roughly half of Massachusetts.) Only then is a trap set for capture.

Setting the Traps

Setting a trap, despite long efforts to condition coyotes to freely enter it, does not guarantee a coyote capture. During a cold day in early February 2003, my colleague Steve Cifuni, took video in Revere of a glossy light-gray adult coyote with a noticeable black stripe on its shoulders entering a trap. It carefully kept all of its weight and momentum positioned backward as it painstakingly removed pieces of bait from the pile, one at a time. Unfortunately, in this instance, that darn trap had frozen anyway, preventing it from firing.

The coyote happily left the trap site with a full belly while the human onlookers were silently cursing (Steve and his sister Rachel were in his house videotaping this all unfolding). "Chalk one up for the Trickster!" I wrote in my notes after looking at Steve's amazing video. "Trickster" is the name that Native Americans gave to coyotes to fittingly describe their intelligence and ingenuity.

Many other animals including raccoons, crows, possums, domestic cats and dogs, skunks, a few foxes, hawks, vultures, fishers (>15 in urban north Boston), and a number of gulls managed to raid the large 60–70 pound traps before a coyote ever got a chance to.

Imagine the exasperation of knowing that a coyote has been repeatedly entering a trap, but the night the trap is set for capture, we capture an angry raccoon. And a 'coon who growls and tries to reach through the trap to swat at its captor is even more annoying, but a common occurrence. Usually I chase these animals away as vigorously as I can, occasionally using the side of my boot on their rear end to negatively condition them to the traps. This usually does little as they commonly are captured in the same trap, often the very next night! Other animals like possums are easier to release, although at times it was necessary to literally roll them out of the trap using a stick, as they grow fearful and faint, which is where they get their reputation for playing dead.

Naturally we have to release all of the non-target animals we catch, but I admit I was initially nervous with skunks. Nevertheless, I quickly found that a slow and deliberate approach would calm them enough so that I could quietly wire open the front door without having them turn their rear-end toward me and release their foul smelling-odor. Due to the nature of the situation, it didn't exactly prove to be a feather in my cap. Some became so comfortable with this release strategy, they came back to the traps night after night.

One instance of an aggravating trap check involved approaching a sprung trap with nothing inside. We weren't sure if a small animal escaped, if someone had released whatever was captured (like their dog), or if a coyote were involved in tripping the ungainly device and managed to stop the door from shutting completely as it exited the trap.

Raccoon in trap

Skunk in trap

Dave Eatough, a 6'4", 43-year-old science teacher from Revere High School, spent three frustrating years trying to capture a coyote at Belle Isle Reservation, a small marshland on the north edge of Logan International Airport in East

Boston. Many nights he found the traps empty and was convinced that the coyotes, probably working in pairs, took the bait from the back of the trap without tripping the trap or by escaping when they did. In addition, every non-coyote capture is a night that a coyote cannot be captured. To compound the dilemma, Dave suspected that rats often fired the trap then slipped out through the narrow bars to escape. We were convinced we would probably never be able to capture a coyote in that location. "Grrrrrr.... Frustrating indeed," I wrote in my notebook after another fruitless trap check. We only captured coyotes about 1% of the nights that we had a trap set.

Trapping Injuries Uncommon

One of the benefits of using box-traps is that animals are rarely injured when captured. In fact, chipped teeth and superficial cuts on paws were the most serious injuries that coyotes inflicted upon themselves. These types of injuries are generally regarded as minor injuries in other traps, since leg-hold traps can cause compound fractures to an animal's leg. Unfortunately, some non-target captures have suffered worse injuries in our box-traps.

One possum, captured in Saugus on a wet, icy, winter day, nearly died in the trap. There were no visible injuries and we assumed that the animal was sick and wandered into the trap to get a last meal. Efforts to revive him inside Steve's home did not work. Possums are migrants from the south and are poorly adapted for winters in the northeast as evidenced by many who have lost their ears to frostbite and another one whose tail was broken off, likely during a frigid night.

In the worst instance that we experienced, a red-tailed hawk bled to death in the trap. It either fought with other animals or greatly thrashed around to escape before we rechecked the trap at dusk. Dave and I each felt very guilty for the animal's demise, and as a result, we wired traps open during the daytime at sites where birds were causing problems. Other animals, such as raccoons and foxes, occasionally chipped their teeth on the trap like some of the coyotes did. These injuries, although very disheartening to the research team (especially the hawk), were few and far between as most captured animals left with a full belly and no harm. When we identified problems, we tried to minimize our effects on non-target species by modifying our trapping schedule, such as wiring traps open during the day or checking traps more than two times per day where we thought we would capture an animal.

A Grueling Schedule

Trapping, coupled with late-night tracking sessions, is rigorous work. We always tend our armed traps twice a day, once at dawn and once close to dusk, which varies depending on the time of the year. This is especially difficult when working alone.

On 17 December 1999, I had tracked coyotes during the night and finished with the location of "Snix", the first adult canid captured in our study site on Cape Cod in West Barnstable. I rolled into bed at 3:46 AM and still exhausted, I got

Red-tailed hawk playing dead

myself up at about 8:30 AM. After checking other sites, I arrived at the location of the Cummaquid Cemetery trap at 9:45, only to find it gone. I could only stand there looking around and scratching my head. To this day, over six years later, I still get visibly annoyed when I think about this. While the chance is small that there was a coyote in the trap, it was set for capture and someone possibly could have taken a trapped animal before I got there. I can only hope the trap was pirated by a mistaken animal-lover who came across it and thought they were saving lives by removing it. A call to the Environmental Police never yielded any evidence of its whereabouts.

Despite the prevalence of non-target captures and human disturbances, our study group was the first to report capturing coyotes in box-traps in the scientific literature. The significant amount of calories provided by us placing two to three days of food in each trap turned out to be irresistible for the coyotes; some even repeatedly entered our traps. We proved that it was feasible to catch enough coyotes to obtain a significant sample size for a study using box-traps, although the technique is largely inefficient because of cost, time, and the difficulty of catching numerous animals at one site. We have captured all sorts of coyotes ranging from young pups to very old adults. One female coyote, Mole, was captured when nine years old and died when 11.5, judging from counting the annuli—annual rings on teeth similar to what a tree has—on a canine tooth. We have captured small coyotes, such as a 27-lb adult male aptly named "Tiny", as well as the heaviest female coyote ever documented, 55-lb Casper.

Old coyote Mole in trap

All our coyote captures are exhilarating after spending literally hundreds of hours repeatedly baiting and checking a trap. At this point, an actual capture can cause a seemingly sane person to do wacky things. When I first saw Snix in our trap on a remote stretch of land about five miles from the nearest house on 19 June 1998, I will never forget high-stepping it back to my car with my finger up like I had just won the 100-meter dash in the Olympics. I couldn't wait to call my colleagues to report our first adult coyote capture.

While some coyotes have proven difficult, if not impossible, to capture even once, others have been caught numerous times. These coyotes appear to be food-conditioned to the traps, which makes them susceptible to repeated captures. The 55-lb mammoth female (called "Casper" both because we trapped her in a cemetery, and because her body was notably a ghostly white) was originally one of the first animals that we collared back in 1998.

We recaptured her for the fourth time in March 2004 when she was about nine years old and collected a boatload of data on her over a total of eight years (1998–2006 at 1,800+ locations). Her collar had been dead for about two years and for a while we did not know her whereabouts or even if she were still alive. Data only available by using marked animals via radio-telemetry had allowed us to discover that she had given birth to her sixth documented litter in 2004 and then stopped reproducing in 2005 and 2006, possibly due to her advanced age.

The author holding Casper

The North Boston Site

We had a much more difficult time catching coyotes in Boston than on the Cape. Boston coyotes were very hesitant to enter our box-traps even though we expected them to be human-acclimated since most of the surrounding landscape has a dense human population. It may be just that smart animals in urban areas survive and reproduce, and the genes responsible for things like avoidance get passed on to offspring in places of high hazards such as people and cars. However, our northern study is relatively young and by using methods similar to our Cape Cod study (that is, typically having as many as six operable traps set at any one time), we expect to capture additional animals over time.

Two of our captures in north Boston involved mangy males (in the true sense of the word, not just straggly). One such animal designated as "Bart" was released after capture and was later found dead, we assumed from starvation. To avoid the same mistake when we caught another sickly coyote that we called Notch, we brought him to a certified rehabilitation facility some 30 miles from his capture location in Malden. Unexpectedly, he escaped from his chicken-wire rehab cage there after just three weeks.

This individual was larger than the previous one, probably at least 40-lbs at the time of his break. I wasn't informed of this until I called the rehab facility a full week after it occurred, by which time it was too late to even attempt to retrieve him. Because we spend months and sometimes years trying to catch these animals, you can imagine the frustration and disappointment when we learned of the escape. We never observed Notch again.

One of the females, 30-lb Fog, was actually captured in a very large hog trap about twice the size of our average traps. It was actually designed to capture feral pigs in Texas. Although you'd expect we would have more luck with a larger trap, we had difficulty even getting coyotes to go inside this one. Plus, that trap did not fire well and often sprung without an animal getting captured. We never had success capturing any other coyotes in that cumbersome trap.

The Cape Cod Site

On Cape Cod, many female coyotes have been captured when they are finishing nursing their pups in mid-to-late May. The stress of raising pups must catch up to them and they commonly enter traps to get a "free meal," even more than in the wintertime. In 2001 on Cape Cod, we captured five lactating adult females in less than three weeks, using only seven box-traps. Between tracking them and checking traps, I barely slept.

On 8 June 2001, it was the third anniversary of our first coyote capture (Pon). Having stayed up for more than half of the night tracking the ten radio-transmitting coyotes in the Cape Cod study site, I went to bed exhausted after 2:00 AM. I woke up at about 6:00 AM to track again and to check traps along the way. To my surprise, I found an old 39-lb female coyote whom we soon named "Mole", in the Marstons Mills Dump trap. Upon collaring her at the Hyannis Animal Hospital, I brought her, like most coyotes that we catch, inside the box-trap to my grandparents' garage to allow her to wake up in her trap in relative peace and quiet.

Never a Moment's Peace

After putting Mole in the garage, I took the opportunity to catch a short nap, only to be roused about 20 minutes later by a call from Charlie Lewis, Barnstable's Animal Control Officer. It was news I didn't want to hear. He had called to inform me that a collared coyote had been hit by a car and killed on the mid-Cape highway. From his description of where it happened, I assumed that it was a breeding female we called "Skunks" who used portions of the villages of Centerville and West Barnstable within the town of Barnstable. I was not looking forward to retrieving a dead coyote's carcass, especially not one whom I had hoped would fill my notebook with several more years of data before the batteries in her collar expired.

My suspicions were well-founded because I picked up Skunks' collar signal loud and clear as I drove up to the town of Barnstable's Natural Resource office. Skunks had apparently tried to cross the highway at noontime on a Friday, which is one of the busiest traffic times of the week during the summer. She normally foraged in the more residential areas of her range south of the highway yet had her pups north of the highway. We later found that her mate and her helper coyote, probably one of her previous offspring, successfully raised her four pups during the summer. This substantiated that coyotes other than the mother can be very good nurturers. The father was likely "Jog," collared in December 2001, six months after the death of Skunks. One of those pups was probably one we named "Carm" whom I collared later that winter as a full-grown pup.

We used our Cape Cod late spring trapping success as a core time for also trapping up in Boston and managed to catch all three adult females there during this same period of the year. Two of the three were lactating females and I remember getting Dave Eatough's excited call at 6:05 AM on 17 May 2004 to tell me "Get your butt over to Everett. We caught a coyote in the cemetery." He mentioned it was much healthier than the ones Steve Cifuni had caught before, referring to two of our last three captures that were severely infected with mange. Dave and Steve each regularly checked two to three traps in north Boston and Dave had baited that particular trap for about two years before finally catching our first adult coyote there, a 32-lb female we named Maeve. To say that Dave was elated would be a gross understatement. Most importantly, that catch marked the start of our research with a very urban coyote.

David Eatough releasing the coyote Maeve in Everett

Net-launching

Aside from box-trapping, another novel capture technique that we were attempting to use on coyotes for the first time, was net-launching. This involves shooting a ground-based net, which is roughly 20 by 20 feet, from three barrels over an animal strategically positioned at a pile of bait. The two big advantages of this method are: 1) a skittish animal like a coyote can walk in and eat bait without entering a restricted area like a box-trap; and 2) the method is very selective. The net can be manually detonated to catch a particular individual. This avoids ensnaring non-target, that is, non-coyote, animals and radio-collared coyotes.

Net launching has potential, as a similar technique to using a net-gun or dart, described in detail by Doug Smith in his co-authored book *Decade of the Wolf*. It has been successfully demonstrated to capture wolves and coyotes in open, usually snowy, areas such as Yellowstone Park and Alaska. However, in that situation, the net-gun or rifle-powered dart is deployed from a helicopter, which is maneuverable enough to literally drop down on top of (10 feet away) a running canid, an option we do not have.

In our case, after a few frustrating misses involving coyotes running away from under the nets, we managed to figure out how to successfully operate the ground-based device. Canids have about 1,000 times more olfactory receptors than humans do, and a coyote's sense of smell is so keen, they can easily recognize when the device is at a site—even *before* walking in close enough to see it. So just as some experienced coyotes are shy to enter box-traps, it is very difficult once a coyote has been missed using the net-launcher to get the same coyote(s) to come in close enough to attempt to catch it this way again

One coyote, dubbed Chew, was almost captured in Melrose. This individual confidently walked up to and bit the string leads that tethered the net-launcher to the ground. Watching him with night-vision, I debated scaring him away so he would not ruin the mesh. I assumed he did not do much damage, however, because he finally quit biting the trap and walked to within firing range over the bait pile. Steve and I then watched with disgust as I detonated the device and he just ran off, avoiding capture because the side that he chewed never fully extended to land on his back.

The methodology for using the net-launcher is very precise. It involves getting the coyotes to come to bait less than 10 feet from the device, funneling them in with two-by-fours laid on the ground. These function like mental barriers causing the target coyote to avoid stepping over them to escape, and instead to run backwards or away from the device when it is fired. This usually results in a successful capture. After netting a coyote, we then restrain and sedate them. Of course, this is easier said than done.

We initially (wrongly) believed that we would be able to capture multiple animals at the same time. As it turned out, this method was really quite time-consuming. Since the bait site had to be clearly visible in order to precisely deploy the net-launcher, good binoculars with low light capabilities and night vision equipment are required. Then we had to wait in the car about 50 feet away in extreme silence. Maintaining such a vigilance for over four hours was very tedious.

Also, radio-telemetry equipment is needed for packs which already include some collared individuals. When two or more animals are together it can be difficult to determine which individual is collared solely from listening to the signal. My notes from a capture attempt with Dave Eatough during January 2003 illustrates some of the flavor of net-launching:

It is very dark and we need the aid of a binocular or night-scope to make out the bait pile in front of the net-launcher. As the car gets colder, our need to piss increases. We decide to wait another 15 minutes before quietly sneaking out of the car. I use the light from my cell phone to write. Another hour and a half pass and few words are said.

Fearing that the slightest sound could disturb a coyote, who needs to get within 50 feet of the car so we can see it, we optimistically believe that one is just out of our limited range of vision. The temperature in the car cannot be much warmer than 20° Fahrenheit as the temperature outside has dropped to near 10°F. We have to keep the windows cracked open to avoid fogging them up with our breath. We are bored out of our minds. This is self-inflicted pain as it is so uncomfortable waiting in the dark and being frozen to the bone!

Net-launching is a time-intensive endeavor involving over 90 hours of sitting time per capture, not including set up and practice. After three misses with the net-launcher, we successfully captured a coyote on 29 June 2004 on the fourth firing. Our capture, whom we named "Jet", was the mate of a collared female "Maeve," who was rearing pups. Jet was captured at the Jewish cemetery in Everett.

Jet had approached and withdrawn from the bait pile an amazing 22 times before finally settling down to stand over the pile for just a few seconds. Before that, he was repeatedly lunging at the bait, snatching single pieces and running, then eating outside of firing range. He had managed to eat over half of the six pounds of meat scraps without spending more than a second at the bait pile each time. It was frustrating watching him that close to firing range around the bait and not being confident that he couldn't escape if we launched it. Dave's limited range of sight and depth perception from 60 feet away, even using binoculars, made it more difficult than we expected.

On Jet's 22nd approach, Dave whispered to me, "Fire it, fire it!" I detonated the net-launcher and we jumped out of the car and ran to the site with gloves, nets, and sedatives. It was so dark, that even when we got within 10 feet of him, we were not sure that we had netted anything until we saw Jet struggling in the net. After subduing him with hand-held nets and a blanket, I injected a prepared dose of sedative in a syringe into his rump. It took 10 minutes, but finally he was out and we were able to untangle him and drive him to Steve Cifuni's basement. The wide-eyed look on Steve's face when I pulled into his family's driveway with a sedated coyote in my lap was priceless. The following morning we released Jet back at the capture site with a newly affixed radio-collar.

Judging from my experience with box-trapping, Jet would have been nearly impossible to catch in a box-trap since his mate, Maeve, was captured in one about six weeks prior to his ensnarement and he undoubtedly saw her in the trap. With our refined method of funneling the coyotes in with two-by-fours, we found that although this was very expensive (the net-launcher alone cost the research program about $4,000) and time-consuming, it was practical and may one day be very important to our study as a different or alternative capture technique.

Netlaunch practice at Revere High School

Releasing the coyote Jet in Everett, MA

Chapter 2

Handling, Collaring, and Weighing Coyotes

Up Close and Personal

It has been very important for me to see my study subjects up-close in an intimate fashion. Their allure is incredible and completely captivating when they were right in front of me. Many researchers, such as Doug Smith in *Decade of the Wolf*, were mesmerized by the beauty of the wild canids they were studying. There is something about their piercing eyes that evokes a sense of wildness, even in our urbanized study areas.

During the past years of our study, I have handled about four dozen of them, which afforded me the truly unique opportunity of knowing exactly what my subjects look like. I can mentally picture them crisscrossing through neighborhoods, waiting to cross main roads, howling with their pack, resting in the shade near their puppies on the relaxing days of midsummer, and feeding on prey just out of sight of my limited night vision.

Handling

Learning how to handle coyotes under different circumstances is always a challenge. Once we capture coyotes, they are sedated, weighed, measured, have blood drawn, and are radio-tagged either by a collar or an implant. Most of the time, we transport the captured coyotes in their respective box-traps to the veterinary clinics we work with. Once there, we sedate the animal and conduct the routine handling procedure with the animal fully tranquilized.

During clinic business hours, we are often given strange looks by the regular clientele who are probably wondering what we are doing with sedated coyotes and if our study subject might be a danger to them or their pets. When the patrons

Trapped coyote Sog staring at camera

are informed of our operation and intentions, they often become very interested and fascinated with our work.

We only process a small fraction of the coyotes in the field, usually when the animal hospitals are closed, our veterinarians are away on vacation, or when we capture a coyote via net-launching. The strategy for handling trapped coyotes involves four simple steps:

1) Sedate the animal where captured or at a veterinary clinic.
2) Do the necessary handling to take measurements, video, and put a collar on.
3) Put the animal back in the trap, and
4) Supervise the animal (with a blanket over the trap to calm it) until it is fully recovered and ready to release.

Capturing a coyote via netlaunching is the only scenario when I am put in the bizarre situation of driving with a sedated coyote in my lap. Because we only net-launch coyotes at night, we do need to drive the animals to a well-lighted working location to collar them, usually inside a house. As funny as it might appear (and I hope I am never stopped by the police at such a time), it is actually the safest way to transport the animal because it enables us to ensure that its head is upright and it is breathing in its motionless state. In addition, the animal is usually out cold for an hour or two making a short ten minute drive to a secure location safe for all concerned.

Collaring

For tracking purposes, all of the adult coyotes we capture are fitted with radio-collars. For young pups (before mid-summer), who would be too small to collar, we surgically implant radio-transmitters into their abdomen at the veterinary clinic. It is a simple procedure where a trained veterinarian sterilizes the abdomen and implant, makes a small 2-inch incision, places the implant inside the pup's abdominal cavity, then finishes with a 3-stitch closure. If done on an afternoon, typically by that night, the pups are safely released back to the wild.

We have yet to encounter any problems with this technique where the coyotes are concerned. For our part, however, the implants do not work quite as well as a collar for several reasons:

1) They have a smaller range so we have to be closer to them to detect their signal, which sometimes amounts to exponentially more driving.
2) The batteries only last about one year.
3) The tiny 2-inch incision on a pup's abdomen is impossible to recognize as the fur grows back on its stomach, therefore, unless we use an ear tag (and if it does not get ripped off), implanted coyotes are regrettably unrecognizable as one of our study subjects if recovered by an uninformed person.

Because of these drawbacks, we try to attach radio-collars to most animals we capture, including mid-sized (about 15-lbs and up) pups. For adults, we take great care in attaching the collar and usually put it on with a finger space between their neck and the collar. This ensures that it is neither too tight, nor loose enough to fall off.

For young coyotes, we use a collar that is adult-sized (usually 32–33 centimeters in circumference), but insert foam in between the collar and their necks. The foam prevents the collar from being lost while the pup is immature and compresses as they grow to adult size, precluding the collar from getting tight enough to endanger their health.

Finally, we take lots of video and pictures to enable us to remember individuals and to study all aspects of our handling protocol. This has proved invaluable, such as when Dr. Larry Venezia watched the video of how we released Snix, captured five miles from the nearest paved road, wake up from the sedatives and stagger away on her own. He quickly told us of the danger to an animal of doing that, ranging from putting her at risk from cars, dogs, or people, to her freaking out some people who might see a coyote acting like that.

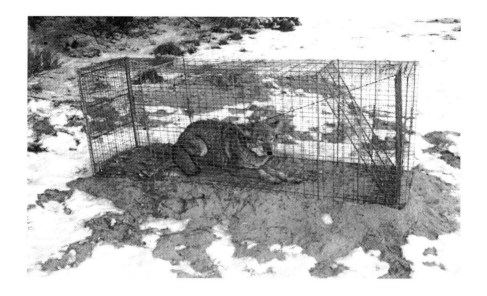

Coyote Snix in box-trap

Accordingly, we quickly revised our sedation and release protocol and now put all anesthetized coyotes back in their cages and release them only when they are fully awake and alert. Most studies, in more remote locations, process their study subjects where captured, then leave them to wake up and fend for themselves. The members of our research team, determined to exhibit the highest level of responsibility for our subjects, felt that leaving them to wake up on their own would provide unnecessary dangers to coyotes in urban areas.

Many people ask me why we don't use GPS (global positioning system) collars on the coyotes. There are several good reasons for this:

1)   GPS collars cost over $3,000, while conventional collars range between $180–$270, depending on the manufacturer and the collar options, such as 'mortality mode', in which the collar emits a rapid series of beeps when the collar does not move for more than four to six hours.

2)   The limited life of GPS collars is less than a year, while conventional collars are active for three to five years on a coyote-sized animal. Larger collars last longer because they have additional batteries, but the biggest collars are too heavy to be placed on coyotes. Due to the accessibility of our animals residing in developed areas near where we live, we track our animals a lot and in the long-run we get just as much data over a longer period of time.

3) The weight of GPS collars are just now becoming small enough for use with coyotes. GPS collars require a lot of battery power and thus are usually much heavier than a conventional collar. The weight could handicap a marginally healthy coyote, impacting their hunting, mating, and general health, and thus the data we collect on the animal.

4) With all of these factors, it was a no-brainer to bypass them with our almost laughably limited budget. If this study ever expands to include more sponsors, however, and the technology of the collars improves, I would certainly entertain the use of GPS collars. It would be fascinating to use a GPS collar to track a dispersing coyote over time, as those animals are difficult, if not impossible, to keep up with in a vehicle.

Weighing

After collaring coyotes, we then take standard body measurements such as weight and total length. When in the field, the simplest way to accomplish this is with a bathroom scale on which I weigh myself holding the coyote. I then subtract my weight from the total. I take three or four of these combined measurements and average out the totals to avoid any error associated with using a cheap scale. While some might think I am anal-retentive with that procedure, I call myself a scientist obsessed with accuracy! When we bring coyotes to a veterinary clinic, the weighing technique is much simpler because we use a digitally calibrated scale and obtain measurements accurate to a fraction of a pound on the first measurement.

The adult female coyotes we have captured have ranged from 29 to 55-lbs (averaging about 35), while males have weighed from 27 to 49-lbs (averaging about 40). These coyotes are often over five feet long from nose to tip of tail. The northeast consistently reports the largest, heaviest coyotes found anywhere in the United States.

Our data has been quite variable, however, with some females found that are heavier than most males. For instance, we captured a dispersing 42-lb female we named Sog, within the territory of a local collared breeding pair (Mizz, 29.5-lb female and Jog, 40-lb male). This large female was traveling through the territory of her smaller conspecifics and continued westbound where she was struck and killed by a car off-Cape, in Bourne.

Several other animals we acquired considerable data on showed a similar pattern of weight variation. Casper was a large female that eventually mated with Sly, a male of 38.5-lbs when he was captured as a yearling. The lightest Casper ever weighed during the three different times that we handled her was 43-lbs, and she was noticeably skinny at that time from raising a litter of at least four pups during that summer (1999). The heaviest male we have captured to date (Glope), was 45-lbs when captured and 49-lbs when recovered, killed by a car, in Hyannis in August 2001.

Mizz in snow with author (on right) and Roswell Joseph (deceased)

Surprisingly, we had monitored Glope tending two dens, feeding many mouths in the process. One of these dens consisted of pups born to Mizz, a collared female also in our study. It is always a blow to lose a coyote whom you have tracked and gained knowledge from; and particularly in this case, because I lost the opportunity to follow up and document the survival of this unusual pack consisting of a double-litter. Further on in another chapter, I'll discuss Lupe, a robust captive coyote even bigger than Glope, who weighed in at 55-lbs at his heaviest.

Preliminary data from our Boston study indicated that coyotes there might be smaller than on the Cape. Of our three healthy adult females, two weighed 30-lbs and one weighed 32-lbs. The only healthy male weighed 35-lbs. The two sickly males, Bart and Notch, were likely 40-lb coyotes when healthy.

Often during our research in eastern Massachusetts, people inform us that they saw a wolf, or a coyote that was 60, 80, or even 100-lbs. While this is unlikely, the weights of coyotes in the northeast (probably greatly exaggerated in people's minds because of their tall stature and thick winter coats), are still considerably heavier than coyotes reported from other regions of North America. We believe that the main reason for this large body size is because they are hybrids between the western coyote (*Canis latrans*) and the wolf.

Other researchers hypothesize it is because there is more food in the Northeast and that coyotes can select larger prey such as white-tailed deer in this locale. There may be some accuracy to this hypothesis, although their normal food of choice, small prey such as rabbits and rodents, often live at lower densities in the northeast compared to other regions. Deer are also common throughout the United States, not just in the eastern part of the country.

Theory of Evolution

The evolution of the coyote in the northeast dates to around the turn of the twentieth century when humans killed nearly all of the original wolves living in New England and southeastern Canada. The theory is that some of the remaining lone wolves may have mated with some of the dispersing western coyotes gradually colonizing the East.

Until the late 1990s, the gray wolf (*Canis lupus lycaon*) was originally believed to have historically been present in the northeast. However, recent DNA tests by Brad White's laboratory at Trent University have revealed that the original wolf in New England and southeastern Canada was probably the red wolf (*Canis rufus*). This same species was originally thought to have only existed in the southeast and was believed extinct in the wild before being successfully reintroduced to the wilds of eastern North Carolina during the 1980s.

It has been proposed that the wolf in eastern North America now being called the eastern timber wolf, eastern Canadian wolf, or simply the eastern wolf, be scientifically dubbed *Canis lycaon*. The end-product of the probable hybridization episodes between this species of wolf and the western coyote is believed to be the eastern coyote.

The eastern coyote is thought to have reached northern New England by the 1930s and 1940s and is believed to have moved steadily southward, now occupying virtually all suitable habitats in the northeast. Many people in southeastern Canada call this same creature the Tweed wolf.

This "Canid Soup" is interesting because one of the main threats that red wolves and eastern wolves face, along with habitat loss and persecution, is hybridization with eastern coyotes/Tweed wolves. However, scientists like Brad White's team believe that the ability of the hybrids to adapt to human-changed landscapes is more important than them remaining a pure species, especially considering that the hybrids still have much of the DNA from their wolf kin. In a co-authored peer-reviewed paper, *Genetic Nature of Eastern Wolves: Past, Present and Future,* White's team noted that, "Hybridization may be enhancing the adaptive potential of eastern wolves, allowing them to more effectively exploit available resources in rapidly changing environments."

Out west it is rare for large wolves and small coyotes to mate. In fact, in many areas where wolves exist, such as Yellowstone and northern Minnesota, coyotes are commonly killed by wolf packs, especially where human persecution is rare. In the east, however, where wolves are smaller and coyotes are larger, it seems that eastern wolves are more closely related to coyotes than they are to the larger gray wolf.

Around the turn of the 20th century, wolves were nearly driven to extinction. Because these small wolves have a close genetic relationship to coyotes already, it is logical that coyotes and eastern timber wolves might mate and produce hybrid offspring. Most researchers believe that this hybrid species called the eastern coyote started colonizing northern New England in the 1930s. They then reached western Massachusetts in the late 1950s and eastern Massachusetts, including Cape Cod, by the late 1970s.

It is likely that coyotes reached Cape Cod either by swimming the man-made Cape Cod Canal or by crossing directly over one of the two bridges that connect the Cape to the mainland. One theory, however, asserts that these canids (also called 'Brush wolves' in this context) have always inhabited New England and managed to survive at very low densities since the early 1900s. Our data, however, does not support this theory.

During our study, we have found that coyotes are generally able to colonize new, even disparate areas rather quickly. Indeed, their colonization of eastern North America after the extirpation of the wolf, took only about 50 years. Biologists know that coyotes settled these new areas, including New England, with their own four paws. There is no evidence that there was human involvement or a documented release program, so they are not some exotic or alien species as some people seem to think.

Rather, as Gerry Parker, in his book *Eastern Coyote: The Story of Its Success*, explains, this probable hybrid between wolf and coyote, which we call the eastern coyote, started breeding true somewhere in northern New England, and with no competition, it quickly spread throughout all the available habitat. With their tremendous range expansion in a relatively short amount of time, coyotes proved that it is unnatural not to have a predator in most ecosystems. With a territorial species like a coyote, any land that does not have other resident coyotes might as well have a "For Rent" sign out.

We are fortunate to currently be collaborating with Brad White's research lab at Trent University in Peterborough, Ontario, by taking advantage of their genetics research. Their lab is analyzing tissue samples for us from our study animals as well as road-kills we have obtained, to uncover some of the secrets of this relatively large-bodied canid. Tissues from our study and from other regions may provide definitive confirmation about what the eastern coyote actually is.

Preliminary evidence indicates that the animals called Tweed wolves in Ontario may be very similar to what we call eastern coyotes or sometimes Brush wolves in New England. Despite probably being the same animal, it is ironic to compare the different connotations of the words 'wolf' (majestic, rare, mythical, pack animal) and 'coyote' (cunning, Trickster, lone animal, smallish predator, common). Some of these claims are probably substantiated (e.g., wolf = pack animal) while others are not (e.g., coyote = lone animal).

They are really very similar creatures, as you will see in the following pages. Pending additional data, it will be interesting to see if this creature is ultimately called the 'eastern coyote' or dubbed some type of wolf, like the "New wolf", originally described by Ray Coppinger in the early 1970s, or even the "Coy-wolf," to potentially describe its mixed-species heritage.

Chapter 3

A Night in the Field

A Winter Adventure

Our quest toward understanding coyote ecology and behavior began with a typical adventure—tracking one of our radio-collared eastern coyote packs on a quiet, cold Cape Cod evening. For the purposes of our study, this event could have taken place virtually anywhere. This particular example occurred during the middle of winter in Barnstable County.

It was Sunday, 25 February 2001 at 8:30 PM. The temperature was 33° Fahrenheit with biting wind gusts up to 40 miles per hour that drove the sleet noisily against my windows. I'd been parked in my pickup truck with the lights off for 20 minutes, facing a golf course that borders the back of an apartment complex in Mashpee, Massachusetts.

I noticed movement periodically at some of the lighted windows as people looked out, apparently wondering what I was doing in their parking lot with my driver's side window rolled down in such miserable weather. But bored by my stillness, they almost simultaneously closed their curtains to seal themselves off from the dilemma I posed, and the cold, stormy night.

I, however, was hot on the trail of a four-legged quarry, and the receiver I had out my open window indicated that something was very near. I used my binoculars to scan the nearby fairway covered with three inches of slushy snow. The full moon, although partially blocked by heavy clouds, provided a pale light that illuminated the open landscape of the golf course.

Suddenly, there they were. Materializing from the dark backdrop of the nearby woods, three large figures emerged like ghosts, moving stealthily onto the back of the fairway. After a moment, the coyotes I was watching loped gracefully across the golf course together. Then the two animals out in front noticed something ahead and bolted after it at full speed. The third animal pursued them about 100 feet behind. When the last animal was out of sight, I started the truck and drove to a trail a short distance away that led in the direction they were heading. I left the vehicle and grabbed my receiver. From there, I located the fresh, dog-like footprints in the snow and began tracking them on foot.

The weather was truly miserable. The wind was piercing and I reminded myself how much I loved my chosen profession as golf ball-sized chunks of hail hit me in the face. Depending completely on my receiver to guide me, the chase led me across a main road to a different section of the golf course. I tried to walk quietly in the wet slush along the south edge of the fairway, very close to the houses that border it, while staying out of sight of my quarry. Inside the houses, people watched television in their living rooms, completely oblivious to the wildlife drama taking place right outside.

After following the three coyotes for half a mile, I suddenly saw four canine figures running back and forth on the fairway and realized that the two lead animals had been chasing a member of their own group. In the midst of this nasty winter storm, these four animals were all wagging their tails and appeared to be playing and having a great time chasing one another around.

I was amazed to watch these creatures frolicking so freely seemingly unaware of the harsh weather. The wind was in my favor, so none of my subjects noticed me standing at the edge of fairway; they were too intent on releasing excess energy. After their game of tag, they casually trotted off together into the darkness. Watching the animals dashing about for those few minutes, displaying such exuberance, it was easy to think that they were just excited to be alive.

I tucked the receiver into my waterproof jacket to protect it from the elements and continued to follow the animals' 3-inch long tracks. They led me down a slushy neighborhood street, then onto another dirt trail covered with more fresh tracks. Concerned that I might lose them, I started jogging, but after 150 meters, I stopped short. I was suddenly only 12 feet away from them!

I could see that the largest animal was wearing a radio-collar. Another sensed me and trotted out of sight and the collared animal followed. The remaining two animals paused, then decided to investigate. Each went into the edge of the woods and I stood there and watched them as they silently passed within eight feet of me. When they got downwind behind me, they walked out onto the trail and sniffed the air. It was then that they realized I was a human and they wanted nothing to do with me. They retreated into the woods and quietly but swiftly all four hightailed it out of sight.

I trudged the mile back to my truck, drenched and nearly frozen to death. After I started the engine and turned the heat on, the first thing I recorded in my notebook, with very numb fingers, was: "Wow, what a night!"

Recording Data

This little adventure was typical of many of my night tracking forays that have provided me with the bulk of data I have recorded during my ten years of

research on eastern coyotes. In this instance, I was following them in a typical suburban area on Cape Cod, specifically radio-tracking a 44-lb adult male coyote
named Kett.

The author holding sedated coyote Kett

To conveniently identify and remember individual animals, we name our
study coyotes based on capture events and/or local features. Kett was named for the
Cotuit Kettleers, a baseball team from the Cape Cod Summer League, because he
was first captured near where they play. The scientific community is, in my opinion,
a little uptight about the use of names in technical publications, so we also assign
numbers to each coyote we capture. Males are given odd numbers and females even
numbers, with the last two digits of the year as a prefix to their capture numbers.
North of Boston coyotes also receive a BN (Boston) before their capture number.

Kett was given an identification number of 9805 because he was the third male captured in 1998 on Cape Cod. When the narrated incident took place, Kett had been radio-collared for two and a half years. At this writing, I am not sure if he is still alive because the batteries in his collar have expired, but we guessed his age to be about two or three years at the time of capture, so today he sure would be an old coyote.

Diary of a Wildlife Biologist

In addition to their formal education, wildlife biologists are molded by the factors of their background and environment. For instance, many have the heart of an animal rights activist and want to help the creatures they study, yet they not only have to learn about the wildlife, they have to cultivate the skills of a hunter or trapper to do so. In order to protect wild creatures from those who would willingly harm them, biologists typically need to gain a vast amount of knowledge of an animal's behavioral patterns and how and where to locate them for biological study.

Then, in between the extremes of society, is the general public that typically does not fully understand either those who would harm the wildlife or the biologists who study them. One thing is for certain: data must be collected on a species in order to learn about it and make accurate and humane management recommendations. That is the job of a wildlife biologist.

Radio-telemetry is a technique used by biologists to monitor animals by remotely tracking a radio signal emitted from a transmitter (normally a radio-collar) on the animal. A researcher can track the signal, and the animal's location, by tuning a specially designed receiver to the transmitter's specific frequency and scanning the surroundings with a directional antenna. I typically affix the handle of the small antenna to my car by manually rolling up the window to secure it. Then I drive until I "pick up" the cluck-cluck sound that the transmitter emits on the receiver. The closer the receiver is to the transmitter/animal, the stronger the signal reception.

A signal can generally be detected from up to one mile away (radio-collar to receiver) but this varies with interference, such as trees, hills, and buildings, and by collar manufacturer, as some are better than others. Sometimes signals are faint from less than a half mile away in a location with lots of ground clutter. They can be relatively strong from over two miles away when the locale is elevated, or over 10 miles when finding signals via airplane.

Regardless, a search pattern for particular coyotes is employed to try and minimizing travel time by maximizing the efficiency of finding it. A coyote with an established range is easier to find when its home range borders are known, yet even finding a coyote within its range can sometimes take well over an hour. When coyotes are outside their normal range, it is more than challenging to drive around for hours without hearing the locating ping-ping of the receiver.

In a forested environment typical of the northeast United States, we usually do not observe the animals directly. Instead, we listen to the signal that is released from the coyotes' collars as our typical mode of data collection, especially when it is dark and difficult to see or during the daytime when they generally are not active and are sleeping in the woods. That leaves crepuscular times around dawn and dusk as the best times to get a decent view of a coyote in the wild. Still, sightings are erratic at best and the researcher must become familiar with an individual animal's activity patterns as well as how to use radio-telemetry accurately if they hope for visual appearances.

The power of radio-collaring cannot be understated. It is truly amazing what you can discover about a study animal by using this relatively simple technology. Collars normally broadcast 24 hours a day (there are exceptions to this) and those designed for a coyote-sized animal last around three to four years, depending on which brand and model are used. By radio-collaring animals, biologists can identify individuals and follow them at virtually any time.

In our study, we tried to sample location points of radio-transmitting coyotes relatively evenly throughout a 24-hour period, which required us to work many graveyard shifts. This unpredictable schedule makes the life of a coyote researcher very demanding and time-consuming, but has provided key insights into our nocturnal study subjects.

A typical night of tracking may last within a range of one to ten hours, and consist of many different location finds. The initial bearings of a coyote's location are often obtained from a researcher triangulating from at least two different places. If the signal is very strong, one location fix would be appropriate. Because the goal of a research project should be to not disturb the study subject in order to obtain the most accurate information on its behavior, tracking can be strategic.

The researcher needs to be able to predict where the animal is moving and monitor it while staying out of its way. My field notes commonly depicted that type of scenario. As an example, the following is a section of my data from tracking Sill, an adult male breeding coyote, in Marstons Mills on 2 May 2005:

11:20 PM—He is at the south-central part of Lovell's Pond northeast of Lovell's Road.

11:27 PM—He is now at the southwest part of Fox Den Bog. Judging by the change in signal, he is moving east at a trot.

11:34 PM—He is now traveling north on Curtis Path, a dirt road in a watershed.

11:38 PM—He is right around the north bog at Katie Jo's house (a former high school researcher whose family lives on these bogs). At this point I immediately drive three quarters of a mile to the junction of Wakeby Road (a main thorough-fare with heavy traffic) and Old Post Road (a dirt road with just a few houses) and turn my car off facing that junction. I assume he was heading back to the den at a brisk rate for the past 20 minutes and I am trying to get ahead of him. I am parked about

50 feet east of the junction on the north side of Wakeby, facing west. Judging by his medium strength signal he is now right around Patty's Pond, about a quarter mile away, and heading this way. A street light illuminates the junction.

11:44 PM—The signal is getting stronger.

11:52 PM—Sill comes out onto the street and fast-feets (shuffling his feet) across Wakeby. When he gets to the north side of the road he stops at the base of a long driveway, sniffs around, then, instead of continuing north, he heads west on Wakeby! He then recrosses the road and goes into the pine forest south of Wakeby, just east of Newtown Road (another main road in the study area).

11:53 PM—A second coyote, smaller and more cautious, stops at the north edge of Old Post Road. It looks like Sill's mate who is similar looking with a grayish body and a silver stripe on her back behind the front legs. She looks around, does not see Sill who is OOS (out of sight), but does catch sight of me waving my antenna as I try to locate Sill from within my vehicle. At that point she turns around and trots back down Old Post Road. Sorry girl, I didn't know you were there!

11:56 PM—As I summarize my notes, the same coyote comes back out and crosses Wakeby, this time right onto the driveway that Sill was sniffing four minutes previously. Judging by their movements for the past hour I bet the two are on a territorial patrol to scent mark the cranberry bogs around these ponds. (These areas contain a high density of rodents and the coyotes spend a lot of time in them.)

The total distance Sill traveled in this instance was about a mile and a half. By the following morning, the two were back with their litter of eight or nine pups about a mile from that last location. These field notes of my observations are typical for an average tracking expedition. Since my undergraduate days at UMass Amherst, I have filled 15 large notebooks with research data and six small journals with data that solely describes the captive coyote project.

The one drawback to studying coyotes in urban areas, especially near my own house, is that my office is my back yard, my neighborhood, and my town. I feel like I should always be out there tracking since the coyotes are always nearby. When I have conducted brief periods of research elsewhere, like in Yellowstone Park for a week or more, there is usually a mental line drawn between doing research and going back to a field station or camp. However, when I am heading home from a night out with friends at 2:00 AM and am traveling through a collared coyote's range, I have many times stuck the antenna out my window and tracked those individuals. When I quickly find my study subjects, all is well. When I have trouble locating them and a simple spot location fix turns into a 4:00 AM adventure, that is a different story, especially to the poor passengers, or should I say prisoners, with me.

The more animals that we catch and the more often we are in the field tracking them, the more we learn about the overall system. Probably the most difficult part of a study is the biologist's nightmare that the minute we look away for a moment something important is going to happen. Rolf Peterson, in his book *The Wolves of Isle Royale*, talks about the "nagging uncertainty" of not figuring out the fate of some of his study subjects. I call this the 'soap-opera dilemma'.

Nothing substitutes for being in the field. When I have not conducted research for a few days, I feel like a viewer who has missed a few episodes of his or her favorite show. I then have to "watch" or track my study subjects more frequently to try and get caught back up. I certainly would never have produced the story of Kett and his pack if he were not radio-collared. Sometimes we never find out what happens to our collared coyotes as they die out of our sight—or they travel out of our study site.

Alternatively, one may think of their study subjects as pieces of a jig-saw puzzle. The more animals who are collared, the more study subjects we have, the more results that we obtain. Therefore, by analogy, the more pieces of the puzzle we can put together. However, this puzzle can be transformed over time as animals potentially change their habits. Hence, the power of using good science is apparent in the short-run to fit as many pieces of the puzzle together as possible to get an accurate portrayal of the system. The value of having long-term studies becomes obvious when looking at changes over time.

The soap-opera dilemma, coupled with multiple concurrent studies, has resulted in a lot of sleepless nights for me. Having an adaptable schedule and being able to fit in enough catnaps on a daily basis to survive, has probably been one of the most important, albeit unanticipated, outcomes of this research. After a night of unsuccessful net-launching that kept us up until 4:35 AM on 26 August 2004, Dave Eatough told me "I don't know how you do it. That's truly a gift, especially for this line of work."

Dave was referring to how I slept in my car for only two and a half hours before waking up around 7:00 AM to go to the Stone Zoo to interact with the coyotes whom I hand-reared. After that, I joined Dave in Everett at about 9:00 AM to collar a 22-lb pup coyote, Jem. My commitments for the date met, I was then able to go home and literally pass out for an additional two hours in my apartment, before heading back to the Stone Zoo in the late afternoon. (Many people inaccurately think that I live with wild coyotes because they see pictures of me with the captive group of five coyotes whom I raised, posted on my web site, and they assume that is what I do in the wilds of north Boston or on the Cape. These captive animals were with me as study subjects for three years, and are the subject of the second half of this book. They currently reside at two zoos under the jurisdiction of Zoo New England.)

Simply put, if you have or need a predictable schedule, then this vocation probably isn't for you. Tracking nocturnal animals like coyotes requires sleeping during the day and being more active at night. Fortunately, for me, I have a problem. I admit it; I am a coyotaholic.

Chapter 4

Coyote Range Requirements, Causes of Mortality, and Social Classes

Tracking Kett

Driving around Mashpee, Massachusetts on another cold, winter day in late-February 1999, I was tracking Kett to determine if he were part of a social group of coyotes. I captured him originally in the town of Barnstable, yet we regularly found him near Otis Air Force Base in the town of Falmouth—two towns and about seven air miles away. His range was so expansive that on some days I would have to drive for up to two hours just to pinpoint his location. I determined he had been using a very large, nearly 20-square mile area consisting of most of the town of Mashpee and some distance beyond. At this point in time, I was attempting to identify his social status, so I had to observe him with other coyotes. This day I had an easy time finding him at 6:10 PM in the central part of his range near the Mashpee dump.

At 6:15 PM I parked my car across the street from the landfill on the southwest edge of the junction of the dump and the main road to take a radio-fix. Kett was due east of me but was difficult to track in the darkness due to his high level of activity and the fact that I was just getting the knack of tracking these swift moving urban predators over long-distances. I decide to pull into the dump, and when I did I saw two pairs of shining eyes on the top of the capped landfill. As I watched, the creatures paced along the top of the hill. Despite the excitement of the sighting, I still did not think I had a complete tally of animals on that hill. From 6:25–6:50 PM I waited by the southwestern edge of the dump. Kett's signal, as I pointed the receiver toward the dump, was still very strong but I couldn't see him.

Coyote Kett traveling in Mashpee, MA

I decided to howl twice about 30 seconds apart. The literature recommends doing a series of three separate howlings, approximately one to two minutes apart. I heard no response but I knew that there were at least two coyotes up in the dump, so I decided on a bolder approach. I stepped out of my vehicle and walked quietly up the access road. I howled twice more, approximately 30 seconds apart, since I was not patient enough to wait the full several minute period.

The moon was bright on that crisp, clear evening, but initially I saw nothing. Then a few minutes later at 6:55 PM, I noticed a ghost-like silhouette on the road just north of me. A coyote looked right at me for a long moment, then disappeared. I was sitting on the ground and down-wind of a slight breeze, so I didn't think that it really noticed me. Once the creature was out of sight, I sprinted up the hill, as quietly as the urban phantoms I was trailing.

I placed my feet carefully to avoid making the slightest noise. When I reached the top of the hill, which took about 15 seconds, I spotted three coyotes about 20 feet away. Completely shocked to see me, they immediately turned and fled. "Wow," I thought, "How amazing! I just drew Kett's pack right up to me by howling!"

The coyotes fled back up the slope to their original location. One of them immediately disappeared over the hill; the other two, including Kett judging from the loud signal, stayed on top of the hill looking back in my direction. It probably was a good thing that I had no light to shine on them, because they lingered on top of the hill as if I couldn't see them.

For the next 15 minutes I watched both remaining coyotes alternate from running back and forth on top of the hill to bedding down for several minutes at a time. At 7:10 PM I got up as quietly as I could and dashed back to my truck for my binoculars, cursing myself for not bringing them with me initially. When I returned, the coyotes were still in view, watching me from about 50 meters away.

The binoculars worked very well amplifying the available light. Little did I know just how often over time I would use binoculars for nighttime observations, especially under street lights. I continued to watch as both the coyotes loped around on the hilltop with their tails below the horizontal plane of their spine, indicating possible nervousness. They did not seem to be focused on me as they made no noise or signals that they were distraught by my presence. Their actions perplexed me, a seemingly bizarre waste of energy. Bored by the lack of interesting movement and in an attempt to forget the cold, at 7:25 PM I became just a tad greedy and tried two more howls 30 seconds apart. The coyotes got up and looked at me, but did not respond. They appeared to have had enough of my antics for one night.

I watched them for 33 more minutes, but by then my freezing body was succumbing to the cold and the thought of going back to my car to warm up became more appealing by the moment. I was poorly dressed for the conditions, wearing just a fleece jacket, and the temperature was well under 20° Fahrenheit. I made my way back to the car and finished summarizing my notes with the heat on, "Thanks Kett," I wrote, "and your friends, for an amazing hour plus! Wow!"

Home Ranges of Breeding Coyotes

I eventually discovered that Kett was the breeding or alpha male of the Mashpee pack of three or four adult coyotes. To gain insight into canid behavior, capturing dominant canids in a given territory is very important. These animals are typically called breeding or resident coyotes. They determine what the social group does, such as where they travel, where they den, where they sleep, and where and what they eat.

There is nothing more satisfying from a research standpoint than to capture the many lactating females (breeding females) that we have found in our traps during the month of May. Breeding coyotes, also called the alpha pair, determine the size and location of their group's range, while juveniles and helper coyotes live within those borders, as they are usually offspring of the mated pair. The inclusion of alphas, helpers, and juveniles is what forms a coyote pack.

The home range of Kett's pack was a chunk of Cape Cod real estate that extended from Falmouth clear across Mashpee to the Barnstable town line, an area covering approximately 15 square miles. His group regularly traveled across that large range in their nightly activities and I often sighted him traveling with the same pack members in various parts of that territory.

When tracking this and other groups, I have become more careful of when and where I howl, because howling too often can disturb canids and potentially desensitize them to responding. For instance, I completely avoid howling around any den sites for fear that a mother coyote may associate the sound with an unfamiliar coyote, a threat which could further stress her during this demanding time.

A coyote's home range is the area that is used during typical and regular activities. Outlying locations where they might be found, which comprise 5% of an animal's fixes, are excluded when calculating home ranges. Breeding coyotes have large home ranges on suburban Cape Cod. This has been one of the biggest surprises of our study, as other biologists predicted that coyotes in urbanized areas might have smaller ranges compared to coyotes inhabiting more rural landscapes. The average home range of adult resident coyotes (that is, the breeders) in our study was 11 square miles, and varied from 6–18 square miles.

Juvenile and Helper Coyotes

Juveniles, which is the term used for pups up to their first year of life, generally have smaller ranges than resident adults and nomads (or transients). This would be expected as they travel within portions of their parents' home range until they approach full size.

The 'age of independence' is between six and nine months old. We have monitored a number of new litters during our studies and tracked eight radio-marked (implanted or collared) 'juvies', including Pon, Poo, Cup, Kash, Hap, and Cix on Cape Cod, and Jem and Cour in north Boston. When these adolescents matured, if they survived they became either transient coyotes who dispersed into new areas or resident associate coyotes. Resident associate coyotes are also called helper or beta coyotes.

Resident associates or helpers, like the coyote Sill on Cape Cod who stayed with his father Kett for nearly two years, remain with their parents to help raise the next year's litter of young. Food supply and sibling-acceptance are often the determining factors for how many and how long grown juveniles choose to remain 'at home'. During good food years and assuming friendly sibling interactions, more juveniles might remain in a given territory. These remaining offspring, with their parents, are what typically form a pack, defined as at least three coyotes.

As far as biologists can tell, parent coyotes do not actively kick their offspring out or drive them off their home range. It is more likely that the lack of food being delivered to them generally by early to mid-fall when they are five or six months old plays the largest part. Additionally, if no strong bonds are established with littermates, or if enmity occurs due to dominance issues, this is often enough to trigger dispersal by late fall or early winter of their first year.

Technical Difficulties

Radio-tracking coyotes can be a challenge. I have often driven around looking for a single coyote for over an hour without detecting that individual's signal. Still, it was rewarding to finally locate them on those difficult finds, especially when they were documented in new areas. This meant either a range increase or a new area of use within an established range. Unsuccessful finds are an annoyance to most researchers but especially to someone like me who is "just a tad" competitive. I can hardly count how many times I have been late to a friend's house or missed a sporting event that I wanted to watch on my day off because I had to make a quick check on one of my subjects and a simple search for a coyote turned into a mini-project.

Other seemingly simple issues can cause tracking difficulties as well. Coupled with a coyote's large home ranges is the fact that the collar's frequency is affected by weather. During extreme cold, an inexperienced tracker might have the fine tuning of the receiver off just enough that they have no chance of detecting a signal. When the fine tuning is properly dialed in, there is also the chance that the animal might be out of range and, as simple geometry and mathematics tell us, the larger an area that you search the more driving and time it will take.

In early March 2006, I passed the 200,000 mile mark on my truck, averaging 25,000 miles a year, mostly related to this research. I am normally environmentally conscious and try to minimize my use of energy and to recycle the products that I use; however my conservation efforts are limited by the amount of carbon dioxide that my truck generates during my daily travels.

Radio-Collars

The tracking process usually involves listening to or for the ping of the transmitter. Different collar manufacturers, such as Telonics and Advanced Telemetry Systems (ATS), produce different signal strengths. On some tracking occasions, a surprising twist to the normally mundane task occurred when we had members of the same pack deployed with different collar brands. For instance, Jet was fitted with a Telonics collar and was often very easy to find, while his son Cour, wearing an ATS collar, often had a much fainter signal even when the two were right in the same place.

We found that often the variances in signal strength between different brands of collars made it difficult to know precisely if two coyotes from the same group were together. Thus, to accurately determine how close collared coyotes were to each other, it made it necessary to triangulate a location by taking multiple fixes from different angles in a short amount of time. It consistently took more time pinpointing a group that had animals collared with different brands of transmitters compared to a group with multiple animals wearing the same brand.

Why would we use different collar companies? It comes down to pure economics. A coyote-sized ATS collar, with no special features costs about $180. A Telonics collar is about $260 for the same specifications. Both collars are warranteed to last three and a half years. While both types of collars work just as well when you are close to the animal, Telonics collars have proved to be more sensitive and allow us to detect signals from much further away than ATS collars. For research purposes, this can make all the difference in the world.

When animals are more nomadic, or when they are traveling fast, the weak signal of an ATS collar can result in exponentially more search miles daily. Unsurprisingly, there are many more days when a coyote fitted with an ATS collar rather than a Telonics collar cannot be found at all. Naturally, if one studies a species with

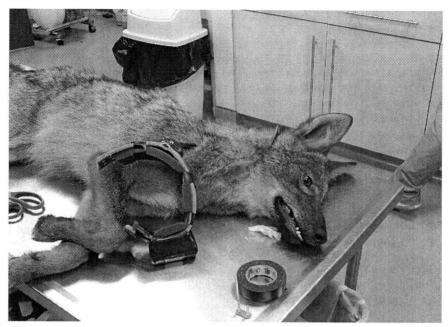

Coyote pup Jem given an adult-sized radio-collar with foam inside it

a small territory, then the reliability of the cheaper collar, even with the short range, might be perfectly adequate. There are many different types of telemetry manufacturers and I described only two of them. Appropriate technology and functioning equipment are some of the many different factors that impact a wildlife study.

An example occurred on 21 May 2005 when I was again tracking Sill, in the village of Marstons Mills. I wrote,

> "Sill's collar is so aggravating. With a Telonics collar I probably would have seen him several times already. With ATS, I am constantly trying to catch up to him rather than predict where he is going to go next. The much weaker collar makes it difficult to know where/in what direction he is moving."

However, over time, I eventually became adept at locating Sill with that collar.

Highway Fatality

Even when using the best type of transmitters for signal detection, unexpected events can cause problems. One such tracking adventure on 9 July 2002 involved Maple, a breeding female and the first coyote we had collared in the north Boston area. After many busy days on her trail, we observed her with three very healthy pups at a rendezvous site situated among natural fields and regenerating aspens near Steve Cifuni's home in north Revere. We tracked her during that early morning as she left her pack's rendezvous site and traveled a few miles east-southeast. That night, we were exhausted and decided to leave her to herself and instead get some much needed rest.

The next morning Steve set out after her, but could not find her. Dave and I joined the search a little later on, but for three days she eluded us. I remember this quest well because at the time I was in the middle of leading a three-day coyote expedition sponsored by Massachusetts Audubon's Wellfleet Bay Wildlife Center. This consisted of ten people, and most of our work focused on watching wild coyotes at rendezvous sites on the Cape. Activities included taking a van up to the Stone Zoo to see my captive coyotes. This two-day time period was the longest I had been away from them for their first year of life. The zoo trip went well, with the puppies playing and howling and the crowd laughing as the young pups competed for my attention after not seeing me for all of 48 hours.

But the subsequent search for Maple did not go well. We drove around for an hour and a half in north Boston and could not find her. Between people getting sick in the back of the van, getting scared from being in inner-city type areas, and doubting if we actually had a collared coyote in this type of environment, I had a lot of skeptics on my hands. To make matters worse, we never detected Maple's signal that night at all.

In the past we had lost her for a day or more a few times as she tended to move quite a distance in her urban range. By July, however, we were beginning to understand her pattern of movements and this disappearance was atypical, so we were apprehensive. True to our worries, my heart sank when three days later the Division of Fisheries and Wildlife informed me that a coyote, and it turned out to be Maple, had been killed crossing Route 107 in Saugus.

A thunderstorm in the early evening may have been partly to blame, as we noticed that other collared adult breeding coyotes, including Glope, who was struck by a vehicle 100 meters from Barnstable High School on Cape Cod, seem to lose their bearings in bad weather. Maple was hit on Route 107, a road that is notorious for speeding and accidents. Her collar was so badly damaged that it could not emit a signal.

She had been struck multiple times, probably after she was dead. It is safe to assume she died quickly, but the view was dismal, even for a seasoned biologist who has seen many such dead animals. My feelings alternated between sadness and anger for the next week. We had had the thrill of seeing her three pups after a couple months of knowing that they existed, but never having been able to find them. Then we lost this matriarch of that social group who lived within a few miles of downtown Boston and was the first coyote to be captured in our north Boston study site.

The call from that Massachusetts state official indicated why our three solid days of looking for Maple had been in vain—she was lying dead in a freezer some 20 miles away. She was probably searching for a new mate, since the male coyote who regularly traveled with her had mange, which was noticeable even in summer, when coyotes normally have short coats. We assumed that because the animal had mange, he was sick. Maple was probably able to sense that, or directly experienced his illness by his not being able to provide for their litter. It is likely that she was searching for a more capable provider.

We never managed to capture that sickly coyote whom we dubbed Scruffy, but he (and potentially others) may have managed to raise the pups through their first winter, as six coyotes were documented on infrared video behind Steve's house in Revere during January 2003.

Causes of Death

Road-kill, it turns out, accounted for about 60 percent of coyote deaths on our study site, especially on Cape Cod. Human hunting was the second-most frequent cause of death. As we captured more coyotes during the study, we learned that coyotes can die in many different ways, as detailed elsewhere in this book.

Two youngsters from the same litter were among the first to go. One early October morning when Pon, a juvenile, and the initial animal we monitored, was six months old and three-quarters grown (35-lbs), I was standing at the shoulder of a road where I often watched his group during the summer. I was excited and sure that I would see him when first light came as his signal was strong right near my car. But as light gradually emerged from the fog-filled cranberry bog that I was watching, I noticed he was not active.

Indeed, I found him lying dead in the road about 50 feet away. Judging by tracks in the sand, he was hit attempting to cross the street behind two or three others as they exited from a narrow wooded patch of woods behind some houses to make their way out into the bog. His brother Poo had made a similar mistake a few weeks before as he tried to cross a different busy road a few miles away at 10:30 AM. That cost him his life as well.

One reason why coyotes, especially pups, get killed by cars is that they have to cross many roads to traverse different sections of their large ranges. Scientists believe that the size of coyote home ranges vary based on the degree of urbanization. In urban areas, there is assumed to be more food and resources to support their populations enabling them to live in smaller territories. Our results, however, contradict that, as many of our coyotes throughout suburban Cape Cod have large ranges similar to more forested areas like northern Maine.

However, as predicted by other biologists, the coyote with the smallest home range in our Cape Cod study lived in Hyannis, the most urban part of Cape Cod. This female Hyannis coyote, whom we named Mizz because she was captured at the Cape Cod Melody Tent in Hyannis during a blizzard, was regularly documented as having traveled throughout her established home range, which abutted the Cape Cod Mall area. When she eventually left her territory, we believe it was because an uncollared female, probably an older daughter of hers, forced her out at the end of summer 2001. And a five to six year old breeding female coyote that we captured on 15 June 2006, 37.3-lb "Raider", in the woods at Barnstable High School may be that same female coyote from five years before.

The author holding sedated Raider captured in Hyannis, MA

This is not a common occurrence and has not been previously reported in the literature about coyotes. During that summer I confirmed that Mizz's radio-collared mate Glope bred with two females and attended both den sites before himself being killed by a car a couple of hundred meters from Barnstable High School, my alma mater.

Mizz was a small, 30-lb odd-looking adult coyote, mostly white with blotchy chunks of brown. Her almost cow-like color pattern was combined with the look of both a bat (her face and ears) and a fox. We assume she was a full-blooded coyote as she gave birth when normal wild canids do—although on the earlier side, in late-March. Her offspring looked like coyotes and always associated with coyotes.

Research has found that coyote-dog hybrids, called coy-dogs, do not have the same reproductive cycle as wild canines. They mate in the fall and give birth in the winter, making it almost impossible to mate with coyotes, who are only in season during the winter. Plus, the prospect of a coy-dog (or any wild canid) raising a litter in the dead of winter is slim. Despite being in a heavily suburban setting, I never saw Mizz interacting with dogs, which were abundant in the study area, and the local foxes avoided her group.

Mizz acted like a typical urban coyote, usually sleeping in wooded settings in sizeable areas. Sometimes I also located her, via radio-signal, in unusual places, such as a sewage treatment plant bordering the Cape Cod Mall, or in bushes within a residential area. Like an apparition, she was hardly ever seen in these odd locations, despite bedding in many of them for the day. She gave birth in wooded areas in the more wealthy parts of her range (like Hyannisport), but regularly traveled to low-income housing areas. I suppose one could say that she moved easily between the social-classes.

Once being displaced from her Hyannisport range, Mizz traveled widely and I located her only intermittently thereafter because her collar malfunctioned. She eventually was shot and killed on a private island in Yarmouth in fall 2002, reportedly in the company of other coyotes, all of which were shot by a landowner just for being on the island. I am, admittedly, always distressed when we lose a collared animal I had come to know so well.

Coyote Mizz and her bizarre coat pattern

The Real End of the Story

The story of Mizz does not end there, however. After her death, an obscure hunting journal called *Woods and Waters USA* produced an article criticizing my team's research. The title of the article, "Is He Kidding About Coyotes?," claimed that my population density data for coyotes living on the Cape was ridiculously low. It was obvious the author had no introduction to the scientific method of determining population numbers nor knowledge of how field estimates were made based on resident coyote territory and group sizes.

This individual called me a "self-described expert on coyotes" and complained about the use of tax-payers' money for my research (even though I never received any). While many people might argue that it would be wise to publicly fund this work to provide information to the public on how to coexist with coyotes, to date that has not happened in Massachusetts.

This writer from *Woods and Waters* bragged about his hunting friend, a taxidermist, who 'bags about 30 coyotes a year on Cape Cod', and that apparently included Mizz during fall 2002. He had no idea of the difference between resident and transient coyotes, nor the fact that because his hunting friend left rotting carcasses in their yard and every coyote who was in the area was shot when they approached the food source, that there were probably no resident coyotes left in their area at all. This probably resulted in a continual influx of transient coyotes, yearling or adult coyotes with no definable home range, who were constantly attempting to colonize it, and in turn were also shot for just being there. An area like this is called a sink habitat, which reflects the poor quality habitat; in this case, the area was marginal for coyotes solely because of the actions of one or two humans killing everything in sight.

To add insult to injury, the article further claimed that the 'collar was strangling her' since I 'collared her as a pup'. Contrary to his deductions, my file on Mizz showed she was first collared as a pregnant two- or three-year old, who was subsequently re-collared two years after the initial collaring, and then shot two years after the second collaring. Thus, she was collared for four years before "being put out of her misery" and her most recent collar was only two years old and well-fitted to her as an adult animal. The author concluded with: "I can't even imagine the suffering this animal went through during the year or so that this collar nearly suffocated it. If you get a chance, email the aforementioned web page (my site) and report sightings and let them know how you feel about this work. Personally, I think the only way to kill a coyote is a clean shot to the head, not slowly strangling it for many long months. But, who am I to say anything? I'm not the 'expert' here."

Upset by this negative article, I contacted local environmental groups, advertised the article on my web page, and contacted the state to see if they would help. The Massachusetts Society for Prevention of Cruelty to Animals (MSPCA) and other concerned individuals sent numerous letters to the magazine in support of our study and condemned the way the article attacked me personally as defamatory and reprehensible. But the state, content to sit on their haunches, did nothing.

This incident, and the state's apparent policy of coddling the 1.5% minority of the population who hunt, led me to formulate my idea for no-hunting National Wildlife Watching Areas. I'll discuss that in detail further on.

Home Range Dynamics of Breeders in North Boston

Although our Boston study covered only three and a half years and involved just eight animals, we found some similar patterns of behavior in this coyote population compared to our Cape Cod group. For example, Maple had approximately a 10-square-mile territory that involved parts of five towns from Revere to Peabody—impressive for the amount of urbanization tolerated!

She gave birth in Revere to at least three pups during 2002 but was killed by a car later that summer. Her offspring stayed in the territory so that we regularly saw five full-sized coyotes that winter. This indicated that the pups probably remained with their father and either a new mate he found or a resident associate who remained on territory but whom we did not detect before Maple's death. We never did determine what happened to Scruffy, her former mate infected with mange.

We also deciphered diverse patterns of coyote behavior in very urban environments like north Boston, mainly, the mated breeding pair Maeve and Jet. This pair was tagged during spring/summer 2004 in Malden and Everett on the north edge of Boston. Both used a surprisingly small area consisting of roughly one square mile, concentrated around four abutting cemeteries. They raised four pups within this small range and made it through the winter of 2005 before being found poisoned shortly thereafter. Our tracking data indicated that this smaller area put them at less risk from cars, yet I suspect that had they not died, they eventually would have expanded their range to explore new areas.

For a mobile species like a coyote, one square mile is not a large area. As a famous Russian proverb says "A wolf is fed by its feet." I would like to add that this applies to all wild canids, but I would modify it slightly for coyotes, in that a coyote is fed by its feet, its adaptability, and its curiosity. Nevertheless, having other coyote groups nearby may have ultimately kept this particular group confined to this small range. Our late-night observations of Jet, who spent a significant amount of time in areas at the northern (railroad tracks) and southern (a large cemetery) part of his range, seems to indicate that he heavily marked his scent in those areas, no doubt to notify other trespassing coyotes that this turf was already claimed.

Transients

It is fairly straightforward to collar resident animals and guess how many live within a given area, but it is very difficult to obtain any concrete information on transient coyotes. Locating and tracking transients is expensive and time consuming, and I have to agree with such recognized experts as biologist Dave Mech, that they are the most difficult type of canid to obtain accurate data on. To catch and mark the pups, document when and from where they disperse, and ultimately determine where they end up is a formidable task. If the animal dies before breeding successfully, which has to be verified, then the biological life cycle data is not complete.

In our study, some transient coyotes roamed in relatively localized areas of 100 square miles, an area larger than most Massachusetts towns. Other individuals were difficult to ever find again, since some of them dispersed to locations far from Barnstable. However, some eventually returned to localized areas almost as if they were waiting for a territorial opening. Bob Crabtree in Montana calls these coyotes in Yellowstone 'solitary resident coyotes' because they do not actually disperse. Instead they appear to travel consistently throughout a sizeable range of their own, which overlaps the ranges of multiple resident packs. These individuals are likely looking for a vacant territory or breeding opportunity.

Glope was observed traveling in this manner during 2000–2001 before eventually narrowing his range to the Hyannisport area when he mated with Mizz. He traveled throughout the town of Barnstable but focused most of his movements in the Hyannisport area. We never documented what happened to Mizz's previous mate, but he might have been yet another casualty of the heavy Cape Cod traffic or hunting, or his position may have been aggressively taken over by Glope.

Normally, dispersing or transient coyotes make a beeline to a new location rather than taking the risk of floating in a large, but relatively localized area like Glope did. One young male coyote named Glif, was shot by a policeman in Chatham, halfway down the Cape, after being observed having seizures in a resident's backyard. We did not perform a necropsy on Glif so the cause of his seizures remains a mystery.

Another young adult named Fog dispersed over 60 straight-line miles through eastern Massachusetts, traveling from Revere south to Dartmouth. We think she possibly came from New Hampshire or Maine and we captured her as she was moving south. There is no doubt that her actual movement down to Dartmouth was not in a direct line as she would have had to dodge traffic at major interstates and secondary highways all along her southern sojourn.

Snour, another young male, wandered throughout the Cape and traveled 45 miles from West Barnstable to north Wellfleet on Cape Cod during a record snowfall of over three feet in February 2005. On his solitary travels, he may have trotted by Henry Beston's famous *Outermost House* in Eastham before getting shot by a hunter two weeks after I found him in Barnstable. He was nomadic, easily traveling the length of the entire Cape looking for a vacant territory until he made the mistake of investigating a predator call, which is a small device that simulates the squeal of an injured rabbit. No doubt he was hungry from the long winter and was simply following his predatory instincts. He paid the ultimate price.

Ironically, Snour was taken (legally as far as I could tell) on National Park Service lands. (Cape Cod National Seashore is one of the only national parks that allows hunting). I'm perplexed by how he managed to travel that far, given the deep snow, rugged conditions, and probable lack of food. His pointless death still bothers me.

Reasons for Killing Coyotes

Fur prices these days are low because many people no longer like the thought of killing an animal just to adorn themselves. Perhaps it is a sign that we are an upwardly mobile civilization that people have grown out of wearing dead animal skins. Most coyotes, therefore, are killed for sport. Hunters can use the fur, mount the bodies as a trophy, or more rarely, eat them. The men who killed Kett's long-time mate Gash, used a predator call to draw her within range in mid-February 2005 in southeast Falmouth, and then ate her at a game dinner.

I often wonder if these folks would do the same thing, given the chance, had they known how unique these individual study animals were and how much was known about them. I had the chance to speak with the hunters who killed Gash, and they actually appreciated coyotes, unlike others who simply gut-shoot them so that they die a long, slow death from multiple pellets lodged in their bodies.

These men were amazed to hear how large her pack's range was and that I had her mate, Kett, collared for six and a half years prior to Gash's death. They seemed to understand that coyote territoriality prevents many coyotes from living in a given area; however, the departing comment from one of the gentlemen really struck me: "Hopefully we will soon find out if Kett is still alive," meaning that if they could bag him in the next few days I would be getting another call to retrieve one more collar. Certainly he did not mean that as a personal attack on my work, unlike the *Woods and Waters* article, but nonetheless it gives credence to how wildlife, including study animals, can be exploited by nearly any human being who chooses to.

Releasing coyote Gash

While picking up Gash's collar (the men kept her carcass as their trophy) I couldn't help but wonder how Kett felt after suddenly losing his mate of five to six years, a very long time for a coyote to be paired. While some behaviorists think it is a taboo for other scientists to discuss animal feelings, I couldn't help it. I could feel Kett's sadness knowing that he would never be able to cruise through his range with her and have pups with his former (at least) seven-year-old mate. This

personalized nature of a study is never included as part of typical wildlife management programs when seasons are established on a species, especially a social
one like a coyote.

Navigating the Cape Cod Canal

Coyotes can cross seemingly disparate areas to reach new land. For example, a dispersing 42 lb. adult female coyote named Sog made it safely clear across
the Cape Cod Canal, but was hit by a car on Route 25 off-Cape in Bourne. She was
probably dispersing in a straight line and encountered the water. It seems unlikely
to me that a coyote would successfully cross the bridge, then get hit by a car on that
same stretch of road in a wooded area. (However, to contradict that statement, I
have received reports of coyotes crossing the canal both on foot over the bridge
and by swimming, so certainly both means of navigation are a distinct possibility.)
So here we assume that she swam across the canal and traveled a bit further before
being struck and killed as she tried to cross the highway barely two miles north of
the bridge.

The question is, what happens to the transient coyotes in a population?
Many are no doubt killed by people, whether with vehicles or guns, as evidenced
by the data in our study. Other coyotes likely become temporary or permanent
nomads, crisscrossing in and out of existing territories while searching for living
quarters, food sources, and mating opportunities. On Cape Cod, I surmise with
some certainty that individual transients repeatedly travel the length of the entire
peninsula. If a territory holder dies, then the territory falls to either a strong transient or a resident associate, which is a coyote that travels with the parents and is
probably one of their older offspring. This may entail being successful in obtaining a breeding position, most likely by coercing the deceased coyote's mate to
accept the new pair bond.

Dave Mech and Luigi Boitani, in their landmark edited book *Wolves:
Behavior, Ecology, and Conservation*, describe other ways that biologists have
documented how transient wolves successfully obtain a mate. These include:

1) Pairing during dispersal and traveling as a pair until they locate an
    available territory
2) Hanging around a local area until a breeding opportunity becomes
    available
3) Traveling a long distance to a new and previously unsettled area
    and pairing with an available mate
4) Claiming part of their parents' territory (called 'budding off') and
    attracting a mate by any of the scenarios just described

Many transients probably roam around in a saturated population where all
available territories are claimed, for a long time without finding a place to settle.
On the other hand, in an exploited population (subject to rampant hunting), the
opposite probably occurs, where transients can settle quickly in a territory because

of the high turnover associated with human-caused mortality. These nomads, whether they roam a relatively localized area (maybe 100 square miles) or travel in a straight line to maximize their distance from their natal range, can colonize new areas and also settle in formerly claimed territories where other coyotes have died.

It is very difficult to guess how many transients live in any area, partially because their long-distance movements make them so hard to monitor. One thing is certain regarding transients and reproduction; a heavily harvested coyote population can actually rebound to saturation level within a year or two due to normal reproduction and dispersal. In other words, killing coyotes might regionally, in Massachusetts for instance, reduce coyote numbers temporarily, but does little to ultimately limit coyotes in towns or other local areas. This is due to the way that the surviving coyotes fill in the newly available territories by either the resident coyotes expanding their ranges or, more likely, by transients claiming them. I will explore territoriality in more depth in Chapter 6.

The different coyote social classes mentioned in this chapter are not rigid; in fact, the opposite is actually the norm. During the course of a coyote's life, it may experience being in each of the social classes for some time period as it matures, locates a territory, and mates. A juvenile coyote may remain with its parents during its first winter, thus becoming a beta or associate as it delays dispersal in order to help raise its younger siblings (its parents' next litter of young). During its second fall, now fully mature, the coyote may disperse and become a transient until it finally finds a vacant territory perhaps a hundred miles away where it may settle to become a breeder or alpha coyote.

Chapter 5

Foraging Ecology and Competition

Foraging

The day of 28 July 1999 started out hot and muggy, typical of late summer on Cape Cod. It was already nearly 85° by 5:00 AM when I awoke to begin my day. At 5:40 AM I pulled into the Hyannis Watershed, a wooded area in the most urban part of Hyannis on Cape Cod.

I was on the trail of Mizz, the brown and white Holstein-looking coyote captured nearby at the Melody tent earlier in the year. The Melody tent is an odd location for capturing a coyote because it is an outdoor arena where the majority of the summer concerts take place on the Cape. Even though it is situated right in downtown Hyannis, a small strip of woods bordering these lands makes it a suitable place for coyotes to range.

Mizz had five pups in this watershed near a swamp, in the middle of this quarter-square-mile area. When I stopped my car in the gated driveway that led to the watershed, I realized that Mizz was very close to the road, closer than her wooded den site. The gate is so close to Straightway Road that I could barely get the tail end of my pickup off the main street to park.

As I turned off the ignition, I noticed a fat black cat barely 20 feet away near the roadway, all alone feeding on a mouse. Mizz's signal was very strong so I reached for my video camera and then took several quick paces away from my truck and quietly hid behind a five-foot telephone pole. I used the top of the pole as a makeshift tripod.

Just as I got set up, I noticed Mizz about 75 meters away, close to a water building. She casually trotted down the road toward the cat, which was unconcerned with anything but the rodent between its front paws. I must have hidden behind that skinny pole just in time because Mizz did not seem to notice me. She stopped short and stared at the cat from about 60 meters away. Then she proceeded to crouch down and approach the cat in a stalking position, similar to a lion ambushing prey in Africa.

Coyote Mizz stalking cat

She closed half the distance without the cat noticing while I was rolling the videocam and trying not to shake it during the excitement of the moment. This was the first time I was aware of anyone recording the interactions between a wild coyote and a domestic cat. Don't think me a monster, because I was totally unprepared to witness this drama. But after all, my job is to record what is actually happening with my study subjects and I would have done an injustice to science by intervening.

When Mizz was about 50 feet from the cat, I waited apprehensively for her to do the last part of the predatory sequence before the attempted kill—that is, the rush and chase. However, she continued stalking the cat, approaching to within 10–15 feet before stopping and simultaneously looking at me and the cat. Caught up in the moment she had failed to realize that a coyote's worst enemy, a human, was very close to the cat, who now had noticed Mizz and bristled itself up to twice its size. This cat obviously had no intention of giving up its mouse or its life without a fight!

After noticing me, Mizz looked once more at the cat, which by now appeared much larger, in defense posture, and not too far from me. Making a quality decision, Mizz abruptly turned and headed into the woods that bordered the entrance road. Before sighting the cat, Mizz was probably headed that way to bed down in one of her favorite spots, a thick tangle of vines bordering a small pond less than 100 feet from the main road.

The black cat, barely budging during the stalk and probably annoyed by that 'dog' interrupting its meal, assessed the situation and after strutting around bristled and stiff-legged for a moment or two, unexpectedly dove into the woods after Mizz! I returned to my car and waited for about 30 more minutes, but I neither heard nor observed anything further. The predator and the unknowing prey must be resting, and at that point I wasn't sure which was which.

Mizz trots away from cat

So don't believe everything you read about coyotes being responsible for cat predations. An average cat living in or near the middle of prime coyote country (Mizz's litter of pups was in that patch of woods) is certainly vulnerable to being preyed upon, especially when let out during crepuscular and nocturnal time periods to do its own hunting. Indeed, a couple of weeks later I saw fliers posted on telephone polls of a missing cat in that neighborhood. This filming however, underscores the importance of 'innocent until proven guilty'—that is, observing a coyote in the act of killing a cat.

I frequently show that remarkable video during the public seminars that I speak at, and without fail people come up afterward to ask me why I did not do anything to prevent that near attack. I explain that we are doing this study to investigate the effects of coyotes in urbanized areas, and we certainly learned something positive about coyote-cat interactions by observing this unstaged incident. I can't imagine that I would learn anything from attempting to stop a predatory attack and it would defeat my purpose for being there. Further, if Mizz were not collared for the purpose of tracking her movements, I absolutely never would have been in that place at that time.

Anyone seeing my film would agree that that cat intended to defend itself—and may very well have been capable of doing so. Nonetheless, responsible pet owners should themselves try to prevent such confrontations if they are concerned about the outcome for their domestic pets. An obviously simple way to avoid predations by coyotes is to keep pet animals inside, unless completely fenced in, or on a leash and attended to, especially at the times of day when coyotes are most active. It is my considered opinion that unless one lives near a coyote denning location there is a small chance that a cat would be killed if left out for one night, but because of the large ranges and impressive movement patterns that coyotes display on a nightly basis, it logically would be only a matter of time before coyotes came into contact with a nocturnal outdoor pet.

Another benefit to leaving domestic felines inside is because many authors, including Michael Woods in *Predation of Wildlife by Domestic Cats in Great Britain* and Martin Nogales in *A Review of Feral Cat Eradication on Islands*, have found that cats can have devastating effects on wildlife, even causing extinctions of species. Although cat-caused extinctions have only occurred on island settings where birds or rodents have not evolved with predators, the domestic feline can also cause chaos in more mainland settings by preying on literally millions of animals per country, especially songbirds. Cats often live at unnaturally high densities due to their association with people and should be considered 'part of the food chain' the moment their owner lets them outside unattended. For a domesticated species, cats sure are amazing predators!

Researchers, such as Kevin Crooks and Michael Soulé, have found that coyotes can actually increase the diversity of species living in an area because they decrease cat and other small predator abundance (weasels, foxes, fishers, etc.) through either direct predation, avoidance by the smaller carnivore, or because they provide a strong incentive for people to keep their cats inside. Small breeds of dogs that must go outside to do their business do not fall into the predator status like cats, but they are at risk in many suburban areas and need to be well watched when outdoors as well.

Food Habits

One of our findings regarding coyote food habits, through direct observation, radio-telemetry locations, and scat analyses, is that coyotes have a mostly natural diet even in urbanized areas. They mainly feed on rabbits, voles and other rodents, not pets. Other researchers, such as Stan Gehrt in the Chicago metropolitan area, have also discovered that coyotes mainly eat natural foods in urban settings. Their fondness for rodents is obvious as coyotes commonly enter traps to feed on road-killed squirrels and woodchucks.

Coyotes also eat just about anything people eat, as well as many things we do not. In addition to small prey, eastern coyotes have been known to take young ungulates in the early spring, or weak adults, in the same way that wolves hunt them. Adult deer, and certainly moose moving into suburban east coastal regions, are generally too large for even eastern coyotes, except after severe winters that

Coyote eating a rat

have caused the ungulates to become malnourished. Livestock however, especially sheep, chickens, and tame waterfowl may also be attacked, as well as small pets.

While they are classified as carnivores, coyotes are in practice omnivorous. These wild canines are important scavengers, eating all forms of carrion, as well as garbage, human food discards, and fruit and berries. Local droppings are often riddled with wild raspberry and blueberry seeds in mid-summer. Out west, in one Arizona study, 99% of the coyote scats collected during September contained prickly pear cactus fruit. In the southeast, farmers complain of coyotes eating too many of their watermelon!

One old coyote, Mole, appeared to have a football in her stomach when captured, as she had consumed two whole squirrels and a few pounds of meat scraps that we used baiting the trap. Mizz was recaptured on one occasion using a large road-killed woodchuck as bait. The prey item was so large, in fact, I was able to reuse it in a different trap after catching Mizz. While I have not observed coyotes capturing prey that often, I have often seen them with rabbits and groundhogs in their mouths.

In one such instance in July 1999, I was with three middle school students tracking Casper in Cummaquid. She was away from her pups when we drove up to her strong signal at a dead-end road by two houses. No sooner had I turned my car off, than Casper trotted by about 50 feet away with something in her mouth. Excitement turned to frustration as one of the children with me yelled through the rolled-down window, "There she is!" Casper immediately turned around and bolted into the woods with her prize in her mouth. At first I thought it was one of her pups, but upon reflecting how dark the large critter was, I realized it was a woodchuck that she was carrying back to her pups over a mile away.

We usually discover what coyotes have eaten by gathering samples of their scats, a term used for their excrement or waste droppings. Lab results show that other animals besides rodents and rabbits, like deer for instance, are consumed where available. We hope to eventually institute a sorely needed coyote-deer study on the Cape and/or in the Boston area at some time in the future. It would likely be the first of its kind in an urbanized area, and would provide some important data in these days of increasing wildlife populations in urban centers.

We know that deer often live at very high densities in suburban areas (although not yet on the Cape) and coyotes might be a good source of control for deer numbers, at least to ensure maintaining them at habitat-carrying capacity. In most areas that do not experience heavy snowfalls, deer can live at high concentrations amid healthy coyote populations. A coyote pack is generally no match for a healthy deer, which can be quite dangerous to a coyote. In fact, many wolf researchers like Dave Mech, Rolf Peterson, and Doug Smith even find some of their study subjects dead, having been trampled or kicked to death by ungulate prey (deer, elk, and moose).

It has been a long time since the bulk of the American population lived off the land, so we have lost our natural wisdom about how wildlife lives. Because we are most familiar with the hunting concepts of human beings, some people today believe that wild canids also kill for the fun of it and do not consume all of the prey that they kill, especially when they may kill more than one animal at a time.

Scientists call this 'surplus killing'. It often happens with livestock, especially sheep, who have lost their ability to act in self-defense through domestication. Occasionally, multiple wild ungulates such as deer can be killed at once in deep snow conditions that renders them incapable of flight or defensive action. But it is highly likely that coyotes would not leave a good meal behind, and would continue to visit the carcasses and consume them until they were gone.

Roger Peters, studying wolves in Minnesota, demonstrated that the coyote's larger cousin has a well-developed cognitive map which helps individual wolves maintain their sense of direction and find their way throughout their large hundred-plus-square-mile ranges. Thus it is foolish to think that they or other wild canids which normally eat both fresh kills and carrion, would kill for fun and ignore the protein packed, nutrient-rich carcasses that lie within their territories.

If they are left, it is more likely that people or other large predators disturbed them at a kill and they returned later, even days afterwards, to finish it. I have documented this at Sandy Neck Beach on Cape Cod where hunter shot-deer have been left behind. Once coyotes discover these all you-can-eat buffets, they repeatedly return to devour them even up to a month or two later, until only bone and fur remain. This is their job and they take it very seriously, removing carrion and rotting carcasses from the landscape that might otherwise cause disease in ecological settings that could impact both wild creatures and humans.

Coyotes have been known to feed on garbage like raccoons do, but only rarely. One time I witnessed this in a low-income area in Mashpee. The neighborhood had trash overflowing the limited number of dumpsters in an apartment complex. I watched as Kett dragged a full trash bag across a neighborhood road into someone's front yard at about 1:00 AM. The dragging noise scared him every time he moved it, so he repeatedly dropped it.

Each time he bravely went back and picked it up again until he finally got it completely across the road where he proceeded to rip open the bag and tear apart diapers, crunch down chicken bones, and shred plastic items. While I had my binoculars trained on Kett that night, I remember thinking that the residents who observed the mess the next morning probably blamed raccoons or the neighbors' dogs for it.

Besides such food items described above, coyotes may also become adept, and even specialize at, catching other animals like cats, especially where locally abundant. Coyotes are intelligent creatures and if they could make the connection that preying on pets cause them to run afoul of humans with deadly consequences, they might even learn to avoid them. But since both cats and coyotes are often nocturnal and there are rarely humans about when cats are left out at night, it's hard for that connection to be reinforced.

From a wild coyote's perspective, those animals we consider to be our pets, mainly cats, if left outside to roam around, appear as feral animals who are part of the food chain and thus, fair game. Cats are not the world's easiest prey, since they have the potential to bite, claw, and fight back when being attacked. From a loose pet's point of view, coyotes are yet another risk in their outdoor world, as well as cars and a whole slew of other predators. I often try to explain when I give seminars, that it is neither animal's fault when a cat gets into a tango with a coyote, but rather the pet owner who chose to let it outside in the first place.

My coyote tracking has enabled me, in a number of instances, to observe coyotes trotting in a zig-zag fashion through neighborhoods. While it might have been for other reasons such as dog-avoidance, I could only guess that they were "cat-ing" or looking for any stray *Felis catus*. This hunting technique appears different than the typical "mousing" method of jumping high in the air and pouncing downward on an unsuspecting rodent. Since I have actually never witnessed a successful coyote attack on a cat, but assume they likely do occur, I will plead the fifth and not name which individual coyote(s) I have observed exhibiting this behavior

Interspecies Competition

One thing that wild dogs commonly do not eat is each other; i.e., other canids. In areas where wolves rule the land, they often kill each other and coyotes in territorial conflicts. However, it is virtually unknown for them to eat their competition.

Similarly, coyotes tend to dominate foxes, yet have not been known to eat any that they kill. In rural locations, research has discovered that coyotes lower the abundance of foxes in a given area. No research has been conducted in an urbanized area to see if the same principles of land ownership and interspecies aggression hold true.

For instance, foxes might be able to live in neighborhoods, especially at the edge of established coyote territories, as well as other areas where coyotes spend less time. Foxes can hide close to houses and den under human structures, something most coyotes avoid. It is possible that the more stable the coyote packs (when people are not killing the breeding coyotes) the more likely it would be for foxes to establish relatively secure territories. However, there might also be coyote groups, particularly well-fed ones, who do not mind the presence of foxes as long as they do not forage too close to them. This is known in the biological world as interspecific tolerance or indifference.

In addition to studying deer-coyote interactions, investigating how small wild canids such as foxes manage to survive in the presence of coyotes is a very intriguing question. Our research to date has focused on an in-depth study of coyote ecology and behavior, but we hope to expand this to study how coyotes interact with other canine species.

Some researchers believe that gray foxes, who climb trees, are more abundant around coyotes because they can avoid them. These types of community-level interactions are important to address and poorly, if at all, understood in urbanized areas. Only long-term research studies can paint a picture of the delicate and complicated web of interactions here.

Possible Fox Study

I became interested in foxes early in the coyote study, as I commonly sighted them on the Cape at night. In 1999 I managed to capture a number of red foxes there during summer months. Because we were curious how foxes survived among coyote territories, my colleagues and I requested a permit for collaring foxes, in addition to the permit that we had for studying coyotes.

After submitting a proposal and laboriously reworking it through two revisions and numerous delays, the Massachusetts Division of Fisheries and Wildlife (MDF&W) rejected our request. They claimed the rejection was because that was not part of my graduate study, in spite of the fact that my advisors, the faculty who determined my course of study, disagreed. And we all wondered then why the MDF&W required us to go through multiple drafts of our proposal request.

My study team and I believed that if enough foxes were collared, then I might secure a doctoral project immediately following the completion of my Master's degree. To this end, I kept several traps unarmed and waiting for what turned out to be a pre-determined rejection. Nonetheless, I still feel that a multi-species canid study in an urban ecosystem is a vital project and would certainly give us a better understanding of how coyotes affect closely related species.

So as it stands now, even though a permit for us to study fox behavior and interactions was denied by the MDF&W overseeing authority, they still freely authorize a four-month canid hunting season in Massachusetts every November, and anyone may buy a $30 hunting license to kill unlimited numbers of them.

Red fox in a box-trap

Dogs and Coyotes

Domestic dogs also sometimes come in contact with coyotes. Although we think of dogs as domestic house pets, it is most likely that coyotes view them as another canine threat much as they would wolves. Thus, if coyotes were to kill a dog, it would not be for food. They don't eat their adversaries.

Understandably, people are disturbed when coyotes attack or kill dogs, but the coyotes probably see most dogs as serious competition, especially average-sized versions. A larger dog might resemble a wolf to a coyote, and is usually left alone because of the obvious risk of confronting a larger adversary. Most wild animals, given the opportunity, will try to avoid any confrontations that are not directly motivated by protecting their young or mate, their food, or themselves; and coyotes are no exception. Much like our storybook heroes, they live by the old saying "He who runs away lives to fight another day."

Possibly due to the subliminal propaganda of cartoons and misinformation in nature shows, there is a general conception of coyotes as cowards because they generally avoid such confrontations. This behavior, however, is indeed wily, because one such interaction could result in a fatal or otherwise serious injury to a coyote whose continued existence depends on their peak health to catch prey.

This avoidance is also fortunate for pet owners, considering that coyotes are generally well-muscled and likely better practiced at canine sparring from pack living, so even a brief 'dog fight' with a domestic opponent could cause severe injuries to almost any size dog. Coyotes live nearly everywhere in the country now, and with the large and growing domestic dog population it is amazing how relatively few coyote-dog interactions there actually are. However, every spring there are a number of confrontations where dogs are chased away or attacked by coyotes. Almost without fail, these incidents occur near where coyotes are protecting their young-of-the-year.

Coyote and dog interacting in Marstons Mills

The interaction between domestic dogs and coyotes is not one-way. Dogs probably also see coyotes as either competition or a threat. I inadvertently gained some humorous first-hand experience of this over the past few years. From 2002–2005 I suspect I often smelled like a coyote, living with the captive coyotes during that time and often handling the wild ones. A dog's keen sense of smell could no doubt detect their wild brethren's scent on me even after I had showered and washed my clothes, as evidenced by quite a few dogs who have been completely terrified of me.

A friend of my sister and brother in-law owned a Rottweiler who was supposedly amiable with everyone, but this dog visibly shook in my presence. We could only surmise that she smelled the coyotes on me and either may have previously had a bad experience with one, or simply abhorred their 'wild odor'.

Another dog, a golden retriever named Cassie, hid from me when I approached her, while her brother loved me and always sought my attention. Eric Strauss, the dog's owner, explained that Cassie was once attacked and pinned by two coyotes while on a spring hike. While Eric could not figure out why the coyotes did not kill her, Cassie certainly did not forget the experience and I was not a pleasant reminder whenever I visited them.

Hunting and Eating

Individual variation in canid behavior is another factor to consider when dealing with any type of social animal. While some dogs were terrified of me, others could care less about my coyote-scented clothes. Likewise, some coyotes seem to specialize in a particular prey item while others eat a variety of food. This can be due to dramatic differences in hunting ability.

For instance, while all of the captive coyotes at the Stone Zoo were good hunters and regularly attempted to make kills, one of the females, Cane, was by far the most polished of the pack. She would often sit on my lap and greet me in a docile manner as if she did not have a care in the world. However, the moment she spotted potential prey in the exhibit she became extremely alert and went into stalking mode.

About twice a week she would catch something, normally a bird, by sneaking around the sparsely vegetated exhibit area and springing or darting at her unexpecting prey. Then she would trot around the enclosure carrying her prize in her mouth. The other coyotes followed and instantly pounced on the prey for their own games once Cane was done with her sniffing and chewing. For some reason the captive coyotes hardly ever ate the items that they captured. They preferred to eat their usual food items consisting of frozen mice and rats, or the dog chow that we normally fed them.

Coyotes are possibly one of the most adaptable of all animals and probably the most adaptable North American canine, as evidenced by their colonization of all of New England in about 50 years. However, they probably do not eat absolutely anything, as many sources like Frank Dobie's classic *Voice of the Coyote* claim. While they may try every food available to them at one point or another, many other animals also do that. For example, deer have been observed eating fish on beaches, but we do not call deer piscivores on this account; instead they are classified strictly as herbivores or plant eaters.

There have been many times when I have put out road-killed raccoons and possums near, but outside, a trap in an attempt to entice coyotes to come into the area. Often those items dry up and are "maggotized" (devoured by maggots), without even being touched by the coyotes. In other instances, such items (especially raccoons) were taken the first night that they were put out.

At one rendezvous site I had the occasion to watch coyotes feed on what looked like a freshly road-killed raccoon. It was not far from a stretch of road where they were frequently killed by passing vehicles. Through my spotting scope, I watched as an adult fed on the raccoon and a pup tried to drag away the carcass, which weighed about as much as the youngster did. Just like humans, there is individual variation in a coyote's dietary preference, with their hunger level playing an important role in what and when they eat.

Coyote Sill carrying a squirrel while a helper coyote
for his father Kett in Mashpee, MA

Chapter 6

Territoriality

Where Did They Go?

My journal entry read:

June 1998. Marstons Mills, Massachusetts. This month, I captured my first three coyotes on Cape Cod. Two of them are male sibling pups and we have radio-implanted them with finger-size transmitters; the other one is Snix, an adult female, from nearby Sandy Neck Beach. The pups, Pon and Poo, are part of a litter of five and judging from sightings of adults coming and going to feed them, there are at least two adults raising them, with probably one or two more whom I have not observed yet.

In early to mid-June these coyotes were located in the southern part of a large swampy conservation area bordering a residential neighborhood. During that time, neighbors from this vicinity commonly reported to me that 'coyotes were everywhere' and that they heard them howling, sometimes multiple times, nearly every night.

After capturing and subsequently releasing Pon, I tracked him day and night for the first few weeks so I could vouch for the neighborhood's claims. Indeed, the coyotes were very prevalent around that area. Unfortunately, during one of the days tracking Pon, I intruded too close to the pack. The parents most likely were not used to human scent in the immediate vicinity of their wooded den site by an old overgrown cranberry bog. Within a couple of days the adults moved the pups to a new location.

Coyote pack howling

The new puppy daycare area was a large cranberry bog complex near my parents' house that eventually became a benchmark location for the coyote study, as this site has now been used for puppy rearing for at least 10 years in a row (1997 to 2006). Frustrated that I had caused that coyote family to move its base of operations, I quickly improved my operation by not being so "sloppy" when I tracked. I thereafter made a very concerted effort to avoid displacing family groups by respecting them and keeping a reasonable distance from their den and rendezvous sites.

Being a novice at tracking coyotes at the time, it took me a day and a half to verify that the coyotes at the cranberry bog were the same ones I spooked from the conservation area. I found the pack again at the bog site by pure dumb luck as a friend of mine, Ron Tauro, and I were driving less than a mile from my parents' house. He was totally perplexed when I yelled "Holy cow, there they are! An adult and five pups—over on that large sandhill!" My foot abruptly landed on his as I jammed on his brakes (it's fortunate we are good friends!), and I directed my shaken driver safely over to the shoulder of the road so I could conduct my observations.

I never thought that I could have been looking at Pon because the two sites in question are over two miles and many neighborhoods apart. I was pretty sure that the pups were simply not able to move quite that distance yet, even led by an adult. I had searched unsuccessfully all around the original rendezvous site for a few hours, and finally went home discouraged. It was then that I made an Einsteinian decision—"Gee dummy, why don't you go back to the cranberry bog rendezvous site and see if you receive Pon's signal."

Sure enough, when we got into the area, I dialed his frequency and instantly detected his strong signal. Two days after confirming their move to the cranberry bog complex on 15 June 1998, I captured Poo, Pon's 15-lb brother, at that location and then followed them both for the rest of the summer.

Residents around this new site reported to me that they were hearing howling all the time and that the "coyotes were everywhere." Knowing that it had to be the same group that had been at the previous neighborhood, I returned to the old area and asked some of the people I had spoken with if they had heard the coyotes recently. They responded with a resounding, "No, we haven't heard them in nearly a week now." I was able to explain to them that the coyote group had moved to a new rendezvous site a couple of miles away and they nodded their heads, understanding why the howls had subsided.

After a few weeks, the pups were moved to two additional sites, the furthest one nearly three miles from the bog complex and even farther from the original wooded rendezvous site. Thanks to the ability to track Pon and Poo via the implants, I discovered that residents in vastly different parts of the village of Marstons Mills were apparently hearing these same coyotes. Every night that I documented the pups at a given locale, a resident would report to me that they had heard howling the previous evening. Apparently, this group enjoyed howling more than most, which made it easy for the local residents to know their whereabouts.

Most of these observations, remarkably, were of the same litter of young pups moving around in an area of about five square miles, which is not even that big for a coyote family. I eventually discovered that this preliminary data on pup activity was just a prelude for what would come, along with some impressive adult coyote movement patterns we recorded that will be presented in the next few chapters.

The Value of Data Gathering

The data obtained on this first radio-monitored pack that we studied provided an important find. Early on I had suspected that there were not that many coyotes living in any specific area despite most neighborhood concerns that we were being overrun by them and the numerous newspaper reports touting the 'growing coyote population'. The published literature indicates that coyotes are territorial, meaning that they have specific territories that they consider to be their home range and that they guard from other coyotes. But the question we had was, would they behave territorially in a suburban area?

This initial data I just cited supported the fact that a family group of coyotes could be observed in relatively disparate locations in a given area, sometimes during the course of one night. What I needed next were more coyotes from surrounding home ranges to make a case for territoriality in urbanized coyotes.

After a few more years of field research following that June 1998 story, including catching more coyotes and intensively radio-tracking them, I was able to learn some interesting facets about coyote behavior. Some researchers had speculated that in an urban landscape with good food resources, coyotes might abandon territorial behavior to freely intermingle with other coyotes. We collected convincing evidence that this was not so; and in general, a coyote pack excluded other coyote groups from an area of approximately 11 square miles on Cape Cod, through means such as howling, scent marking, and direct encounters.

Indeed, one thing that our research has demonstrated is that coyotes are definitely territorial even in suburban areas with a good food supply of both natural and anthropogenic foods. An important finding from our study, consistent with the literature describing coyote natural history in various areas of their North American range, is that radio-collared coyotes avoid areas used by collared resident coyotes living in adjacent areas. This categorically documented territoriality in an urbanized landscape.

Repeated Contact and Observations

Although we have had a relatively low sample size of radio-tagged coyotes per unit of time (for example, it took us six years to catch our first 25 coyotes on Cape Cod), we did manage to locate each coyote an average of over 400 times. A couple of the collared adults were located more than 1,000 times each.

The large amount of data recovered per animal has given us a good perspective on how individual coyotes move through a fragmented and human dominated landscape. During some of these spot fixes, I have witnessed transient coyotes chased out of a resident coyote pack's territory, usually by the breeding male of the local group.

One of these encounters I observed involved Mizz's group of at least three adults on the Hyannisport Golf Course on a cold February day in 2000. I witnessed her probable mate (uncollared) take chase after Glope, a collared transient at the time. He was obviously attempting to drive Glope off that golf course which was in the core part of their territory.

Glope, who was on the same golf course during the initial sighting of Mizz's group, immediately chased and pinned one of the other coyotes from her group. We surmised that the pinned coyote was a female whom Glope was attempting to mate with. When the pinned coyote made a loud whining sound, Mizz and the uncollared second coyote—assumed to be the breeding male—ran to her aid. The assumed breeding male chased Glope for greater than a kilometer. Afterward, Glope left the golf course and crossed a major road during broad daylight at 8:30 AM to get away from him.

The next day, Glope was again located at the edge of Mizz's home range, and was sighted three days later and appeared to be uninjured. A few months later (upon my return from my seven-month stint at the Bronx Zoo), we discovered that Glope had somehow taken over as the breeding male of that group. We don't know what happened to Mizz's previous mate. He may have died or Glope forcefully evicted him. In either circumstance, it's apparent that Glope's persistence paid off.

In another instance, at midnight on a frigid winter night in 1999, I watched Casper and Sly and at least one other coyote approach a pond where there was a collared coyote from another pack. Snix (one of our collared coyotes) and her companion were milling about near the edge of the pond by Route 6A, a historic road in Barnstable Village.

These three animals I've named were all well-known to me because they were some of the first coyotes that we collared in our study, and they have all provided us with a wealth of knowledge about coyotes on the Cape. All were dominant breeders in their respective territories, making them locally important coyotes. Snix, a female, was our first adult coyote capture. Casper was the very large female captured in Cummaquid, while Sly, a male, was captured as a yearling in Centerville, and eventually dispersed five miles to the east to pair with Casper.

I observed the mated pair Casper and Sly at the west edge of their territory centered in and around the village of Cummaquid in Barnstable, while Snix's group, which frequented the Sandy Neck region of West Barnstable, was trespassing about three miles outside their normal range. The area by Hinkley's Pond was a sort of no-man's land between two known coyote territories (and may have been on the radar of one of the two groups to appropriate it), but it was closer to the edge of Casper and Sly's.

Casper and Sly's group was traveling that night along the edge of Hyannis, starting about four miles away and on the south side of Route 6, the only major highway bisecting the study area. Within 30 minutes they had crossed the highway and traveled directly to the pond. They appeared to be on a territorial patrol and were probably pausing for a drink on the way. Moments after seeing Casper's pack cross the main road to go toward the pond, I observed Snix escaping alone along the edge of a lighted part of that street. She quickly fled toward the nearby railroad tracks and hightailed it back in the direction of her own territory.

Patrolling coyotes in a neighborhood in Marstons Mills

Fifty minutes later I saw her again, back in her normal home range with a second coyote, approximately seven kilometers from her close encounter with Casper and Sly. I surmise that the two groups randomly stumbled upon each other and Snix et al., realizing their mistake of trespassing, wanted nothing to do with the other pack.

In addition to such direct encounters, I have seen alpha coyotes double-scent-marking strategic locations within territories. Double-scent-marking is done by a mated pair and it solidifies the pair bond while also passively defending their territory. Places marked with urine are probably areas that:

1)   have a greater chance of advertisement where other coyotes are most likely to travel through, and
2)   are prominent places such as golf courses, elevated areas, and power lines, among others.

I once watched Casper, Sly, and a third coyote, scent-marking on the Hyannis Golf Course off Route 132 on a snowy January night. With the snow helping illuminate my view, I watched the third coyote mark a shrub through my binoculars. It was likely a resident associate because Sly, immediately noticing the action (it was probably one of his offspring), ran to the spot, sniffed it, then raise-leg urinated over the spot, and finished with intense rear-leg ground scratching of the area. They all then went on their way at a brisk trot, no doubt on a territorial boundary patrol.

Coyote territories are not bounded by iron walls and many young coyotes will disperse through or along the edges of these territories. Most will move on when they encounter the presence of a resident group. John Theberge, in his book *Wolf Country*, describes nomad wolves as having a "free pass" because resident wolves do not seem to threaten them. When there is a direct threat to their territory from another pack, however, those same resident packs might fight to the death, especially with the dominant members of a bordering group.

Transient canids probably act submissively in the presence of residents and spend little time in a given occupied home range, making it easier to avoid death from the fangs of over wolves. I even suspect that some of these nomad coyotes, like Glope was during the summer of 2000, are active during the day to avoid resident coyotes.

Some nomadic coyotes may purposely linger in an area in order to try and lure a mate from a given territory (for example, a helper or beta from a neighboring territory), just as Glope appeared to be doing in Hyannisport during late-winter 2000. These individuals may stay nearby if an opposite-sex member of a resident pack shows interest in them. Alternatively, they may move on if unsuccessful and travel until they find a suitable area without a resident pack.

The journeys of transients can potentially lead them hundreds of miles from their place of birth. Life is certainly easier if a young coyote colonizes a new area that has many vacant territories. It is much more difficult to find and establish a home range in an area with a saturated population, which is currently the case for coyotes in much of North America. This applies everywhere except in places where coyotes are heavily hunted because territories in those regions are commonly left temporarily vacant because of human killing.

Dispersing to new areas is precisely how coyotes have colonized new territory over the past 100 years, including Cape Cod and the Northeast. If a territory is vacant (that is, not actively defended by resident coyotes), dispersing coyotes can quickly move into it within days. Because so many transient coyotes are waiting in the wings to colonize vacant areas, it is fruitless to kill coyotes in a specific area simply to get rid of them. It may however, sometimes be necessary to kill specific problem-causing coyotes if they threaten human safety or create problems for other wildlife populations.

'Problem-causing' is a subjectively-defined term varying with the specific situation and people involved. In my perspective, the only problem coyote would be one who was rabid, or for some other reason was threatening and/or attacking people. Aside from these extreme situations, I feel that our studies have shown how easy it is to avoid unnecessary encounters with them. After all, I outweigh an average coyote by a little more than four times, making me question whether a non-rabid coyote would ever pose much of a threat to a half-capable human. Obvious things like leaving pets and food/trash inside can further alleviate any potential coyote-human encounters. Removing coyotes that are actually causing problems, such as stalking people, would not leave an area "coyote-free" for very long, but it would open up that territory for non-problem coyotes to settle into.

Killing Coyotes Increases Their Numbers

Coyote territories appear to be relatively stable on Cape Cod, as we have documented a high survival rate of many radio-collared adults. Tradition can regulate their numbers as other coyotes may learn to avoid certain areas that are habitually used by specific packs. However, in one instance, the death of a resident mated pair (Skunks and Jog, who were both killed by cars in separate accidents), caused an influx of transient coyotes into their original area that completely changed the canine socio-ecology of the area.

Carm was a 35-lb young male, probably a pup of Skunks and Jog, who was captured before his first birthday off territory in Cummaquid. He regularly traveled with Jog throughout the original territory in Centerville and West Barnstable before Jog's demise. Within two months of Jog's accident, Carm, now alone, was only using the northern part of the territory. Cake, a young female coyote collared nearby, immediately claimed the southern half.

Cake got her name because she came awake at the animal clinic while being handled. Dr. Larry Venezia was low on Telazol®, the usual narcotic that we use to sedate animals, so we used an alternative drug. Since our goal was to simply get a collar on the small 30-lb female, we used half of the recommended dosage. Twenty minutes into the checkup she came awake. With collar safely secured and enough blood and measurements taken, I bear-hugged her and quickly walked her outside to my car to safely place her back inside her carrying cage.

Normal release time for a coyote following such an exam is four to six hours, but Cake was ready to go only two hours later.

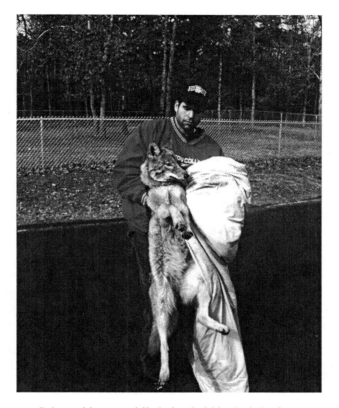

Cake waking up while being held by Rob Proietto

Both Cake and Carm became breeding members of their respective packs for at least two years. Winter pack sizes in both groups consistently numbered three to four members, which is average for the region. Thus, a year after the deaths of the original territory holders, two family groups—twice as many coyotes—inhabited this area. Monitoring of both groups ended in early 2005 when two events occurred:

1) The batteries in Cake's old collar died, and
2) Carm and his probable mate were shot by a hunter on 28 February, the last day of the 2005 Massachusetts coyote-hunting season.

Both coyotes were called in to the hunter's range with a predator call. Carm's mate was following her instincts to search for prey, while Carm was probably instinctively trailing his recently-impregnated mate. Both paid for their actions with their lives. Two days later, I retrieved Carm's collar.

Without a collared coyote in the group, contact with them abruptly ended. It is highly probable that within a few weeks new coyotes colonized the area. However, these new animals wore no radio-collars, and my motivation to spend several more months to collar a new animal had ended. On a happier note, we caught and re-collared Cake on 7 May 2006. She was healthy (37-lb), clearly middle-aged (worn teeth), and lactating.

As the previous anecdote demonstrates, coyote numbers can often increase following the death of a breeder or breeding pair. Bob Crabtree first formulated this theory from his research on coyotes out west. The logic behind this is that older, well-established coyotes guard large areas from other coyote packs. Young coyotes find out rather quickly through scent-marking, or lack thereof, and howling from other coyotes, if there is a vacant home range.

Because competition is intense for new territory, the new groups settle for part of a given territory, as their ultimate goal is to quickly establish a home range of their own in order to breed and establish a family group. If resources are plentiful in an area, new coyote families might be able to survive in a smaller range. As in the case of Skunks and Jog, the original pack territory was about eight square miles and each new pack claimed half and remained in their respective smaller areas of about four and a half square miles rather than risk fighting for the entire area. I am convinced, from my years of research, that coyote numbers would actually remain at lower densities in localized areas if these old alpha coyotes were not removed from the population in mankind's mistaken attempts to 'control their numbers'.

Usurping a Territory

The young female, Cake, that claimed the second portion of the larger territory, may have been a disperser from a nearby area. Another way that a dispersing transient acquires a territory is to simply wrest it from a resident breeder. In fact, in undisturbed populations, researchers such as Dave Mech have discovered that the primary cause of death in wolves is getting killed by other packs. While difficult to document, because both the breeding animal and the incoming transient need to be radio-collared and tracked simultaneously during these events, it is assumed that many coyotes may lose their territories in a similar way.

For unknown reasons, and unlike wolves, it is thought rare for coyotes to fight to the death over territorial issues. This is unconfirmed because there are few published references that describe such fatal encounters. We hope to uncover a more definitive answer to this question and others posed by the relatively high population density of coyotes in our study area.

I suspect that two of our collared coyotes were displaced via this non-lethal but aggressive method of territorial ownership change. One was the case of the breeding female Mizz whose story is described in the previous chapter. We believe that it was one of Mizz's own female offspring that, at about two years old, had become dominant in the pack and mated with the breeding male, Glope during the summer of 2001. This dark brown female possibly evicted Mizz in the latter part of the summer. Mizz seemed to be submissive around her when sighted at night, and her nomadic movements (which ceased when she was shot by a landowner during fall 2002) seemed indicative of this.

The second instance was Casper, the dominant female of the Cummaquid pack for at least six years. She was collared for nearly the entire time, a long tenure for any coyote, let alone in an urban landscape filled with people. This older female started behaving in a bizarre manner in early January 2005, when I began finding her bedded under houses at the very southeast part of her range. It is very uncharacteristic behavior for a coyote to do more than even briefly visit human habitations while hunting. Yet she repeatedly rested in such places, moving from under residential decks to sheds, finding a new location almost every night. Surprisingly, landowners never noticed her in these locations, probably because she wisely chose unoccupied seasonal houses, showing an impressive knack for avoiding people.

I initially assumed she was sick and desperate to find shelter from the elements, including some major snowstorms during the Cape's record year of snowfall. It later became more probable that she was avoiding interaction with other coyotes. Casper was now at least nine years old, had most likely lost her place to a more vigorous female coyote, possibly one of her offspring, and might have been shell-shocked from the whole ordeal.

A wound on her left flank and a reluctance to move suggested an injury, possibly a bite-wound. And a few days before I documented her off-territory, I journaled a sighting of two other coyotes vigorously scent-marking and ground-scratching sandpits in the southwest part of her former range. All of these events provided some evidence to support the theory that the new coyotes had forcefully evicted her (subsequent observations indicate that these coyotes may have been Raider and associates from nearby Hyannis). Alternatively, there is the possibility that she voluntarily vacated her alpha status after many tough years 'on the job'.

Following a major blizzard where three feet of snow fell in mid-January 2005, I could not pick up Casper's radio-signal until 11 March 2005 when I relocated her in the northeastern part of her old range. To find her, I went on a laborious three-hour round trip search that took me all the way to Provincetown and back. After all that driving, and as I was preparing to accept that she was out of range, I finally detected the first faint beeps emanating from her collar back in at the northeast edge of her old range. She remained there for over a year using a very small area of about one square mile.

Casper somehow survived that harsh winter, possibly because:

1) she may have been living off some source of human-generated food (possibly being fed)
2) she lived in a productive salt marsh that was home to a lot of her natural prey
3) she was a very elusive coyote who determinedly stayed out of people's way.

Casper under shed

Most displaced coyotes are not as lucky as Casper and normally do not survive long after losing a territory. Death often comes quickly by any number of means, usually eventful interactions with humans from firearms to automobiles. Casper managed to survive the following winter (2005/2006) in her new range and I frequently observed her with a second coyote, usually at night.

It was not until mid-February 2006 when I was able to observe her during the day with another coyote. To my bewilderment, she was traveling during the day through neighborhoods at the northeast edge of Yarmouth, near the town of Dennis. I usually missed seeing the 'ghost' as I would turn my car off on a given street to avoid disturbing her, and she would usually cross behind a house just out of my field of view. But after the third brief sighting, I struck gold around the next bend in the road.

Hoping to spot her, I had parked and turned my car off just in time to videotape her and her *collared* companion from 50 feet away! "By golly," I said under my breath, "That is Sly." I hadn't known his whereabouts for nearly five years. The fact that her old mate was not only alive but was in Casper's new territory and possibly traveling with her, was significant, as both coyotes may have been displaced from their original territory the year before.

If my suspicions were correct about what had occurred, it would be the first instance of a biologist documenting the behavior of older coyotes after their losing or relinquishing their territory due to aging issues and an inability to defend their range. Most often, since ecology studies are usually geographically-based (e.g., a set study area), if an older coyote or other individual of a species is displaced by new or younger ones, the study goes on researching the replacement animals because the older ones have been killed or chased off and never seen again. Of course, comprehensive results including data on the displaced animals are only possible to obtain during long-term studies, a rarity considering that most studies are funded only for the short-term (two to three years).

After seeing Casper with Sly a couple days in a row, I made a sighting of the two with a very large third coyote on 27 February 2006. They were bedded at the edge of a small pond and immediately behind a house situated on a dead-end street. I walked into a lady's yard to get what I thought was a signal from across the pond. But as I went to take the signal, all three got up and trotted off.

Sly went west and was followed by Casper. The third coyote looked around then ran off in the opposite direction to the northeast. This gray coyote stood even taller than Casper, who, being the heaviest female coyote yet recorded, was big in her own right. I haven't yet identified the sex of that coyote but the next day Casper abruptly abandoned that area and started frequenting the eastern half of the town of Yarmouth on both sides of Route 6.

Until June 2006 Casper survived by traveling in and out of an urban gauntlet of houses and roads, mostly in West Yarmouth around Route 28. Then she abruptly vanished. A recently-collared lanky 36.1-lb young male coyote, Squid, was hanging out near Casper's new range. While I never documented the two together during summer 2006, it was strange that I could not pick up either of their signals anywhere in Yarmouth or Barnstable after being away for a week. I returned on 29 June from nine days in Yellowstone National Park. Although I don't know if they went together, I surmise that they both traveled east from Yarmouth, out of our radio-reception range. (Subsequent tracking indicated that Casper became a transient coyote using at least all of the mid-Cape area). Casper's amazing ability to survive inspired me to write a special tribute to her in Appendix 10.

The anecdotes in this chapter demonstrate why coyotes do not become overabundant in an area. We have clearly documented that territorialism prevents transient or associate coyotes from establishing themselves in a place where resident coyotes already exist, unless they forcefully evict the territory-holder. The general public seems to believe that coyote numbers are always increasing, like deer unsubjected to predation or human hunting.

Deer can become overabundant in productive areas, from 50–100 per square mile, for two reasons:

1) they are herbivores and always live at higher densities than their predators, and
2) except in localized areas where does give birth or near clustered food sources, deer are not territorial, readily sharing space with other deer.

Humans, unaware of biological research data, incorrectly equate the population characteristics of ungulates to approximate those of predator species. This could not be further from the truth. As the story of Carm and Cake illustrates, the death(s) of resident coyotes can actually increase local coyote numbers. Without a doubt, future long-term research is needed to accurately document the impact of coyote territorialism on population figures over time, but we strongly believe that coyote population density would be naturally self-limiting, as it is in any balanced ecosystem, without interference from man either feeding or hunting them.

Chapter 7

Social and Denning Ecology

Running, Climbing and Watching

West Barnstable, Massachusetts. 08 June 1994. After an afternoon of radio-tracking deer on Sandy Neck Beach I took a break for a five to six mile training run. I was 19 years old and ran track and cross-country at the University of Massachusetts at Amherst. I had a summer research assistantship provided by a Research Experiences for Undergraduates (REU) grant with Dr. Eric Strauss, then at the University of Massachusetts at Boston. I was studying white-tailed deer ecology and also trying to learn about the resident coyotes that colonized Sandy Neck in 1992. By studying their scats and tracks and from any direct sightings that I was able to make, I attempted to determine the impact that the new immigrants were having on the ecosystem's flora and fauna.

The evening brought cloudy seasonable 70° weather with 20 mph wind gusts; a perfect time to go running. I budgeted 35–45 minutes for the jog, slower than my normal training speed because of the soft sand characteristic of the area. I exercised with a watch, not because I needed to know exactly how long the run took, but to document when I saw wildlife, mainly deer. I was in the casual part of my training schedule and I would not get that serious about running until around mid-August. My casual exercise program was really just a convenient way to get me to the vicinity of my real goal.

At 7:05 PM I was running on the horse trail, a path that weaves through the heart of the maritime forest in the interior part of Sandy Neck. About two miles away was the cabin that I stayed in a couple of nights a week during the summer, and nearly five miles away was the mainland, making this area one of the most isolated on Cape Cod. There were few campers on the front beach of this barrier island within even a mile of me so I knew that whatever I might see would be a truly wild animal, but I certainly was not expecting what was to come.

Rounding the bend in the trail, I suddenly saw five young coyote pups cavorting around. They didn't notice me so I immediately dove to the ground. This maneuver saved me from detection, but it also spread out an all-you-can-eat buffet for the resident mosquito population.

Being in a bowl of small dunes, the nice summer breeze that I had been experiencing all but dissipated and the bugs were now out in full force. My skin was mostly unprotected because I was only wearing a pair of running shorts and shoes with no socks. However, certain at the time that this coyote sighting was a once in a lifetime opportunity, I stayed remarkably still, with only minor arm movements to swat the bugs around my face and shoulders.

For a good three minutes I observed the young coyotes who did not notice me despite being less than 50 feet away. They continued to play with each other, oblivious to my presence. But the bugs were not, and it became so bad (that general area is basically a large mosquito-infested swamp interspersed with some uplands), that I started moving a little bit to relieve my many itches.

Right when I budged from my statue-like position, one of the pups noticed me. It appeared to be the dominant pup of the litter who seemed bolder and more alert than the others and to have full rein of the group. He ran off into a nearby thicket 20 feet away and, judging from the surrounding open landscape and that pup's movement, I gathered that the den was somewhere in the patch of woods nearest to them. Taking the nervousness of the lead pup as a cue, the others instantly stopped playing and scattered into the woods. They definitely had no trouble running away and I guessed by their size and mobility that they were at least two months old.

Frustrated by my carelessness of being detected, I sat down behind a dune about 20 feet from the woods and waited to see if they would come back. In the meantime, I took the opportunity to stretch my legs to stay loose while waiting. The sweat on my body acted like a sponge sucking up millions of microscopic rock particles as I laid there, effectively engraining the sand into my skin. I was getting less comfortable by the moment. I waited a few more minutes and then decided that I would try howling a couple of times before leaving, just to see if I could entice them back. I just provided evidence for myself that coyotes are such social animals, they can't resist conversation.

The first time I howled, I got a quick reply of a few barks. It was clear that there was an adult just out of sight in the woods that realized there was danger nearby and it sounded an alarm for the pups which were probably hiding no more than 50 feet away in the brush. They were so close, in fact, that I could hear them walking on top of the leaf litter in the woods.

Having probably never observed people before, the pups seemed in a quandary as to whether to obey the adult's warning or to respond to the caller. I howled two more times in short succession and the pups exploded with option number two and came running out of the woods uttering a series of high-pitched baby howls.

Sandy Neck coyote pup sitting alert

Judging from the gradually fading volume of its barking, the adult began moving off as the pups continued to yelp. When they came back out into the open, I hid behind the small dune so only my head was visible. The dominant one, with distinct raccoon-like eye rings, was clearly curious. Attempting to figure out what I was, and with the others right behind, he began to approach within 10 feet of me. When he got to the base of a three-and-a-half-foot sand dune, he suddenly turned and ran back to the edge of the woods. They gave one more howl before disappearing south into the woods.

When they fled, I got up and moved on 50 feet to rejoin the route that I was following for most of my jog. Before leaving though, I decided to do one more bout of howling. Expecting nothing, I was amazed as a couple of the pups actually came back out to investigate me at the edge of the thicket. Another howl by me produced the other three pups, and all five stood and stared at me. This time I was very visible and in awe that they were so casual about my presence. Completely wild, yet oddly trusting, they were probably trying to determine if I were some strange creature, or just a weird looking version of their own species.

When they didn't run away, I decided to do two final howls. On my last "aaaaaahhhhhhh—ooooooooooooooo," they did the unthinkable. Led by the dominant one, they approached closer, astonishingly to within 10 feet of me. Clearly recognizing now that I was a strange animal to them in spite of my coyote-like sounds, they looked visibly nervous and headed back to the woods for the last time. Exhilarated, I ran back to the field station, changed my clothes, and wrote down my encounter in my journal, noting that they were some of the cutest animals

I had ever seen. Still unable to forget the experience, I settled in to watch a few deer from a nearby observation blind—and all of this before dusk!

Over the next half week, I approached the coyotes' den site several times, but very cautiously for fear of disturbing them and their parents, which could cause them to move. In addition, I spent the bulk of my time locating our two radio-collared doe deer. Both still had properly functioning batteries in their collars and were fawning, so I was not able to exclusively dedicate all my time to the coyote pups, even though that was what I wanted to do. The area around the horse trail where I originally spotted them, however, continued to be littered with puppy tracks whenever I walked around there. I dubbed the area "the playpen" and was fortunate to see them there a few more times in the next couple of days.

While everyone else awakened on 13 June 1994 to the latest accusations against O. J. Simpson, I officially began my obsession with coyotes. That was the day I decided to walk through the patch of woods into which the pups kept disappearing when they left the horse trail. I entered the forest at 6:30 AM and located the den with ease, exactly where I suspected it to be, just south of the trail. It was past the brush visible from the horse trail and situated on a small upland about 30 feet in diameter, surrounded by woods—all within 75 feet of the path.

Hiding on a thick branch of a pitch pine 15 feet above the den, I was able to take well over an hour of video of the five pups that day, again using a couple of howls to get them to climb out of the hole in the ground. For the next few hours all the pups came and went so often that it was hard to keep track of their activities. Three of them wrestled on an elevated ridge, consisting of a pine needle-covered dune with some short pitch pines overhead. Two spent more time in the den itself.

At 12:15 PM all but one of the pups, the largest with the raccoon face, were accounted for. I quietly departed 15 minutes later when all of the pups were out of sight. Notebook in hand, I quickly jotted down, *"Did that really just happen?"* No one was within miles of me to answer. I smiled to myself—I was glad that I had the video as evidence.

In Retrospect

Little did I realize at the time that my howling and presence at the den had probably stressed the pups' parents, and potentially their older siblings, because they moved them a few days after I filmed them. When I showed the video to Pete Auger, my former high school teacher, I distinctly remember watching his dumbfounded expression. I think he doubted what I told him in my original phone call that I could have taken such great film footage of wild pups from that close. I still love watching that film even today.

While I have become better at respecting the distances that adult coyotes generally require in these sensitive areas, there is little doubt that this litter, back in the summer of 1994 when I was still a teenager, sparked my fascination and subsequent obsession with these clever canids. It was then that studying coyotes officially became my drug of choice.

It is my desire to pay back those coyotes whom I bothered then, by telling their story—and the story I've learned over the past ten years studying eastern coyotes. The motivation for my current research is the hope that other people will gain some understanding of the amazing uniqueness of coyotes and perhaps also become fascinated, or at very least, more respectful of them.

Pack Life

Most resident groups/packs in our study consist of three to four adult coyotes, which contain a breeding pair, also called alphas, and an offspring or two of the previous year. The yearlings normally disperse, but some delay dispersal in order to help raise the following year's pups.

Although many sightings are made of single coyotes, other members of a resident group are probably close to where an individual coyote is spotted. When individuals get separated, howling is a common method for group members to communicate and subsequently reconvene with one another. In summer, coyotes often hunt alone or in pairs and regularly return to the central part(s) of their territory which contains the den and the rendezvous sites where their pups are.

Coyote pairs often travel together throughout the year but especially in the winter when the females are sexually receptive and the males are doggedly following them. Our research has shown that coyotes mate and breed in late-January or early-February and generally give birth from mid-March to mid-April after a two-month gestation. An average litter consists of five pups, but can vary from two to nine. Occasionally coyote packs produce a double litter, where two females in the same pack bear young, usually to the same breeding male.

Coyote Glope on patrol for a mate

A double-litter situation often involves a mother-daughter pair, as when Glope tended two litters in Hyannisport during summer 2001. One was Mizz's offspring and the other was assumed to be one of Mizz's older daughters from the prior year. The two dens were almost three kilometers apart and pups were observed at both locations. Unfortunately, I was unable to monitor this group in late summer because Mizz abruptly abandoned her rendezvous site in July, and the rendezvous site for the second litter was not located until after Glope was killed by a car in late August 2001.

Denning Locations

Pups are typically not very visible until around June when they are ready to leave the den. Dens are usually in secluded areas under the roots of trees, especially pines growing in sandy soil or up on ridges like the top of pits dug to get soil for cranberry bogs. Less frequently dens are dug under rocks or man-made materials such as plywood boards or concrete barriers. While coyotes usually avoid denning close to humans, individual coyotes do show some variability.

In one such instance in the north Boston cemetery site, Maeve's pups were found several times in very odd locations. At one time four of them were nestled in an old coffin. It was hard to locate them even when we shined a light inside the 'den' because the coffin they were in was hidden inside a tomb!

Another time, they were under a mausoleum in the middle of the same cemetery. While amazing to document, it prevented us from capturing the pups to radio-implant them because it was illegal to dig up the old gravesite. It would have been fairly easy to do, but without digging, the mausoleum had so much cement to support its heavy frame we could not reach the pups.

Maeve and Jet (just before we collared him), eventually moved the pups to a forested site between two of the cemeteries that had a sizable half-mile by about 150-yard patch of woods, within an otherwise very urban area. This stretch of woods consisted of several dens that the coyotes had dug. You would hardly know that you were in the cities of Everett and Malden, Massachusetts.

Maeve and Jet also hid the pups underneath the edge of the concrete canal that bisected the wooded area. They moved them around so much in this area that we could never locate and catch the pups until they entered the baited box-trap placed near their center of activity. We eventually captured two pups from this group: a female we named Jem and a male we called Cour. Denning locations like they chose are the exception to the rule, as coyotes normally choose dens in more natural parts of their home range and Meave's choice of cemetery sites was certainly unusual, but ingeniously protective for her young.

In another part of my study research, I was involved in hand-raising a captive litter of wild coyote pups. It wouldn't have been possible except that we were fortunate enough to locate where their uncollared mother had whelped her pups, underneath a shed in a residential neighborhood. We could only guess that this coyote pair may have felt squeezed into a small territory because they were surrounded by other coyote groups and had nowhere else to den. Another possibility is that, contrary to the norm, some coyotes are not afraid of non-natural objects and do not recognize the difference between artificial sites, such as a shed or a coffin, versus more natural places, like a fallen pine or large boulder, as a suitable place to bear young.

Coyote Cour in Everett

Adult coyotes commonly move pups for either natural reasons (for example, sanitary issues such as to avoid parasites) or due to some form of intrusion, usually human. During our study, coyote parents moved their pups to new den sites after each known case of human disturbance.

The move to new den sites ranged from a distance of 50 meters to one kilometer from the original site. Because of the consistency and correlation of moving to new den sites after disturbances, we think that adult coyotes may dig alternative dens beforehand. This suggests that coyotes can recognize and remember previously excavated dens (and possibly prepare in advance for potential problems) that enable them to rapidly move their pups to other locations when necessary. This facet of their behavior, which provides evidence that coyotes may plan into the future, is significant because it demonstrates intelligence and adaptability in coyotes.

This emerging field of behavior, called Animal Cognition, was initiated by the late Dr. Don Griffin and suggests that non-human animals may be more sentient than previously thought. I was fortunate to have known Don, a down-to-earth guy, and a legend among Animal Behaviorists, while he lived on the Cape studying bats in his later years. He always dreamed of putting a small video-cam on one of the coyotes that we captured to enable us to see up-close what coyotes do, and the noises they make. Unfortunately, he did not live long enough to see that actually happen. With the rapid advances in technology, however, and the shrinking size of complex electronics, it may yet happen, perhaps even in the next few years in our own study.

Moving to Rendezvous Sites

Coyote pups usually grow out of their dens after they are just a couple of months old. Instead; their parents usually choose thick, brushy areas with plenty of cover to hide them from people and dogs during their daytime siestas. Coyotes generally abandon their den sites in late May to early June and move their packs to rendezvous sites.

Rendezvous sites, first described by Canadian biologists studying wolves, are above ground dens or resting sites where the pups learn to become independent. Sometimes a den site is situated within a rendezvous site and other times the pups are specifically brought to a new location.

An ideal rendezvous site consists of thick brushy cover, nearby water, high ground or open areas so adults can spot danger, good hunting, and some alternate dens or areas where they can be created, so the transition to a less sheltered setting is easier. Essentially these areas are 'puppy training centers' where the young grow from dependent pups into independent adolescents—all within a few months.

The location of rendezvous sites is relatively predictable within a given coyote's territory. Woods abutting cranberry bogs are great places for coyotes, because of the high concentration of rodents, mainly voles and muskrats, found in these areas. Not surprisingly, cranberry bog owners typically love having coyotes around because they prey on the very animals who eat their crops.

Some bog owners do not want to give permission for me to trap on their lands for fear that I may scare the coyotes away. I imagine they were initially a little hesitant about sharing the land with coyotes since most workers I have met are the 'good old boy' hunting types. However, the coyote's ecological services, free of charge, rapidly changed their views.

Under favorable circumstances and locations, June-July is the best time of the year to observe coyotes because the adults are returning to predictable locations. The open landscape setting of many rendezvous sites allows an observer to stay far enough away from them (about a quarter mile is a respectable distance) in order not to disturb them, yet still allows a good view using spotting scopes and binoculars.

I have spent a significant amount of time at the Marstons Mills rendezvous site every summer for the past decade. Many local people have learned that when I am parked at the site, I am looking at coyotes. Thus, an amazing number of people stop and ask me if, "I see any," or, "Can I take a look through your spotting scope." Despite getting distracted from my research duties, I happily oblige, hoping to convert more people to becoming pro-coyote fans. Interestingly, very similar occurrences happen in our national parks when popular wildlife is sighted and the traffic (often in larger numbers than in Marstons Mills) created by wildlife sightings create "bear jams," or in Yellowstone, "wolf jams".

Marstons Mills Rendezvous Site

Mid-summer is also a good time of the year to hear coyotes vocalize. It appears that howling is done for four (not necessarily mutually exclusive) reasons:

1) finding or reconvening with another
2) rallying the pack
3) claiming or advertising an existing deed on territory
4) simply for the joy of it—like humans singing.

Tradition

Coyote behavior seems to be fairly traditional much of the time. Even though there has been some change in land tenure over time with regard to how the Cape coyotes divide their territories (see Appendix 1 for Sill and Mole), every year since 1997 I have observed pups at the aforementioned bog rendezvous site in Marstons Mills.

Selection of these areas is likely a combination of multiple things, such as individual coyotes' past experience, learned behavior, and their ability to choose good habitat based on the species' needs. And while the same two coyotes used the rendezvous site in Marstons Mills for a combined decade, the favorable landscape (cranberry bogs, cover, and water) would likely be attractive for any coyote colonizing the region.

Sill and pups at Marstons Mills Rendezvous Site (courtesy of Rachel Cifuni)

On 11 June 1997, I was driving home from a summer job and saw a mother coyote and five pups on a sand hill there at 3:00 PM on a hot 85°F day. It was my first observation of pups at that site. I was a quarter mile away and spotted them out of the corner of my eye while driving, so initially I could not believe my eyes. I had to stop to investigate.

Sure enough, when I got close enough, I spied five small pups with the female. The mother saw me too and let out a warning bark for her young. The pups immediately ran for cover. That was the first of many such calls by coyotes over the years to advertise and warn others of my location. I did not know at the time that this site would become relatively historic, at least in the context of this study.

The next year we captured two pups at this site, Pon and Poo, the first two coyotes radio-tagged in this study. And in 2001, we captured an old breeding female a couple miles from there that we called Mole. I later wondered if perhaps that first sighting was my initial glimpse of her.

Dispersers and Slouchers

By October and November, pups have matured to nearly full size and start expanding their area from rendezvous sites to new places within their parent's home range. They have been found, however, to return frequently to the core areas within their respective ranges such as old denning and rendezvous sites. Being able to return to these places may give them a sense of stability. Likewise, adult coyotes probably use these familiar places to reconvene and socialize with their offspring. Rendezvous sites probably serve as year-round locations where separated family members can reconvene.

By late fall, one or two of the pups usually start traveling with their parents, while others begin the dispersal process. This progression is gradual, with some juveniles strengthening their bonds with the parents, while the more independent ones begin going on predispersal forays before eventually departing.

A third choice for a young coyote is to stay in its natal territory for an extended period of time (over one year) but not in regular association with the others. These lone coyotes are aptly called 'slouchers'. Research by us and other teams, notably Bob Crabtree's crew in Yellowstone, are investigating this peculiar aspect of coyote behavior.

Parents allowing slouchers to remain in their territory makes sense evolutionarily because the adults have a genetic investment in their offspring. It is simply that, as far as the available data indicates, coyote parents are not instinctively predisposed to force their young out on their own. If the slouchers survive and eventually reproduce, the parents' lineage is better represented. Naturally, the reverse is also true. We will continue to investigate the behavior of slouchers. Possibly they stay nearby to eventually challenge the breeders (their parents) in an attempt to take over their natal territories after they fully mature.

In humans, the sloucher would be analogous to a college student who comes home from college and refuses to help his younger brothers or sisters, yet his parents still tolerate his presence. The only time the lazy teenager responds to his family is when his mom yells "dinner," which prompts him to devour his food then head back to his room. Likewise, wild coyote and wolf pups might benefit from parental resources, such as large carcasses, and the protection and familiarity of their natal range, even if they do not help make the kill or assist with other pack activities such as raising young.

Coyotes, especially adults, have amazing recognition systems, both spatially and with regard to differentiating between other coyotes, depending on specific situations (for example, on or off territory, and is it a relative or stranger?). Spatial memory is the part of memory responsible for recording information about one's environment and its geographic orientation. This type of memory is formed after an animal gathers and processes sensory information about its surroundings. In general, mammals require a functioning hippocampus in order to form and process memories about space.

So, once another coyote has been recognized by an adult coyote, they react accordingly (i.e., either accept or chase away an individual). As previously mentioned, adult coyotes do not aggressively displace their offspring from their territories. Leaving the pack is a gradual process after food stops being provided by the adults, which generally happens around mid-Fall. Other factors influencing dispersal occur when:

1) more dominant and aggressive siblings begin to harass lower ranking individuals
2) other coyotes secure more food on natal territories
3) some just do not have or maintain bonds with other pack members

Even with many such causes potentially precluding pack formation, coyotes are normally quite social. The largest group documented on Cape Cod consisted of six adults all over one year old. It was an impressive sight.

Coyotes in Yellowstone National Park live in the largest packs of coyotes
reported nationally, with occasional group sizes of 10–12 adults raising pups. This
occurred before wolves were reintroduced into the park in 1995, and the super-
abundance of prey (mostly wintertime bison and elk carcasses) enabled those
groups to live at the average size of a wolf pack.

In the large group in our study, the breeding female, Mole, was collared.
She was very old and had more than the usual number of her offspring in tow,
many of whom may have instinctively stayed around to usurp the breeding position
from her. It's possible too, however, that the group was so large because they were
all closely bonded to each other and voluntarily delayed dispersal to be with their
natal group. Older breeding females may become more successful with later litters
and thus their pups may be more secure, get along together better, and be better
schooled in the essentials.

With coyotes, as with many vertebrates, the impact of individual animals'
personalities are crucial considerations when studying their social behavior. This
underscores the importance of collaring and tracking individuals of multiple family groups.

Social Ecology During Winter

By winter time, family groups of coyotes are generally seen traveling
together, although the animals that survive are usually savvy enough to cross road-
ways individually to avoid traffic. My first such group sighting was when tracking
Kett in Mashpee after a blizzard in late-February 1999, during the same week I
first captured Mizz. Kett's collar emitted a strong signal very close to a main road.
Because the powdery snow was a foot and a half deep, I walked in virtual silence
and approached to within 20 feet. Then I saw what I thought was a dead body, and
I began to fear the worst; that Kett had perhaps been struck by a car while traveling on the road to avoid the snow pack and he crawled here to die.

My heart sank. But before going over to retrieve his carcass, I decided first
to verify the situation by making myself known. I tapped lightly on my receiver a
few times and after a second or so, to my bewilderment, two coyote heads popped
up from the fur pile I had observed and stared at me. Then the two animals gathered themselves and darted off in separate directions, still leaving a fur mat.

Coyote at home in the snow

Moments later the 'fur mat' stood up and stared at me. This third coyote, bigger than the other two, was Kett; his collar very visible. These three adult coyotes had apparently been sleeping in a pile in the snow (something sled dogs and wolves in cold climates are known to do) with Kett on the bottom. He was awakened by the departure of his 'top blanket', and could not figure out why the other two had run off.

Staring at me from 20 feet away, Kett realized that I was the problem and after a quick look he also bolted off after one of the other two. Of course Murphy's Law was in play, which states (paraphrased) that the unexpected will always happen at the most inopportune time. It did, and I did not have my video camera to document this remarkable sighting.

An additional incident involved walking in on Mole's pack while they were bedded down on a winter day. There was a dusting of snow blanketing the ground. In a mixed pine-oak forest, just uphill from a cranberry bog, I approached her group from downwind and was welcomed by a couple of disturbed barks. As they bolted off, four fresh beds indicated they had all been sleeping within 10–15 feet of each other until being suddenly spooked by me.

Another time, on a winter day in Centerville, a village on Cape Cod, I walked in on Jog and videotaped him and two companions sound asleep in a wooded area where they commonly took daytime siestas. I was filming them from just 15 feet away for about five minutes, until one of them suddenly noticed me and took off, quickly followed by the other two.

When I reviewed the video, I quickly identified Jog by his collar, and then also noticed a weird looking coyote with a familiar brown and white Holstein-like color pattern also in that group. It turned out to be a second collared coyote I recognized as Mizz! Her collar had malfunctioned right around the time she was apparently displaced from her Hyannis territory and at this time she was probably nomadic, except for her brief association with Jog. Shortly thereafter in the fall, she was killed by a hunter in a different town.

Finally, one more unforgettable radio-tracking experience began one night after spending the evening with a couple of friends at a local club. I was the designated driver, and I had my receiver on after dropping off a friend around 2:00 AM. Suddenly I was receiving a signal from Mole's collar.

I traced her signal to a field very near where I grew up and shined my car lights in that direction. There I saw her, along with three others, bedded down in a field at the edge of their territory. They were right on a town walking trail where hundreds of people, including me, jog and walk their dogs daily. The coyotes stood up and looked perplexedly into the car's headlights. Exhausted, I only watched them briefly before deciding that I had really had it for the night and left them to go home and sleep. And judging from Mole's continued strong signal, the pack did the same.

Responsible Research

Direct observation of coyotes is one of the most crucial components of our study project. Although torn between bothering the coyotes and gaining scientific data, I conscientiously try to minimize my intrusiveness and am quick to tell our students, interns, and volunteers to be sensitive to avoid disrupting the coyotes. Not only is it inappropriate for researchers to hound their research targets, but subsequent behavioral changes in the coyotes can result in inaccurate accumulated data.

For example, I typically walked in on individual coyote groups no more than once per week, and often less frequently than that. At other times the woods where I was tracking them were just too dense to penetrate and I gave up without seeing them. Toward the later years of the study, I rarely walked in on them at all, instead preferring to wait and see them when they decided to become active and visible. On other occasions I sat quietly in my car and was able to observe them undisturbed at night crossing roads underneath streetlights.

When coyotes were active, we typically tried to avoid bothering them by shining our headlights directly on them. Rather, we strategically placed our cars in front of anticipated movement locations in order to observe them uninterrupted, like under a streetlight while crossing a road. This strategy often worked well, especially when we learned the routes that particular coyotes most commonly used.

For instance, one winter night in January of 2001, I observed Mizz, Glope, and an uncollared coyote behind the Barnstable Police Department in a new neighborhood. Knowing they were traveling on a dirt path, I drove ahead on one of the streets where the path they were on intersected the road and turned my car off. Barely a minute later I watched the three of them come into view about 15 feet away. They proceeded to trot side-by-side like a small intimidating posse, right by my car.

If it were just too dark to see, we used external lights or a night-scope to view them clearly. If we did shine a light on them, we did so for less than eight seconds and typically left the area immediately after a sighting. Afterward, we made it a habit to stay away for at least one hour to avoid potentially stressing them any further.

Based on subsequent research, we believe that by adhering to these precautions, coyotes only temporarily altered their behavior, if at all, which should be one of the goals of all wildlife studies. However, while we made all attempts to minimize our influence, we did realize that it is possible our efforts to observe individuals may have artificially increased the distance they traveled.

In 2005 I began using a third-generation night-vision scope. This device was a boon for our research as we could see better in the dark and not bother the coyotes we were looking for. After using the scope for a couple of nights I wondered why we ever used anything else as the tinted green glow of the scope's field of view illuminated the entire neighborhood where I was watching a collared coyote and his associates, all while the coyotes had no idea we weren't just another empty parked car.

Occasionally we observed coyotes during the early morning when it was already well light out. Tracking just after dawn often enabled me to get great videotape of them, like the time in July 2006 when Mystic and his smaller companion traveled down the middle of a neighborhood road at 5:30 AM and literally passed by within 12–15 feet (his companion was closer) from my turned off vehicle. They were at the edge of their mutual boundary with Sill's pack and stayed on the move until an hour later when they were about two miles away and back in the core of their territory.

Utilizing Man-Made Shelters

After coyotes abandon their dens and move to rendezvous sites, they almost exclusively rest above ground and in dense thickets in the woods until breeding females repeat the denning cycle the following spring. This behavior was even apparent in captivity.

The coyotes I hand-raised rarely used the kennel boxes that were available in their enclosure after growing up. Instead, even during the nastiest weather imaginable, they would curl up into a ball and rest under a lone pine tree on top of a small hill. It seems clear that coyotes do not like to be boxed in, instead, preferring a commanding view of their surroundings. This is likely an inherited trait for safety's sake and their thick winter coats provide suitable protection in any type of weather.

Coyote Mystic up-close in Marstons Mills

We have observed only a few exceptions to this rule, usually indicating a problem with the coyote we were following, either resulting from illness or some form of present danger requiring the need to stay securely hidden. One such incident was on 18 February 2003 involving a sick, mangy coyote from Saugus whom we called Bart. Dave, Steve, and I walked in on this coyote after tracking his strong signal for some time through the aftermath of an 18-inch snowstorm of the previous evening.

As we approached uphill toward his suspected location, we noticed what appeared to be the remains of some type of structure, with many leaning and downed boards and old logs. After ascending to the top of the hill, I was getting an extremely loud signal, so I turned off the receiver and started walking toward its source. As I continued on, Steve and Dave stayed at the top of the hill overlooking the snow-pack, hoping to videotape Bart or others and also to avoid the deep snow drifts that surrounded the area.

When I crested the ridge I found some fresh, three-inch long tracks and followed them, assuming that they were Bart and his group running away from us. I followed the tracks for about a quarter mile out of the area, down a hill, and into the woods to the east with Steve and Dave now trailing me. When I re-took a bearing on Bart's location using the radio-telemetry gear, it came from the original woodpile we had left behind us. After a confusing few minutes, we realized we were following the wrong tracks and that Bart must have been in the woodpile all along.

We returned to the area and, following a brief search with a flashlight, we found him. He was huddled under a collapsed plywood deck approximately five by ten feet. The enclosure was similar to an average coyote whelping den because it had a narrow entrance. Bart was lying safely in the back of the den although in an apparent catatonic state, clearly frightened by the noise we were making just outside. He was about six feet from us there, but was unapproachable from the other side due to large stumps on top of some of the plywood.

In spite of his apparent weak condition, it was quite dangerous walking in on him like that as we had to negotiate five-foot snowdrifts near the logs. In respect of his obvious distress and poor condition, we took a few minutes of video and then left the area, leaving him some scraps of meat for his trouble. I want to be clear that I recommend never feeding coyotes, but Bart's situation was different because

1)   he was obviously very sick
2)   he was not located near people
3)   he was part of our study, so we tried to help him, hoping he would survive the winter

Immediately after this observation I wrote in my notes that,

"This is one of the first documented instances that I am aware of a non-pup or non-whelping female using a den-like structure. Coyotes do not seem to use dens, except for about two months after females give birth. Bart clearly seemed to be taking shelter in there because of the blizzard. I wish he had needed a new collar because we easily had him trapped!"

The other two or three coyotes whose fresh tracks we had been following were apparently sleeping above ground near Bart. They must have run away, undetected by us, as we approached him, while Bart was lying in the dry den and became trapped upon our approach. The other coyotes certainly seemed to be loyal toward Bart as any good family-oriented animal would be. (Previously a man working at a nearby pig farm saw hairless Bart and three healthy coyotes feeding at their garbage pile set out for the pigs to eat.)

It shocked me that Bart would enter such a narrow, enclosed area as the place where we found him because, in general, coyotes are so difficult to trap even in a far more open-aired structure like a box-trap. I concluded my notes on that day by writing,

"Bart is amazing. On a frigid, dry day we see him lying on a warm mulch pile (a couple of days earlier). On a cool, 25°F snowy day we see him in a dry den. He certainly seems to know how to conserve body heat."

Unfortunately Bart's condition was very serious and it got the better of him, because he was found dead a few weeks later, apparently from starvation. There was little we could have done even though we wanted to and also allow him to continue living in the wild. We actually left food/bait near this location a few times but he may have been in no condition to even get up to retrieve it. We are convinced that the other members of his group ate it instead. They may not be quite as generous with each other as I previously had thought. Then again, it is every coyote for himself during tough times like the snowy winter we experienced in 2002–2003.

All of us involved in this project felt awful knowing that Bart starved to death, and we made a pledge that, although it was certainly was not our fault, this would be the last sick coyote we would release without attempting to rehabilitate it first. The thought of him slowly starving to death on our watch affected the entire research team for months.

Another instance of a coyote choosing an unusual location to hide out occurred when I found Mole, the old matriarch of Marstons Mills on Cape Cod, dead. Because I had been so busy both studying the captive coyotes and trying, but not catching, coyotes in north Boston during 2002–2003, I had not tracked Mole since late fall of 2002.

However, during Father's Day weekend 2003, I located her within a half-mile of my parent's house. The second day in a row of finding her in the same location prompted me to walk into the woods and pinpoint her location. Sadly, I found her. Her decomposed body was underneath a shed bordering two large cranberry bogs. She most likely died over the winter from natural causes related to old age.

When wild animals are deathly ill or sense they are dying, they try to hole-up in a safe hidden location where they will not have to defend themselves in their weakest moments. Dead feral or stray cats are frequently found desiccated in the corners of old barns or under buildings. It is interesting that Mole chose to die where she did, under a shed, because her body was perfectly dry, in a very similar type of location to what Bart had chosen before his death.

I concluded, after having found her some 500 times, that she was weakening and had climbed under the shed for some refuge. She probably never stood again after that decision. I wished I had been there to document it. It's quite likely, given their close bonds to one another, that her group members hung around there for a few days as she was dying. This location was only about 400 meters from the prominent cranberry bog rendezvous site referenced before. This area currently remains a favorite location for coyotes and I now refer to that small building as 'Mole's shed.'

A final example of locating a coyote that's using a man-made structure for shelter occurred in the early morning of 13 November 2005, when I was in the Falmouth/ Mashpee area off Route 151 on Cape Cod. I was on my way home from a college buddy's wedding in Falmouth and stuck the antenna out the window just for the heck of it on the 25-minute drive back to Barnstable.

I was shocked when I obtained a signal near the Barnstable County Fairgrounds for Cale, a skinny, 32-lb collared male coyote that I had not found in over a year. I captured him in Cummaquid, some 20 miles to the east in Casper's former territory. Cale was likely one of Casper's offspring. He probably roamed the entire

Cape peninsula nomadically for some time before settling down in the western part of Mashpee.

After two weeks of tracking Cale, I started to document him sleeping under unoccupied summer cottages near two ponds in the area. He had mange on his rear end and ended up dying two days before Christmas. A gross necropsy found severe chafing from the collar and mange. The poor guy, not belonging to a pack, appeared to have become debilitated from parasites that affected his normal immune response. He seemed to be taking cover under sheds to avoid precipitation and maybe to conserve his body heat. After all, he had no other coyotes to 'pile-up with'. Prior to his death, eastern Massachusetts experienced February-like cold two months early, and temperatures were in the teens for the better part of two weeks. That appeared to have done him in.

The X-Rays taken of Cale at the Cape Wildlife Clinic after his death also revealed that eight pellets (likely from a bird hunter) were lodged in his head and shoulder. That angered me. It is difficult to understand how someone can sucker-shoot any animal in the face.

I tracked him for the better part of that past month after locating him again after the wedding, except for the 12 days immediately before finding him dead as that time was my finals week at Boston College. I had a tough time with the thought that I could have saved him had I been down there a week before Christmas. I likely would have found him half-alive and might have been able to get him to a rehabilitation clinic.

Worrying about each study animal has become a way of life for all of us who are part of this research project. We joke that it is likely to significantly shorten our life spans due to the added stress levels, especially in such situations as this when losing an animal that we might have been able to help.

Other Shelter Options

Although coyotes like Casper (after being displaced from her former territory in January 2005) sometimes make use of man-made structures by sleeping under decks and sheds, it is more common for them to be found traveling on streets and residential front yards at night. This was Casper's usual form of behavior in her subsequent smaller range in Yarmouthport when I observed her on 27 January 2006.

During that time I was monitoring her locations and she had been in the same place for two consecutive days. I intended to track her at night for a few hours to see if she would move. She was about ten years old and apparently living within the confines of quite a small range and I was not sure how long she could support herself within those boundaries. My notes that night beginning at 11:38 PM, happily describe otherwise:

> I park on the southeast corner of Dauphine Road and wait for her as she comes from the north. She just got active and is traveling south through

this neighbor-hood. After obtaining a strong signal for two minutes I see her through my night-scope trotting south down Dauphine Road with a second, smaller (male?) coyote. I notice her collar as she travels in the lead. When she gets within 25 meters of me I have a perfect view of her underneath a street light as I use binoculars to zoom in on her though my front windshield. The moment she appears under the light, she stops, having noticed my parked vehicle. It was not running and she cannot detect my scent as my windows are rolled up, so she briefly looks around then loops to the southwest into a front yard at the bend in the road. The second coyote follows her. Using my night-scope, I watch as they travel south on the raked grass ten feet from the front door of the house and only 25 feet from me. I can tell when they leave the combed lawn as they make a slight noise when they trot on leaves out of the yard and back onto the street behind me. After circling around my car, Casper stops on the street, gives my car one final look, then trots off. I can't believe how robust she looks, given her age and dis-placement from her original territory!

Displaced coyotes such as Casper, along with transient coyotes, appear insecure and seem to go out of their way to hide from resident territorial coyotes. Yet they relax and behave more normally once they are comfortable in a vacant range and neither in danger from, nor in competition with, other coyotes. Casper's varied behavior from 2005–2006 certainly supports that conjecture.

Chapter 8

Movement and Activity Patterns

A Trespassing Transient

We watched in astonishment back in late-April 2004, as Fog, a young, 30-lb female transient coyote, went under the main cemetery fence at the south part of Woodlawn; the south edge of the territory of Maeve and Jet in the city of Everett.

There was about eight inches of clearance, and after circumventing the fence, she trotted right down city blocks before bedding in a very small wooded area bordering neighborhoods less than a half-mile away. The patch of forest, about 100 yards square, contained a small amount of shrubbery where she hid. The new buds had not yet blossomed, leaving the site barren since the previous fall.

On the second day of her being in this unusual location, I walked in to see if she were still alive. When I went into the woods, it took me a few minutes to get close to her and at first I thought she might have shed her collar and left the area without the tracking device. She did not move until I was about 20 feet away, then bolted straight across a neighborhood street where she bedded, undetected, under a relatively large ornamental shrub about eight feet in diameter.

We watched, Dave and Steve perched on a person's porch, in amazement as she ran across the road then found the nearest available cover. Luckily it was a side road that did not have much traffic, or I probably never would have attempted to disturb her in the first place. All of the commotion drew a half dozen of the neighbors outside.

While we feared they would be irate about a coyote being in their neighborhood they were all very intrigued. One lady gave us bottled water and juice, while another individual described how he fed a 3-legged coyote in those woods (one we had never caught sight of).

Steve Cifuni holding sedated coyote Fog

Dave tracked Fog that night and documented her as stationary, never moving until just after dark. That was the last time I ever disturbed her in her unusual sleeping locations, another of which included a small patch of woods bordering Route 93 in the city of Medford.

After reflecting on Fog's unusual sleeping locations when seemingly normal wooded locations were available within a mile of her location, we realized that there were probably resident coyotes in the cemeteries and she was avoiding them by sleeping outside their range. These assumptions turned out to be correct with the collaring of Maeve and Jet in the cemeteries of Everett and Malden, which is chronicled throughout this book.

Fog Finds a Home

On 29 April 2004 I was on my way home from a relatively early night at a club in Boston with a friend. As usual, on my drive home my thoughts turned to my nocturnal charges and I decided to get a location on Fog who recently moved south of the cemeteries in Everett and Malden and into previously uncharted land for her (at least since we collared her).

For the past three days and nights she had been located within a small, 10-acre, weedy field in very urban east Somerville, directly behind the Assembly Square Mall. Fog was very active at night in this small abandoned locale and we obtained many locations per day to verify this. We speculated that she was plundering an abundant rabbit and rat population in the fenced-in area. Nonetheless, it was a very unusual location for a coyote, with only railroad tracks to the south and a bridge over a quarter-mile wide river to the north that connected this patch to others.

Dave, Steve and I suspected that Fog was about to make a precipitous move somewhere new as this location approximated little more than a large-sized zoo habitat enclosure that would only be a brief stopover point for an average coyote. We knew how far coyotes usually moved on a nightly basis, so we were fairly confident about our prediction.

The area was so urban, however, that we also suspected she was building up her courage to strike out and explore new terrain. Despite rigorous academic schedules, the three of us had literally been up day and night, alternating our time so as to keep tabs on her. We realized the tremendous opportunity of monitoring and recording her journeys to new locations in such an urbanized ecosystem. On this particular night I was to have a bit of good luck documenting some unusual movements.

When I arrived at the Assembly Square Mall at 12:20 AM, I obtained Fog's signal with ease, but something was new. Her signal did not place her directly in the field where she had been for the past 72 hours. Driving south, then east, around the mall, I discovered her whereabouts. She was on the railroad lines in east Somerville and moving south. Her signal was extremely loud as I rounded the bend exiting the mall. I parked my car at the edge of the mall because the road turns into a one-way nightmare. Sometimes it is easier to be on foot in the city.

I walked to a bridge literally on the Boston/Somerville line and within a minute of waiting, I spotted Fog traveling south down the tracks. She was on the westernmost railroad track of five parallel sets; the ones least heavily used. Watching her sniff the metal track and the supporting wood beams, it was obvious she was trying to sense what was ahead of her, which might have included aggressive, territorial coyotes for all she knew.

At 12:35 AM, I watched as she traveled south, placing her paws on the railroad ties one in front of the other, and officially stepped a few meters inside Boston's Charlestown section. However, it was almost as if there were an invisible wall right there, because just at that point she got nervous, turned right around, and bounded all the way back to the railroad yard about a quarter of a mile to the north. In other areas, I would have suspected that she had picked up the scent of local coyotes who had marked that as their range—adults potentially large enough to kill her—causing her to turn around. But this area seemed too urban to support coyotes, as there was virtually no cover in the vicinity.

I took this opportunity to call and wake up both Dave and Steve. It was a cool but comfortable 40°F and my blood was pumping as I talked to them. The conversations were very similar, with both of them having been asleep because they had classes in the morning.

"Dave, sorry to wake you, but I'm standing at the Boston line, and guess who just officially set foot within Boston city limits?"

It was a rhetorical question as it was obvious who I was talking about. Most of Boston is heavily urban except for some scattered grassy areas that lack any thick brush, a necessity for coyotes to hide in during the daytime. Whereas other cities may have more semi-natural park-like environments within the city limits, one would have to go outside Boston proper to find such areas located in towns and cities adjacent to Boston, such as Somerville, Cambridge, and beyond.

Steve replied that I was lucky because he had tracked Fog for two whole days in a row in that boring field and I located her in a new location relatively early in the night. While I was certainly lucky to document this movement, I purposely didn't mention to him that I did have a 3:30–7:30 AM shift the previous morning and Fog barely moved the entire time I was there. Because Steve and Dave conducted the day-to-day research in north Boston, he was certainly justified to feel this way.

As I waited, I noticed that people were starting to leave Good Times (a local bar/arcade) and I was literally in that same parking lot monitoring Fog. I had the feeling that she was trying to get enough guts to make a run for it, but the trains were still running and I bet myself she would wait a few hours and cross south into Boston along the railroad lines. I told Steve I would call him with my last location so he could find her on his way into Boston College in the morning.

I stayed for about another half-hour parked at the edge of the winding road that twists between the south part of the mall and the railroad tracks. At 1:10 AM I hit pay dirt when I spotted Fog beginning to move south along the tracks originating from the railroad yard heading toward the bridge again.

That location is sparsely vegetated with only a few shrubs. Surprisingly, she sensed me sitting on the sidewalk and ran north a short distance back to the less constricted railroad yard. In traveling back to her safety zone, she proceeded to trot right by me. I was dumbfounded as to why she would be so nervous about my presence since she was on the opposite side of the fenced-in train tracks.

For the next hour or so, I continued to observe Fog to be active in that railroad yard. From a vantage point of about 100 feet away, I saw her again, and amazingly, she sensed me yet a second time and moved off even more to the north. The fact that I was hanging out near her area of activity must have seemed much more of a threat to her than the cars and people, including a few drunks passing by, in the same location. By 2:15 AM I was exhausted and had to leave her. I desperately needed some rest because my morning schedule started at 7:00 AM.

"Where will she go from here?" I asked in my notes, concluding the descriptions of her activities for the night.

Coyote in the City

That morning dawned beautiful, with the sun warming the air to nearly 70°F, the warmest day of the year so far. After spending a busy morning at the Stone Zoo, I returned to my car at 11:15 AM and found that I had six missed calls and four new messages from Dave and Steve. Something was up with Fog and I was missing it!

The first message I listened to from Steve was disturbing. "Jon, I can't pick up her signal from the field behind Assembly Square. I'm on my way to BC and will check on my way,"

Fifteen minutes later he called back and left a second frantic message. "I'm on Rutherford Street in Somerville and in the worst traffic. I have a weak signal but I have no idea where she is. I'll check again after school but you might want to check for her too on your way down, if you have time."

Steve's third message came in ten minutes later, "You won't believe this, but I'm on the ramp literally 50 meters from the Fleet Center (where the Boston Celtics and Bruins play and now re-named the Boston Garden), and have an extremely strong signal. You might want to look on a map before you head down this way. It's impossible to stop around here.

Steve's fourth message, amidst two other missed calls from him, occurred ten minutes before I got back to my car. He said, "I was just wondering if you found her yet. Call me."

After listening to the barrage of messages, I studied my map and looked for the best coyote route to that location. That thinking showed me a route along the railroad tracks that led to a train station and an associated small open area just north of the Charles River and east of the Museum of Science, west of Route 93. The railroad station was less than a half mile north of the Fleet Center right at the Cambridge/Somerville line and just west of Charlestown. This area was definitely 'as city as you can get' and a place I never thought I'd be tracking a coyote.

My first stop was at Bunker Hill Community College, the nearest green area, consisting of just a couple of ball fields, to the original Assembly Square Mall site. But I obtained no signal. Frustrated, I focused on slowly navigating my way across traffic. The walking pace of the cars got me further agitated so I was nearly ready to pull my hair out. My impatient nature is one reason I typically keep my hair shaved.

I then drove west from where we had tracked Fog the previous three days. Those five minutes seemed to take an eternity, but at last I finally detected her signal! That was fortunate, considering that a task that might have taken me a couple of minutes in the country had just taken me 20 minutes.

Next I had to verify that Fog was not at Bunker Hill, because if she were, it would be even more of a nightmare if I had to backtrack. After 20 more minutes of triangulating her location, I confirmed that, true to my initial prediction, she was in the railroad area just south of the main station where the subway cars run.

To get there, she must have traveled through Boston for about half a mile until she found this small amount of open land. Then, to arrive at this specific location, she had to (incredibly) cross under the Zakim Bridge, in the midst of the several billion-dollar road construction project in downtown Boston. She must literally have walked in the sand piles next to the big work trucks, and moved along the train tracks next to the supporting beams holding up the large freeway. "*I wonder if any other coyote has ever stepped paw here in modern times?*" I jotted down in my journal.

Parking across the street from the Museum of Science, I got out of my car and followed Fog's signal to an abandoned railroad yard about the size of a football field. The area was relatively sizable given its urban location. However, there were only a few meager shrubby areas to hide in, and not surprisingly her signal was coming from the most sizable patch, a cluster of no more than five bushy weeds.

I scanned the location and accidentally walked right by her crouched in the shrubs looking apprehensively up at me. Not wanting to bother her because she really had nowhere to go, I pretended I did not notice her and immediately vacated the area. I returned to my car and called Dave and Steve as I headed back to BC. When I translated my findings to my two colleagues, they were amazed, to say the least. Fog had no idea she was single-handedly skyrocketing all of our cell phone bills.

That night Steve took his shift and tracked her until 1:30 AM, including making two verification sightings at the abandoned railroad site. She apparently set out from there at around 2:00 AM because she was nowhere to be found when I resumed the tracking expedition at 2:30 AM, including doing a fruitless search of most of Cambridge.

The next afternoon, Dave, who is from Somerville, managed to find her in another tiny area, a 50-by-50-foot wooded swamp in Cambridge near Fresh Pond. Dave and Steve verified this location from the deck of a million-dollar house after being invited up by the nice homeowners when they explained that they were biologists searching for a coyote in the tiny wooded patch nearby.

We half expected those kind people to call the police. It wasn't an uncommon occurrence (especially at night) when people saw us driving slowly around their neighborhood streets with a bizarre-looking antenna wedged into the vehicle window. In post 9–11 coyote tracking, we get pulled over much more often than before, because we 'look suspicious'. I have personally been pulled over by local police easily two dozen times and almost always get the same startled question from the officer:

"You're doing what?"

"I am tracking a collared coyote, sir," I say respectfully.

"Okay…," they say. " Well—uh—just be careful," or,

"Why don't you just trap them and kill them?"

I usually say "I actually like them…and how are we going to learn about them if we kill them?" But sometimes the officers don't appreciate that comment so I then mumble something like "I'm just a wildlife biologist, not an assassin."

Many are the times I have also awakened officers napping in their cruisers in empty parking lots. Other times, they or others scrutinize me intensely, as if I'm looking for a drug deal. Nevertheless, I am usually very alert when tracking at night, more fearful of a nocturnal human being than a wild animal.

Regardless of the location, these interactions with the local authorities are only momentary disturbances as I regain the ability to track once the officer moves on. I often wonder, though, what the coyotes think about sudden flashing lights and bleeping sirens in a usually quiet part of their range. I know they must see the lights and hear the sirens because I'm never that far from a coyote when these incidents occur.

As for Fog, being young and possibly born in close proximity to human settlements, she seemed to have a high tolerance for human-induced hustle and bustle as long as she could simply avoid personal confrontations. She must have taken the railroad tracks right through the city, as there is a total lack of woodsy terrain in Cambridge. She probably passed right by Harvard University on her way westward across the city. Finding no comforting brushy hideaways there, she probably had no use for this area of tall towers and barren pavement, and couldn't wait to find a safe resting place beyond.

Coyote traveling down street

The night of 30 April 2004 was the last time we tracked Fog in the area. Dave and Steve kept tabs on her until about midnight and she hadn't moved. That activity was typical of her city travels, as she normally became locally active at dusk but waited to move until midnight or 1:00 AM. She usually became less active again at dawn.

The next morning we covered the entire area but could not find her. After trying intensely for the next week, we gave up searching for her except where we had tracked her most recently. We finally concluded that she had had enough of city life and must have bee-lined it out of Boston that night.

After six months of intermittent searching, we started to believe that we would never find Fog again unless she were found dead. But the night of 17–18 November proved differently. I had taken a red-eye flight home from the

Defender's of Wildlife Carnivore Conference in Santa Fe, New Mexico and arrived at Logan International Airport at 7:00 AM.

After arriving home, I checked my e-mail quickly before going to sleep and saw a message from someone in the town of Dartmouth in southeastern Massachusetts, only a few miles from the Rhode Island border. His name was Gary Clabaugh and he briefly stated that he was sure he was seeing a collared coyote in his yard. He had randomly found my web site and had the wisdom to contact me. I sent an equally short note, listing my phone number and requesting that he please call me immediately as that might be one of our dispersing coyotes.

When I talked to Gary, he sounded confident enough that the coyote he had seen was collared, so I arranged to meet him the next day near his house. After an hour and a half car ride to his home, I quickly did a few scans of different frequencies, and sure enough I picked up Fog's signal.

Gary and I pinpointed her location about a mile away in a watershed in Dartmouth. She was 60 miles (straight distance) from her capture location in North Revere and nearly just as far from her last location in Cambridge. Of course we do not know the actual route she took to get down there, which surely added miles to her journey.

Fog's location was actually considerably closer to Cape Cod than Boston, and at first I thought that the signal might be from one of our collared Cape coyotes that had gone missing. To get from Cambridge to Dartmouth, Fog had to cross many major highways, including Rte 90/the 'Mass. Pike'. Routes 90, 95/128, 495, 24, 195, and hundreds of secondary roads wind through and across that intermediate area.

What an amazing trek she made (north to south) across nearly all of eastern Massachusetts! After this event, I thought that if such a small inexperienced animal could manage to travel through that much of eastern Massachusetts and arrive safely to set up shop, then it was likely that coyotes as a species could go nearly anywhere.

Although coyotes have dispersed 300–400 miles in other locations, the precise detail we recorded while monitoring Fog's dispersal is right up there with some of the best documented reports of coyote travels in today's highly urbanized landscape. There is little doubt that the urban gauntlet that she ran forced her to take a non-linear path down to her eventual destination in Dartmouth. Additionally, we do not know where Fog originated; rather, we assume that we captured her as she was moving south. She potentially could have come from New Hampshire or Maine about 50 miles north of her capture location.

Fog eventually settled by Gary's house and paired with a handsome red coyote, whom I was lucky to get on video on a late-spring morning in 2005. The two traveled in a several-mile radius around Gary's home, and we know that she gave birth to an unknown number of pups near Dartmouth High School in April 2005.

Dave and I made the trip down to track her on an irregular basis until the beginning of summer 2005. On 23 June, I traveled down there to check on her once again. I had returned a little over a week before from a 10-day trip to Yellowstone National Park with Steve Cifuni.

I picked up her stationary signal in a mosquito-infested swamp within a quarter mile of Gary's house, and when I investigated (in complete darkness nonetheless), I found her there dead. Her body was too decomposed to even determine the cause of death, so we guessed she had most likely died within the first few days after my departure. The odor was so bad, it was literally painful for Gary and I to retrieve her collar, but getting it back gave us the option of getting it refurbished for a future capture. This was certainly another sad and anticlimactic end to an otherwise fascinating life.

Impressive movements

Now that coyotes are seen regularly in Massachusetts, I frequently read in newspaper articles that they appear to be 'everywhere'. One of our study objectives was to assess the validity of this impression. All of our collared adult coyotes have been confirmed to move at least ten miles a night, which in a suburban setting involves traveling through many different neighborhoods.

A single animal or pack of coyotes can be seen and heard in widely diffuse areas within a respective territory during the course of one night. By using simple math, it is presumable that a pack of coyotes can leave over 50 miles of tracks per night in a given home range. This, combined with their increasing boldness around humans, may lead to more sightings (and howling heard) by the general public, and the inaccurate belief that coyotes are more numerous than they actually are.

Sill, when he was around ten months old in February 2000, displayed a dramatic example of long-distance movement. In a 25-hour span, he traveled from Hathaway's Pond near Hyannis, way off his natal range, then back to his family's home range of about 15 square miles. During the course of his travels, he rejoined his collared father Kett in the central part of their range near the Mashpee Dump, then traveled together with him and his probable mother over to the west side of their territory in the Otis Air Force Base.

This movement was fairly atypical in that he traveled well over 20 miles in one night and moved through five towns—Barnstable, Mashpee, Falmouth, Bourne, Sandwich, and back to Mashpee. Sill was captured and re-collared in May 2004 and eventually established his own territory in 2001–2002 adjacent to his natal range. From our tracking data on him now, we are seeing him regularly move around in this smaller area of about seven to eight square miles.

I often laugh when I hear the media's 'heightened awareness' warnings or view the fear-generating local news station 'neighborhood interviews' on TV regarding coyote sightings and the potential risks they present. Coyote boldness is rarely unmotivated, often caused by people actively feeding coyotes or leaving food outside, whether for pets or in garbage containers. These newscasts are based on lack of scientific information and rarely document actual coyote behavior, such as these impressive movement patterns through the maze of suburbanization, and how coyotes actively avoid people.

Coyote Sill sitting at the edge of a cranberry bog in Marstons Mills

When Glope was a transient in 2000 (remember, he eventually became Mizz's mate in Hyannisport) he traveled about 25 miles overnight, going through the areas of at least four or five different pack territories in very diverse locations. He went from his capture location in the southwest part of Barnstable all the way to the northeast part of town almost ten miles away, then concluded his activities by moving through the northwest part of town and continued west, to eventually bed down in the adjacent town of Sandwich.

I was lucky to be tracking Sill and Glope to document those striking movements, mostly because they acted out those travels within my study area. Other coyotes just disappear from our radar and the data we could obtain on them is lost. For instance, Dave and I tracked a female pup, Jem, in Everett and Malden everyday from her late-summer capture until 2:30 AM on 11 December.

We returned a little over four hours later and could not find her in her parent's territory or anywhere nearby. Judging from her sudden disappearance, as well as that of another uncollared pup, for the rest of the winter, it is likely that this eight-month-old juvenile hightailed it right out of her natal range and out of our study area. Coyotes such as Jem are often not found, unless tracked by airplane, or until they turn up dead from a human-related cause.

Spatial Memory

A coyote's spatial memory for traveling throughout large areas is quite impressive when you consider that they move 10–15 miles a night within an average ten-square-mile territory. Canids probably know a given landscape better than nearly any other resident animal.

I vividly remember camping near Casper and Sly's (before his collar malfunctioned) den and rendezvous sites and losing their signals for hours at a time as they left and returned to the den area. Five years later, I tracked Casper via car in those same locations, including other locales radiating three to five miles out from the den in all directions. Over those years her range spanned over 15 square miles of Cape Cod real estate, which she traversed nightly.

While coyotes travel throughout their range, they remember key attributes of their domain. Although food and water may be the first things that people think of as most important to a wild animal, Sill's behavior shows how coyotes assess their environments with a view toward safety and shelter.

In Sill's territory, there is a dense protective stand of cedar trees that shelters the ground from snowstorms. On three occasions I documented Sill and his pack at this location among the cedars both before and after major snowstorms. It is an unusual location, close to a small neighborhood and a main road, yet the nearly impenetrable woods limits human activity and likewise, potential disturbances.

There is no question in my mind that Sill senses the incoming storms and deliberately travels to that protected location. In October 2005 I saw him lead four juveniles and another adult (not previously identified) to that location where they bedded down for the day. He showed his wisdom as a pack leader by bringing his family there during heavy storms, making their lives more comfortable during inclement weather.

The ability of coyotes to move around freely, even in an urbanized landscape, is the aspect of their behavior that most impresses me. I began to really appreciate this after following them on foot. It's similar to trailing a human runner training for a marathon.

There was an incident on 16 March 2002, a mild, early spring day on Cape Cod. Barnstable Natural Resources Officer Russ Keyes dropped me off at the eastern-most part of Sandy Neck Beach, five miles from the nearest permanent human dwelling, to track a coyote. My receiver told me that the small fellow, aptly named Tiny, was bedded down in a patch of cedar trees. Tiny was part of a group residing in and around Sandy Neck Beach at the time.

It was still light so I settled in and waited on a sand dune downwind and south of him for about two hours before he finally became active at 6:12 PM. For the next four hours I trailed him in the dark from a distance, trying to stay downwind of him on the quarter-mile wide south side of the barrier beach so as not to alter his normal movements. Because I knew that conservation area like the back of my hand, having tracked deer and coyotes there since high school, I didn't get lost or stuck in thick brushy areas.

It was very dark because the stars were hidden by clouds and the low-lying fog. The visibility was so poor I had trouble accurately sensing where Tiny was going, and several times the ping of his collar signal became so loud it turned into a loud clucking sound, and I had to turn the receiver's gain dial almost off. Under those circumstances he probably came within 20 feet of me before he sensed me and trotted off.

He must have been baffled and frustrated that he had such difficulty scenting me until he was right next to me due to the strong ocean-driven north breeze. Those same techniques I used are often used by predators, which have far better eyesight than I do, to sneak up on unsuspecting prey.

At 11:00 PM my tracking session ended when I returned on foot to my car. Once back on the mainland, I spotlighted Tiny and a second coyote in the western-most part of the marsh immediately south of Sandy Neck. It was so dark I actually never saw his companion despite trailing them for about six miles.

As I left them, they still had six to seven hours of activity left, which took them off the barrier beach and a few miles onto the mainland to the neighborhoods that overlook this beautiful peninsula. I often wonder if the people in that area realize that the coyotes in their backyard are often the same canids found way out at the end of Sandy Neck.

Use of Corridors

Coyotes also cleverly use travel corridors to move around expeditiously and avoid contact with anything from humans and dogs to other coyotes that might prevent them from getting to their intended destinations. The ones in our study were documented traveling through human-altered areas such as dumps, cranberry bogs, and golf courses more than were expected when compared to residential or natural areas.

This differs from recent studies in the western United States by Seth Riley and colleagues that found that urban coyotes prefer to use the few remaining natural areas. Some of the altered areas in our study that coyotes used for travel were narrow corridors that hosted bridges, narrow footpaths, railroad tracks and areas under power lines. I equate these areas to coyote super highways. Compared to traveling through the woods, these structures allow coyotes to move in relatively straight lines without much resistance.

In fact, traveling on linear pathways is a widely recognized pattern in both coyotes and wolves and enables wild animals to reach ostensibly unreachable diverse locations in a short period of time. These travel routes are very important in connecting coyote populations. For instance, our coyotes Sill, Glope, and Fog used these corridors for much of their movement. To the untrained observer, it would be mind-boggling to believe that one coyote could do all of the traveling that we documented for each of these animals.

We have further identified "micro-corridors" that allow coyotes to travel to otherwise separated landscapes. For instance, in Everett, Maeve and Jet's pack routinely crossed a street connecting two cemeteries via a nine-inch opening in a metal fence located at the north edge of the southern cemetery. They also used a seven-step staircase on the southern end of the north cemetery. In a second narrow area, they passed under a gated road in the south cemetery and crossed onto the main access road to the north cemetery.

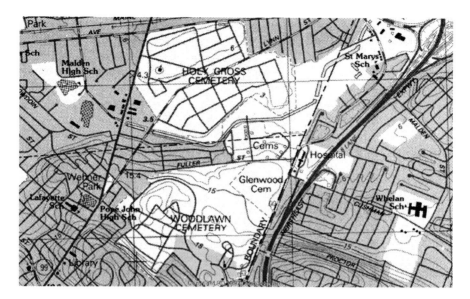

Map of the territory of the Cemetery Coyote Pack (courtesy of Terrain Maptech)

They were further observed to look both ways before dashing across the road when it was safe. When we got radio-signals from Maeve and Jet in that area, one of us (Steve, Dave or I) would drive to that spot, park about 50 meters away, turn off our car, and wait for them to cross. A nearby street light perfectly illuminated the road for us to observe.

In less than 24 hours over 29–30 July 2004, sixteen-year old Jill Moore, Steve Cifuni's high-school age cousin, and I saw seven different coyotes cross through that micro-corridor. From my car, we had quietly watched as Jet, Maeve, and a small uncollared, grayish adult each crossed there separately multiple times that night.

We periodically observed that same uncollared gray coyote, whose origin we never identified, within their territory, but never traveling with either of them. We presumed it was not one of their offspring because both Jet and Maeve were young adults themselves and most likely had not bred yet. We think they produced their first litter in spring of 2004. Verification of a third coyote, not an offspring of one of the two breeders but helping to raise pups, would be a rarity indeed. It may have been a sibling of Maeve's or Jet's, but because we never captured it, we will never know.

The final few sightings that night began at 11:25 PM on 29 July. Jill initially spotted Maeve because Murphy's Law reared its ugly head again. When Jill noticed a collared coyote coming out onto the road, I was looking down trying to figure out why the receiver was acting kooky—it turns out the batteries had just died.

It was Maeve that Jill saw, and she was very casually crossing from the Jewish Cemetery south into Woodlawn Cemetery. Before going through the hole in the fence and out of sight, Maeve stopped on the sidewalk and looked back around. I quietly said out loud, "That is bizarre. Is she looking at our turned-off car or is she sensing some cars approaching from a distance?" Perhaps she was just being wary, but while we pondered that, she trotted through the fence, vanishing like a phantom to the south.

Just as Meave disappeared we had our answer as two pups suddenly bounded across the road in pursuit of her, with a couple of cars only about 100 meters away. Maeve must have been scanning the road to ensure it was safe for her pups to cross. Jill and I both wondered why the other two pups were not with her since Dave had seen at least four pups the night before. As we were theorizing that Jet or the elusive gray adult might have had the other two puppies, they suddenly appeared too. We observed them run south across the road following Maeve and the first two pups through the fence and into Woodlawn.

The fourth pup, which looked fairly small, began crossing just as an oncoming car was heading east. The driver clearly saw them and slowed. If the car had not braked it would have been a very near miss; certainly too close for our "objective" comfort. Objective, meaning that we biologists should not take sides or have biases as to what happens with our study subjects—we should just record what happens. This belief implies that scientists must act like machines and are not permitted to have personal viewpoints. Many biologists and ethicists such as Marc Bekoff and Bill Lynn, respectively, are now becoming aware of the importance of being advocates for the species that they study. I am certainly one.

I often sit in the car muttering directions as if the coyotes in our study could hear me in the car with my windows rolled up. "Be careful Maeve, it is only 9:00 PM. There are still a lot of vehicles out there.... What are you doing crossing the road with your pups at this hour? Watch out little guy, you almost got hit. Okay, good, now pup number 3, go. Go now before more cars come. You too, number 4!" Anyone listening to me would think I sounded like an avid sports fan yelling directions at their favorite player from the balcony, where there is no possibility for the athlete to actually hear the heckler.

Although we were impressed that the last two pups waited for at least five cars to pass by before they crossed the road, the fourth pup appeared to blindly follow the third pup. It made me wonder if that is how young coyotes, such as Pon back in 1998, commonly get killed.

After the five young ones crossed the road, I said to Jill "How cool would it be if the city of Everett put "Coyote Crossing" signs along this stretch of road with small speed bumps on both sides to slow cars down?" That thought underscored the importance of flagging the most-used road crossing areas to prevent coyotes from getting hit, which in Maeve and Jet's territory consisted of this three-foot wide and thirty-foot long tiny corridor connecting the two cemeteries.

Coyotes typically trot or "fast-feet" across the road rather than sprint. "Fast-feet" is a term that I coined based on my many observations of coyotes in different situations, specifically those where they are not in a rush but want to quickly get from one place to another, such as crossing roads. In this form of loco-motion, they travel at an energy-efficient gate similar to a trot, but the movement is somewhat different, consisting of their feet touching the ground in an extremely rapid shuffle-like motion.

While they are on the alert for movement or threats around them, their legs move quickly like they are sprinting, yet the pace is actually trot-like and effort-less. I consistently observe this shuffle-run on hard surfaces such as roads, while the stereotypical bouncing motion of the lope is the norm for coyotes moving through woods where they are more at ease.

Because coyotes usually cross streets when traffic is relatively light, they do not need to expend that much effort doing it. However, there are certainly exceptions to the rule, such as when Mizz, in Hyannis, became impatient during a hot summer night in 1999 because of considerable traffic. I was observing her from my car in a nearby pizza parlor parking lot with my high school assistant Roswell Joseph.

To our amazement, to deal with a never-ending line of cars, Mizz sprinted across the lawn of a funeral home and shot right across the road between two mov-ing cars. It seemed like she was running fast to get perpendicular to the road so she could see traffic coming from both sides while she bolted across the pavement. It all happened so fast the drivers never braked, probably in disbelief that something had actually moved that fast.

We were in awe that she was still alive after that maneuver. Tragically, just over six years later, I paid my final respects to Roswell himself at that very same funeral home, the victim of a fatal automobile accident. An eerie feeling came over me as I thought about Mizz's activity on that same lawn where I mourned with my brother Jeff and Roz's family and friends.

Non-Corridor Habitat

Some human-altered areas that are not corridors, such as golf courses, cranberry bogs, and dumps, provide coyotes with places to hunt as well as travel. These areas may be locations where adults and pups rest when they are at summer rendezvous sites. Residential areas are routinely used as well, although rarely in proportion to their availability.

There is little doubt that coyotes find this type of habitat important for hunting as we regularly observed coyotes foraging at night, zig-zagging in and out of backyards at a trot, searching for such prey as might be found on or near mowed lawns and shrubs, like rodents, rabbits and domestic cats. Residential and human-altered areas provide coyotes with an abundance of prey (such as rodents), making it attractive to them to forage in human-dominated areas especially at night.

Nevertheless, the coyotes we tracked rested primarily in wooded areas dur-ing the daytime. These were also important seasonal locations where they denned and gave birth to their young. Coyotes seem to live well in a combination of altered and natural areas, interspersed with residential areas.

Because the adaptability of coyotes is well-documented, land managers should consider strategically integrating natural areas in human-dominated landscapes when designing wildlife reserves for two reasons:

1) It can provide important buffer zones between humans and wildlife.
2) There may be a proximity threshold beyond which predators such as coyotes cannot withstand human development.

For example, collisions with cars proved to be the highest cause of mortality in our coyote study population. Other factors, such as human hunting, poisoning, and starvation were causes of mortality but they were not as significant as vehicle accidents. (An exception to this was during the harsh winter of 2005 when hunting accounted for the majority of dead coyotes.)

As we continue to keep our records, additional research should shed some light on whether improved wildlife reserve design might increase coyote presence and survival in urban areas. The use of wildlife-friendly tunnels or overpasses along strategic areas of major roads and highways could be tested to determine if increased connectivity to natural and/or altered areas would prove beneficial by decreasing the chances of both animal and human automobile accidents and fatalities. And because urban areas have such a high density of roads, it just may be that certain animals learn to avoid urban hazards, survive, and reproduce regardless of any human-induced changes.

In our study populations, we have had a couple of older coyotes (eleven years old), plus a few animals that were collared as middle-aged adults that may still be alive (the batteries in their collars have expired so we are no longer able to track them). These long-lived animals must have crossed roads tens of thousands of times if they behave everyday as we observed them doing during a typical radio-tracking session. But without doubt, the highlight of our radio-tracking escapades on urban coyotes was Fog's dispersal during spring 2004 as related at the beginning of this chapter. Fog was initially captured in Revere, and dispersed through all of Boston and even parts of Cambridge, before heading south and ending up in Dartmouth by the Massachusetts/Rhode Island border. This area is about as urban as one can get!

Activity Patterns

Evident from many of the documented accounts that I have weaved throughout this book is that coyotes are mostly active at night. Statistically speaking, coyote activity increases greatly with nocturnal time periods. All of the long distance movements of coyotes noted during our study took place during nocturnal hours. That is not to say that coyotes were not sometimes active during daylight hours; they were, especially in the early morning. We also occasionally sighted coyotes during daylight hours throughout the year. We noted a dramatic change, however, during the pup-rearing period of April to June, when breeding females were more diurnal than average and tended to be as active during the day as at night.

Once pups are born in the spring, because they are vulnerable to cold and predators, adult coyotes must alternate hunting and regularly return to the den to provision and protect them. In fact, unlike domestic dogs, father coyotes have a very strong role in raising their offspring. By June I often located males with the pups more than females. I believe this is partly because females are worn-out from several months of non-stop nursing, protecting, and feeding their litters of from four to eight pups. That's enough work for a domestic dog who doesn't have to hunt for her meals.

No doubt this role change in coyote parenting is part of the weaning process, and as with all mammals, the females might be a bit irritable as hormones change and lactation is decreasing or ceases altogether. Coyote moms might also just be tired of being near the pups constantly, and getting bitten and licked for their last supply of milk. At this time of year it is common to notice mother coyotes growling at their pups, an obvious indication of how the females feel. She has to get across to them that the rules are changing and soon there will be no more free milk.

In my observations of Sill with his pups, if I had not had him collared, I would have thought that he was the mother, not father. By mid-summer I would see him with the pups almost every day despite watching him also doggedly patrolling his territory at night. When we re-collared him in 2004, he had an open wound in his rear right leg, probably a result of a coyote fight or even a gunshot wound (it healed by that autumn). I expected him to be struggling for survival so I was shocked to discover a week after his mid-May recapture that he was the breeding male of a pack of three to four adults who were raising *eight* pups! I documented him visiting his favorite rendezvous sites well into February and March, often reconvening with his full-grown offspring. The time he always put into caring for his young was certainly a testament to his great paternal skill.

Activity during the Breeding Season

Every spring I read newspaper articles describing the 'strange, bold demeanor' of certain coyotes. Most people do not realize that this is completely natural behavior to be displayed by coyotes, especially females, during breeding and pup-raising season. Because the need to provision a den site at regular intervals forces them to be more visible during daylight hours, coyotes may appear to act boldly around humans and dogs during this period, while they are simply being diligent about attending to business. There is, however, a big difference between acting indifferently (or boldly) toward humans and being a legitimate threat to people; the latter is rarer than getting struck by lightning.

The majority of complaints probably come from neighborhoods that have active coyote den or rendezvous sites nearby. Knowledge of their activity and movement patterns in local contexts may allow for the implementation of preventative measures to limit human-coyote interaction and protect pets and livestock from coyote predations.

Coyote Sill traveling in his territory

Households in areas where coyotes are frequently observed, like near rendezvous sites, could be informed to keep domestic pets (especially dogs) inside or otherwise protected, especially at night and during the pup-rearing season. Also, future state and municipal efforts should continue to preserve wooded sites in suburban areas to buffer the distances between potential or active coyote den sites and human housing.

An overreaction to the presence of coyotes occurred in spring 2004 in the South Shore Community of Hull in eastern Massachusetts when they declared a "State of Emergency" after finding coyotes "present near a schoolyard" because it was one of the only areas in that town not saturated with housing. This incident is detailed in Chapter 21 and illustrates the extreme measures that can be taken when accurate information is not provided to members of communities.

Coyote Mizz and her bizarre coat pattern

Four coyotes traveling on Sandy Neck

Fisher, a member of the weasel family, captured in north Boston study site

Carm's mate with pups before she was shot

Coyote Casper in trap

Coyote Casper crossing road

Eastern coyotes traveling in deep snow

Trapped red fox

Coyote Sill in trap

Coyotes play chasing

Coyote Mole submissive in trap

The author holding coyote Mizz, along with assistant Roswell Joseph (deceased)
during a blizzard in Hyannis

Eastern coyote Cake with author and Barnstable High School students

Coyotes love a good howl

Coyote Sly slowly waking up

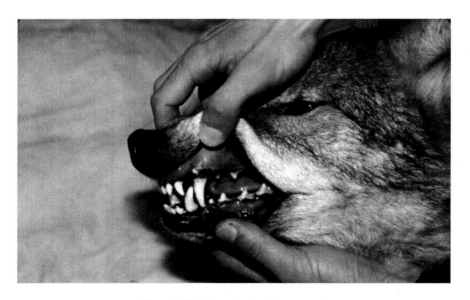

Coyote Kett's canine teeth exposed

Chapter 9

The "Rampant Coyote Problem"

What Are People Saying?

"Coyotes are everywhere."

"Coyotes are as common as tourists."

"If food runs out for coyotes, what will they turn to next our kids?"

"I am sick of the coyote protectionists—what will happen in a few years when coyote numbers triple?"

"Coyotes are increasing on the Cape."

"Something has to be done about the coyote problem."

"Coyote numbers are exploding."

"The increasing coyote population."

"Coyotes suspected in a rash of cat disappearances."

"Coyotes kill a 10-pound poodle let out at 3:00 AM."

"I can't even garden in the backyard because I am scared of running into a coyote."

"Can't coyotes be relocated elsewhere—at least so they are not in my backyard."

"I know I have been seeing 100-pound coyotes in my backyard."

"It is impossible to guess the population of coyotes in Massachusetts without using leg-hold traps."

"Coyotes need to be controlled."

"Coyote season starts November 1; hunters are invited onto my land."

"I pay taxes, so why do I have to deal with coyotes?"

"I came home and coyotes surrounded my car!"

"Jon Way is *Way*-off with his population estimates."

I have read or heard all these and other quotes or headlines, some repeatedly, in local newspapers, magazines, and on television and the radio. The number of uneducated comments, sometimes made by well-schooled and seemingly knowledgeable people, are more alarming than the actual suspected problems. This chapter attempts to address some of these claims and assertions, and comment on them.

First of all, recent articles in local newspapers and stories on the news have indicated that because leg-hold traps were made illegal, in 1996 by Massachusetts voters, it is nearly impossible to accurately measure coyote numbers (as a result of studying radio-collared coyotes) on the Cape or elsewhere in Massachusetts. The contention is that supposedly enough animals will be captured in leg-hold traps (as opposed to box-traps) that they could physically be counted.

I disagree with that haphazard and unscientific assumption. My research group has demonstrated that coyotes can successfully be captured and radio-collared without using leg-hold traps—although it does take more time and effort using box-traps and net-launchers. Furthermore, our study data has very solid scientific statistics on litter, pack, and territory sizes, among other variables, which make it possible to make extrapolations in the first place.

Coyote Population Estimates

Our research team has published an article in a peer-refereed journal that scientifically describes our methods of accurately documenting population statistics, and how we can confidently state that there are typically three to four resident adult coyotes on Cape Cod for every 11 square miles. This estimate, typical of most wildlife studies, was made during late-winter/early-spring when populations are at the lowest ebb of the yearly cycle.

We acknowledge that we cannot confirm just how many transient coyotes there are that are looking for territories of their own on the Cape. All canid studies have difficulty estimating the numbers of nomads, regardless of the technique employed to capture them, including the use of leg-hold traps. In fact, documenting where a juvenile carnivore is born, then tracking it through dispersal to where it settles is one of the most difficult aspects of wildlife research.

The main reason why an accurate, statewide population estimate is difficult to obtain is primarily due to a lack of funding. If the money were available for more traps, it would be possible to collar more animals and cover larger areas. This lack of funding for wildlife studies would make it just as difficult to guess at population statistics even if leg-hold traps were available. However, having the use of leg-hold traps for research purposes would be a welcome research tool. More questionable is the use of these body-gripping devices by commercial and recreational trappers who are killing coyotes, sometimes brutally, for profit or fun.

State legislators introduced bills in 2005 to legalize leg-hold traps in the state of Massachusetts. I wrote to the committee and posited that a rational and integrated management plan should dominate any discussion of coyote population control or recreational hunting. I explained that the proposed trapping changes were troubling for several reasons:

1)   Random removal of coyotes from local populations by trapping will have the unintended consequence of increasing local coyote densities.
2)   Trapping deflects attention and resources away from proven ecological and educational interventions in local communities of the Commonwealth.
3)   Trapping is usually conducted after the fact (for example, after a coyote kills a dog in an area).

Research throughout the country has shown that trapping (especially recreational trapping) increases the wariness of coyotes and makes them more difficult to capture. This is why the current trapping law that allows leg-hold traps only when coyotes present a documented public health hazard (simply being seen in a backyard does not count), is more effective in removing problem coyotes.

Recreational trapping, which causes only a temporary reduction in coyote density, spurs more coyote breeding and transients settling in to occupy those vacant territories, and does nothing to reduce overall population density. Remember, coyotes can cover a 50-mile distance in less than a week. Thus, repealing the trapping law won't result in a decrease in coyote numbers in local areas, and could result in an unwanted increase.

A trapper, attempting to show that he was protecting public safety by trapping and killing several coyotes in Hull, inadvertently supported my theory during his testimony at a state house hearing. At the end of his testimony, he conceded that coyote populations quickly recovered and there were just about the same number of coyotes as were originally present when he began trapping a year earlier.

Non-lethal Population Control Alternatives

One argument used in favor of trapping and dispatching the captured critter is the contention that leg-hold trapping will keep coyotes afraid of people. There is, however, no peer-reviewed research to support that argument. Non-lethal aversion-conditioning techniques, such as chasing, yelling at, or throwing rocks at coyotes could be just as effective at fear-programming in the long run, especially for resident packs in a given area.

Stuart Ellins, in *Living with Coyotes*, devoted an entire book to the prospect of negatively conditioning coyotes preying on livestock by lacing carcasses of domestic beasts with lithium chloride and other chemicals that cause the eater to get violently ill, but not die. Ellins argued that we regrettably spend millions of dollars mired in the use of inefficient and barbaric methods of wildlife management in this age of reason and high technology, and give too little credit to the instincts and intelligence of predators.

In 1996, I actually voted against the leg-hold trapping ban mostly because I was trained in the old-school wildlife management belief at UMass Amherst that trapping is an integral part of maintaining furbearer populations. I now believe that Massachusetts voters made the correct decision. While trapping will not make much difference to coyote numbers because of their reproductive potential and colonization abilities, it will definitely cause undue animal suffering, as ample literature sources demonstrate. The thought of someone dispatching a coyote with repeated beatings of a club to protect the pelt, or with a bullet to the head while it is held in a leg-hold trap is an unpleasant thought to most of us. As of this writing, a decision has not been reached regarding this aspect of 'coyote management' in Massachusetts.

Relocating Coyotes

People ask me, "Why can't you trap the ones on my property and relocate them?"

Considering the biology of coyotes as previously discussed, it is useless to trap and move a coyote to a different area in hopes that it would remain there. This is especially true considering that coyotes have already saturated all of New England (except for a few remote offshore islands like Martha's Vineyard and Nantucket).

And some might consider it unethical to move a coyote to a new place where they might merely end up as an unwanted resident in someone else's back yard. Further, because the new area no doubt already has a resident territorial coyote pack, the relocated animal might have a difficult chance of surviving there. Another valid consideration is the potential for spreading diseases to new areas if coyotes are relocated.

Also, based on what biologists know about coyotes as a species, they have well-developed inner compasses that makes it highly conceivable that a healthy coyote, once relocated, might simply travel back to its original territory. There is no question about their abilities to travel amazing distances. So when you add motivation to return to their family, a coyote might be able to get back to their original location even when moved a couple of hundred miles away.

Coyotes are born to travel

How Coyote Population Numbers Are Affected

Practically speaking, there are two ways that coyote populations can increase at a local (town-size) scale:

1) if something happens to decrease a territory size; and/or
2) if the pack size increases.

In our nine-year ongoing study, we have found no significant deviations from the norm. Slight deviations have occurred such as the larger-than-normal pack of six adults led by Mole that I saw one summer in Marstons Mills (although, the long-term stability of these larger groups is suspect). After Mole died, it was rare for me to see more than three to four adults together in that area, until summer 2006 when I saw Sill and at least four other adults raising pups at the same site. The Marstons Mills Rendezvous Site was a perfect location for coyotes because it consisted of:

- large cranberry bogs to hunt rodents in
- water nearby
- plenty of cover
- elevated views for the adults to spot danger; and
- people in the area probably feeding them

Although the territories of most coyotes, and their associated daily movements throughout their ranges, have remained consistently impressive, there have been some abnormal events that have significantly impacted certain groups. Among them, the case of a mated pair, Skunks and Jog, dying in unrelated incidents within a short interval of time, and two separate packs forming, each taking over half of their original territory.

Interestingly, and I would argue intelligently, the two groups divided their range at the mid-Cape highway. We collared two young adult coyotes in the area, each of which survived for over two years in their new territories. Carm, a young male, remained on the north side of the old range, and Cake, a female transient who previously used the area to the immediate east, claimed the area south of the highway.

Random events could have caused this division of land if each coyote pack formed at the same time and could only claim a certain segment of land before the other was able to. It could also be possible that because both were young adults and inexperienced with cars and highways, it may have been a somewhat purposeful dividing line. In fact, for two years, these coyotes rarely crossed the highway (although in June 2006 I documented Cake crossing north of Route 6 on two occasions).

Nonetheless, even with these smaller territories, there still was only about one coyote per square mile, not including young pups, in areas that averaged well over 500 people per square mile. Furthermore, I suspect that a four to five square-mile territory would be about the bare minimum that a coyote pack could use on a relatively long-term (few years) basis.

It seems obvious that it is humans that have the rampant population problem. In general, we live at amazing densities in which 100 people per square mile would be considered rural to lightly suburban. In contrast, coyotes, like any predator except man, live at very low densities. A very high coyote density in mid-winter, when most population estimates are made, would be less than one animal per square mile. While there might be 35 pounds of coyote per square mile at best, in

Cake sitting alert in her territory in Centerville

many places there are at least 150,000 pounds of humans in those same land-scapes. That translates to 4,200 times more humans by weight than coyotes in lightly suburban areas, and much more in urban areas.

A Little Perspective

Recent comments in many different papers' editorial sections have claimed in one way or another, that since coyotes kill domestic pets, mainly cats, they might next prey upon children. A little common sense and perspective might help this issue. There has been one coyote-caused human fatality in recorded history, which occurred with a 3-year old child in California in the early 1980s.

On the other hand, a survey by the National Centers for Disease Control (CDC) and Prevention in Atlanta reports that there is a dog-bite epidemic in the United States. On average,

- 20 people per year die nationwide as a result of domestic dog attacks,
- About 4,000 dog bites per year occur in Massachusetts alone
- Nearly 5 million people are bitten by dogs in the U.S. every year
- 800,000 of those victims require medical attention

Yet, one coyote bite on a human typically makes front-page headlines regionally and sometimes nationwide. In fact, while the Boston-area news covered the death of a child killed by a dog for one day, those same networks repeatedly, over a two-week period, reported the mere presence of coyotes near a playground.

Data from the CDC indicates that if humans fear coyotes, we should also be terrified of bees, lightning, getting into our cars, leaving our homes and getting murdered, or of getting charged by a deer in rut. Statistically speaking, our commute home from work is a much more dangerous undertaking than walking in our favorite conservation area (in fear of a coyote mauling). Unfortunately, the evening news substantiates that other humans are the worst predators to be feared when out hiking.

When pets are allowed outside, a few simple precautions can quickly make the fear of coyote attacks a relative non-issue in urbanized areas. These precautions will also protect pets from other dangers including those from human predators.

- Owners should not let dogs outdoors loose without constant supervision, unless in a fenced yard with fences at least five feet high, and still checked on regularly. While a fence does not guarantee total protection, it is a good deterrent to coyotes or humans who would snatch or harm pets left outside alone.
- Dogs taken outdoors by their owners should always be leashed unless in a fenced yard, and should still be supervised and checked regularly.
- Dogs should not be tied outdoors unfenced and unsupervised in coyote-prevalent areas. Accidents have happened.
- Cats should be kept indoors unless trained (very difficult) to remain at home.
- Dogs and cats should not be left outside for *any* period of time unsupervised, especially at night, even in a fenced enclosure.
- Invisible fences do not protect your pets from predators. While they may keep your pet in your yard, they don't keep predators or other animals out of your yard.

Is it really that difficult to closely supervise pets or refrain from feeding wildlife to avoid unnecessary confrontations? I am not suggesting that pets are not important or cherished members of the household. As a pet owner, I know the bond and love that exist between man and animal. In late fall 2005 I saved a starving, stray cat who lived most of her first eight or so months outside in the back alleys of the city of Lowell, Massachusetts. I do not dare let "Lowelle" outside anymore and she appears to be happy, fat, and remains safe as an indoor cat.

Many people do not like to acknowledge the serious risks that free-roaming pets face, especially cats. Yes, you have to change their cat boxes if they stay inside, but indoor cats live safer and generally longer lives. And keeping dogs leashed and under close supervision is more work, but it goes a long way in preventing dangerous and unnecessary interactions from ever occurring. Because of the large territories that a coyote pack has, there is a small chance that a cat would be killed if left out for one night (unless you live near a den or rendezvous site), but because coyotes regularly travel throughout their ranges it would be only a matter of time before a conflict occurred.

Now that coyotes are quite well established throughout the state, it may be that pet owners believe that no other forms of fatality for Rover or Fluffy could be possible. Forget about cars, the neighbor's dog (or even the neighbor himself), fishers (large weasels), disease, or other predators, it must be a coyote.

It Was The Coyotes!

In one such instance, I was talking to a very nice lady in Revere who blamed coyotes for the death of her cat. Karen really liked the coyotes of our collared Cemetery Pack. She thought they were beautiful and saw them often from her second floor window. But on 1 November 2004 her cat was killed and she was understandably very upset. "It was the coyotes!" she said.

That morning I happened to be tracking the pack, which, at the time, consisted of six or seven coyotes in the bordering towns of Everett, Revere, and Malden. Four of these animals were collared: the breeding adults, Jet and Maeve, and two of the pups, Cour and Jem.

Karen met me outside her front door and asked if I could please move the coyotes somewhere else because they had just killed her cat. I expressed my sympathy and explained that even if it were within my jurisdiction to do so (which it wasn't), it was not an option for ethical reasons because these coyotes had never caused any serious problems such as threatening people.

I also had to tell her that if her cat was out in the woods in 'coyote territory', the coyotes were just acting naturally. If we moved them, other coyotes would soon move into the area to replace them. Even if it were deemed necessary, the incredible effort involved in trapping and relocating six to seven coyotes would be a daunting task.

After talking with her, I asked if I could see the cat to examine its wounds. Karen told me that it was intact in the field across from her house about 50 meters away. She directed me to where I had just observed three of the collared coyotes within feet of the cat's location about 10 minutes earlier, so I assumed the coyotes had fed on the cat. Upon investigation of the poor critter, however, even I was surprised. Fresh coyote tracks indeed surrounded the dead feline, but the cat was not touched, nor had it been killed by coyotes. Instead I found two paintballs, one which pelted the cat's body with paint, the other had crushed its skull, causing its death. I felt very bad when informing Karen of the actual cause of her cat's demise. Her call to the police to report the incident proved that she quickly and correctly re-channeled her anger from the resident coyotes she had been blaming, to the urban rednecks who cruelly and needlessly killed her pet.

Let's Use Common Sense

The previous anecdote is not intended to dispute that coyotes cause problems, or that they might ever kill a cat. Rather, it is important to realize that coyotes are wild predators living among us and that they are unpredictable and potentially dangerous. Using precautions when in coyote country is always a safe plan of action. The fact that there were two separate incidents in Massachusetts of individual rabid coyotes biting adult humans in 2005 illustrates that we need to have a healthy respect for, and perhaps keep a healthy distance from wild animals (and the diseases they may carry). Watching children and pets when they are outside, for a myriad of reasons beyond worrying about coyotes, is just basic common sense when it comes to preventing dangerous encounters.

A surprising number of people ask me,

"Should I be worried about leaving my small children outside at night? Would coyotes attack them?"

My typical response is, "If you are leaving small children alone outside or in the woods at night, they have much more to worry about than coyotes." I watched the news soon after my conversation with Karen and saw the arrest of a child molester in Malden, just a few miles away from the Cemetery Coyote Pack.

Coyotes in Our Backyards

People say 'coyotes are everywhere', and in actuality, that is not far from the truth. While they are obviously not omnipresent, we know that they patrol their home territories constantly, can travel great distances in a matter of hours, and one could conceivably show up in any location within or around that territory at just about any time. It is important that people do their part to keep coyotes wild by:

1. Getting educated about them
2. Not doing anything to attract them to their property (don't feed them or leave any food outdoors, in or near their yard)
3. Not letting coyotes become habituated to them or their families

Many groups such as the government agency MassWildlife (Massachusetts Division of Fisheries and Wildlife) (http://www.mass.gov/dfwele/dfw/dfwcoy. htm) and the Massachusetts Society for Prevention of Cruelty to Animals (MSPCA) promote the Living With Wildlife program (http://www.livingwithwildlife.org/) and provide advice on how to limit negative interactions with coyotes.

This issue must really be put in perspective. I regularly documented radio-collared coyotes bedded in urban settings such as at the edges of yards or by school playgrounds. I am sure this occurs statewide 365 days per year. As long as I say nothing about the coyotes being there, they usually never make any headlines, except maybe in the newspapers of the local vole population.

Nearly all instances of coyotes harming children are from food-conditioned or sick coyotes, not from healthy individuals. It has become obvious during our study that healthy coyotes very much prefer to avoid people, even though we all co-exist in the same neighborhoods. I can think of two reasons why this would be so:

1. They know that humans are dangerous to them; and
2. With our erect bipedal posture, we do not appear or smell like anything they prey on and thus humans are not on their search radar

At times, coyote indifference to humans can be misconstrued by some as a threat, when the coyote is merely comfortable around people as it goes on its daily rounds looking for food. These bold coyotes are rarely dangerous, and very common in our western national parks where hunting has not been allowed for a long time.

During my ten-day trip to Yellowstone in 2005, colleagues and I watched wolves from a distance of over a mile away, while a coyote family passed within 20 yards of us on a daily basis. Researchers in Yellowstone speculate that coyotes who have learned to stay near human onlookers usually avoid getting killed by wolves.

Considering their ecology, which includes large territories and daily long-range movements, coyotes actually do an amazing job of avoiding people. Collectively, if *C. latrans* wanted to, they could show up virtually anywhere in the state, including cities, on any given night. This is probably true for every state in the Union, except Hawaii and Long Island, New York, where they have not yet colonized because of highly urban New York City in the way. Consequently, since human-coyote interactions are relatively rare, we can only believe that they want it that way.

I cannot even count how many times I have tracked coyotes and located them bedded down within 50–100 meters of houses. In these common situations, I can hear people working or relaxing outside while I am monitoring a sleeping family of coyotes who no doubt is aware of everything going on around them. The following is a typical field journal entry of mine describing such an evening:

31 July 2005. After celebrating my grandfather's 89th birthday, I track Sill, who is at the end of my parents' street (about 200 meters away) in an old overgrown cranberry bog immediately south of Cranberry Ridge Road. The area now contains many saplings and larger trees, making visibility poor.

8:08 PM—Sill is in the central/west-central part of the five-acre bog. I wait on the east side of the access road leading down to Long Pond. I sit under a pine tree to stay out of sight and so I can see both sides of the road in case the coyotes come out of hiding.

8:15 PM—A small adult, probably a yearling, comes up an old sewer gulley and stops on the road about 50 feet from me and looks around. It then shuffles into the woods to the east side of the road. I hear it for about a minute as it moves behind me heading up a slight incline.

—As I sit here, I almost constantly hear people outside on their decks on High View Circle, just up the hill from the wooded bog where the pack is bedded down. It is pretty amazing how quiet approximately 10 coyotes can be (I counted four adults and up to eight pups a couple of weeks before).

8:32 PM—Sill is still in the bog. His signal starts to become variable as he wakes up from his daily sleep. At least a few of the pups are with him as I can hear them growling and whining. No doubt the pups are playing and wrestling, just out of my sight at dark.

Coyotes often become active before dark or after dawn and people see them, especially if their houses are close to a wooded area like I just described. However, a coyote trotting through a field or yard should almost always be considered not dangerous. It might be bold, but being bold is far from being a threat. The average coyote might be comfortable in your backyard, but that does not mean it will attack you.

The "Rampant Coyote Problem"

Coyotes typically show absolutely no interest in human beings unless they have been conditioned to humans by being fed. At the very least, they definitely do not regard people, even children, as their prey. Toddlers and infants, who play or sleep on the ground instead of in a standing position, might be in a gray area since they could be confused with a small animal. Parental supervision of very young children in any area is always wise for other reasons, but they should obviously not be left unattended at camp sites, trailer parks, or even in a rural unfenced back yard in sparsely settled areas where coyotes (or other predators) might appear on the scene unannounced.

Because of my pro-coyote and common sense stance, I am often contacted by the media or local agencies and pitted against angry citizens when coyotes are featured on the news. After a major event involving coyotes, whether directly related to our research (such as a capture), or indirectly related (like a coyote attack on a dog), if it happens in eastern Massachusetts, my team gets a new (unpaid) part-time job. This ranges from fielding phone calls to doing PR work, such as appearing on television or being quoted in newspaper articles.

We always try to be as informative as possible when describing coyote behavior relating to encounters with domestic pets, because losing a pet is very emotional for people. This can be very time-consuming and takes me away from my normal tasks, either much needed field time or rest. Other members of our research team also take their turns performing this needed service.

In spring 2005, after appearing on television a few times, Dave Eatough remarked to me "We need to hire someone part-time to handle all of this media coverage. I just don't have the time or the energy." Dave worked 12-hour days at Revere High School, then always put in a few more hours tending traps and tracking the Cemetery Pack. While we have jobs and classes to attend in addition to the research work we do, people still want information. Since there are few people who can give accurate information in this arena, we feel we need to take time out of our schedules to field questions.

Why Me?

It really sounds like whining when people tell me that since they live in America they should not have to deal with these creatures. In a modern society of skyscrapers and computers and 60-hour workweeks, wildlife has no place. Society's disconnect from nature seems to grow from one generation to the next and could be directly linked to many social ills, including violence, stress, mental illness, and obesity. There is actually a name for this. It has been aptly termed 'nature-deficit disorder' and is described by Richard Louv in *Last Child in the Woods: Saving Our Children from Nature-Deficit Disorder*.

Although not yet officially accepted by the scientific or medical community, Louv details the importance of children experiencing nature first hand and the difference that it can make in their lives. He even goes as far as discussing the importance of creating a zoopolis, or re-creating cities, metropolises that are animal- and plant-friendly. Louv argues that this would benefit people and animals alike.

Coyotes are mostly night travelers

For me, having wild animals around is one of the reasons I love my country so much. Living with coyotes increases the wildness of the landscape and makes it a more balanced and exciting place to be. I strongly believe that accepting all animals increases our moral and intellectual character and increases our chance to prosper as a society in perpetuity. In essence, it displays our humility and forces us to recognize that we are part of this world too, not a separate entity functioning within an environment designed solely for our convenience.

Socio-Ecological Benefits

The presence of coyotes and other predators signals a healthy landscape that also increases property values and improves our overall socio-ecology in the long run. Many of the things we most cherish about comfortable suburban living, such as lush woods surrounding properties and open grassy yards teeming with wildlife, are also some of the key attributes that make suburban areas perfect coyote habitat. Understanding the behavior of coyotes in communities might lead to proactive attempts to avoid negative confrontations from occurring.

In addition to socio-ecological economic benefits, there is also increased belief among many people that having animals around increases our psychological well being. We love seeing animals and many feed them outside their windows and watch them with binoculars. The thrill of observing wildlife is often a welcome distraction from the hustle and bustle of everyday life.

Famous Harvard naturalist E.O. Wilson goes so far as to suggest that there is an instinctive bond between humans and other living things. He calls this 'biophilia' and proposes the possibility that the deep affiliations humans have with nature are rooted in our biology. While I agree with Wilson's hypothesis, I often think that humans are, without a doubt, the most arrogant species to live on this planet. We take land from the animals, and we want them killed or removed when they don't fit nicely into the new systems we create for our own comfort. Then we complain when 'someone' won't kill the pests or when our tax dollars are appropriated to perform some other ecological balancing act, often stemming from the animals we displaced or killed.

This chapter advocates that there are some simple solutions that can be implemented to solve or prevent such problems, but many just will not accept them. With global warming creating flooding from regional monsoons, natural disasters rampant, and a continuing war going on in 2006, coyotes don't look so bad, do they?

Simple Solutions

I know that many people appreciate having coyotes around, as I often receive inquiries about how people can help them by perhaps offering them food. While it is a caring gesture, I always strongly urge these well-meaning people to forego that idea, for several reasons:

1) Coyotes or other animals who get fed by people can become reliant on humans to the point of becoming a public health threat;
2) Human-fed coyotes can potentially become bold and aggressive around people.
3) They are likely to be easier to kill by people who don't like them.

Normally, coyotes live at relatively low densities and, unlike other animals such as deer, they do not become overabundant in an area. However, when coyotes are bold around people, they are not as easily tolerated as deer.

Human feeding can exasperate these types of coyotes, as they then expect food from all humans. It can also expose them to people who might harm them by poisoning or shooting. Throughout the process of my research, I make a very concerted effort not to condition coyotes to me through feeding. Coyotes in our study who are fed are usually trapped and released, and being trapped is a negative experience for any wild creature. We can only assume they fear death at our hands, because they cannot comprehend any other reason for being immobilized in a trap or cage, as evidenced by the way they cringe when enclosed.

Those we have trapped before, run from us when we track them in the field after they are released. On the other hand, coyotes fed by an average homeowner where there is no such negative association might eventually lose their fear of man and become too comfortable in an area. That's when they tend to display aggressive behavior. Coyotes are not stray dogs; they are truly wild creatures and they need and should be allowed to forage naturally. This enables a remarkable predator, who is normally very shy of people, a chance to live a relatively normal life and continue to quietly (except when they howl!) eke out an existence in urbanized environments.

One reason I admire coyotes is because they give a landscape, even an urban one, a sense of mystique. They are the soul of many environments as are many top predators. I am always a little more alert knowing that predators are living in an area. I believe that the more complete an assemblage of species in an ecosystem, including urban areas, the healthier that place is.

Yet, the presence of the wildness component is the very reason so many people are afraid of predators. Living in urbanized areas tends to cause people to lose contact with nature. Based on their limited and often misguided knowledge, people want to control nature by redesigning it with creatures who do not pose a threat. Coyotes can bring the drama of nature right to people's backyards like no other large predator can (except maybe cougars in the western U.S.). It is strangely contradictory that people admire nature and even invite it into their homes (birdfeeders on the kitchen window, or tamed wolves called 'domestic dogs' in the living room), and yet consider other aspects of the natural world to be so fearful and unwelcome.

Many anti-wolf people, such as typical livestock ranchers in western states, despise the fact that most pro-wolf people do not live in areas where wolves range and thus do not have to directly deal with the creatures they are so vocally supporting. In contrast, however, one of the unique things about coyote supporters is that most people who appreciate them do have these wild canids within their regions and locales, with the animals often making their presence known right in their backyards. Thus the pro-coyote voice can potentially be very loud and their arguments easily justified based on the fact that they have to deal with the creatures like everyone else does.

A fact often lost on many urban dwellers came clear to me a few weeks ago when the Boston area networks highlighted an interesting thread of news. Commentators interviewed a number of unfortunate residents living in a particular area where construction, road work, and the inordinate spring rains combined to flush out the neighborhood rat population. Neighbors complained that even their cats were terrorized and their dogs were attacked and bitten by large sewer rats.

All I could think of was that here was a serious inner-city problem, compounded by the possibility of the spread of disease that was just a simple smorgasbord for a coyote family going unharvested. And the only remedies the government problem-solvers could come up with were further perils to the families and their pets, such as rat poison and exterminators. This 'major problem' might simply go away if someone would recognize and act on the ecological value of the natural balance of predator (coyote) and prey (rats).

Chapter 10

Coyote Management

The Redneck Scenario

It is October 2003 on beautiful Sandy Neck Beach, a remote six-mile long, half-mile-wide barrier beach, not far from where I observed the coyote puppies in June 1994. Two hunters are in an open area called the Dromedary, about four miles out and consisting mostly of sand dunes covered with dune grass for about half a square mile. The sun is just peeping over the eastern horizon and the orange glow illuminates the beach.

It is the second week of pheasant season. This part of the hunting season consists of town and/or state employees, depending on location, releasing captive-raised birds into the wild either the night before or the morning of the start of the season. Most hunters already know this but oddly, it never seems to occur to them how ironic it is that they will soon be shooting something that other people were actually holding in their hands just hours before they started hunting them.

Pheasant season has been around for a long time, so non-human predators such as owls, hawks, foxes, and coyotes naturally key in on this abundant, seasonal resource as well. The pheasants were raised in captivity, are unafraid of humans, have few skills for stealth or living in the wild, and are understandably stunned by their sudden release in a foreign area. They are, in essence, 'sitting ducks' for the lamest of hunters.

The two hunters move along and separate, planning to reconvene on the other side of a large dune in the northwest section of the open expanse. As they walk west with the glow of the early morning sun behind them, they have full visibility. Anything to the west would have to look directly into the sun's rays to detect them.

As one of the hunters rounds the bend, he sees a coyote stalking a pheasant. He raises his gun, locks it on target, and takes a couple of shots. The young coyote runs off wounded. The bird shot pellets penetrated her hide and slow her down, but she manages to get out of range of additional shots.

The other hunter comes around the corner and asks his buddy what the heck just happened. The first hunter replies, "Ah, I just saw a damn coyote stalking my pheasant and I took a couple of pops at it."

"Did you get it?" the second hunter asks.

The first hunter responds, "I don't know…who cares. Com'on—let's keep going."

The second hunter shakes his head, realizing that the legal season for coyotes doesn't begin until the first of November in Massachusetts. "I guess there isn't much we can do about it now," he replies, "but one thing's for sure, when the legal hunting season begins I'm going right after Way's collared coyotes."

The first hunter concludes, "Me too. What good is his research anyway? I've been in the woods all my life and I know more about coyotes than he does. There's gotta be five times more coyotes than he claims."

Because of their disrupted focus on the coyote, both hunters totally forget about the pheasant that was formerly the target of both predators, coyote and human. Instead, the two men backtrack their route looking for other pheasants. That pheasant may live yet another day.

Meanwhile, the wounded she-coyote reaches a thick swampy area and hides in the nearby brush, but her time is running out. She is bleeding profusely from multiple small wounds characteristic of birdshot. The bright crimson of her blood blends in perfectly with the autumn harvest of cranberries in the bog where she lies. She beds down for the day but fails to move more than 15 feet. She arises again at dusk, only to move 20 more feet to the middle of the small cranberry bog where she lays down again. The night brings her a merciful peace; her suffering ends with the last breath she will ever take as she finally bleeds to death. Like an aggressively controlled forest fire, the tawny glow of her eyes extinguish. Her body lies intact to decompose by way of the scavenger community.

The Real World

A week after pheasant hunting season opened, I went out for an enjoyable hike, mainly looking for deer before their hunting season started. In the middle of my 10-mile hike, the enjoyment vanished as my random route brought me right to the carcass of a young female coyote whose pelt was indented and dotted with dried blood spots, half decomposed and clearly shot to death. I threw my pocket knife to the ground, stunned and angry that some damned redneck had blasted this animal and just left her to suffer and die in pain.

I did a quick inspection and found it to be a six-to-seven-month-old juvenile female. Her adult teeth were evident and from what I could see, she was a pretty animal with a shiny silvery coat. Had that coyote lived, she would have

Remains of dead coyote found on Sandy Neck

eventually left her family's territory, which includes all of and extends well beyond Sandy Neck, dispersing perhaps hundreds of miles away.

Assuming she avoided cars and people, she possibly would have toured around the Cape and covered more territory and explored more diverse areas than a human could possibly imagine. Her travels might have taken her in a straight-line away from Sandy Neck to maximize the distance from her natal range. Or just as likely, she may have poked around the local area, remaining with her parents as a babysitter for the next year's batch of pups. But she never got a chance because of that early morning misfortune that happened on a beautiful October day.

Shortly after this incident, I learned of another coyote who was arrowed during the deer bow and arrow season on Sandy Neck. Neither was this animal tracked down and humanely finished off by the hunter and it presumably also died a slow death after dragging itself away wounded. My patience was sorely tried when a third incident occurred the second day of January 2004.

It was a cool, crisp winter day. Slot, a beautiful 36-lb red-tinted coyote, hadn't moved in at least two days. He was fairly close, somewhere in the marsh on the south side of Sandy Neck, because the barrier beach was in sight from where I tracked him. I had a difficult time pinpointing him, as his signal was loud and strong in all directions. I assumed he was foraging in one of the creek gullies but I thought that was rather odd during the daytime.

After 30 long minutes of taking bearings, I finally pinpointed him about 100 meters from my vehicle. At that point I became concerned because I didn't see him, and there was nowhere he could hide out in the marsh grass. Sure enough, with some diligence, I found his intact carcass. His distinct red pelage blended in perfectly with the amber-colored marsh grass. He had a broken leg, but otherwise looked to be in great shape. I assumed that he drowned in the creek because of his leg injury.

For routine verification, I brought the body to the nearby Cape Wildlife Center in West Barnstable. The veterinary technician, Judy Ellal, decided that we should X-ray him to see what really happened. It turned out that I was wrong about how he died. He was actually littered with small birdshot pellets, including a couple lodged in his severely fractured rear leg. A necropsy revealed that he sustained much internal hemorrhaging and probably bled to death internally from the damage caused by the pellets.

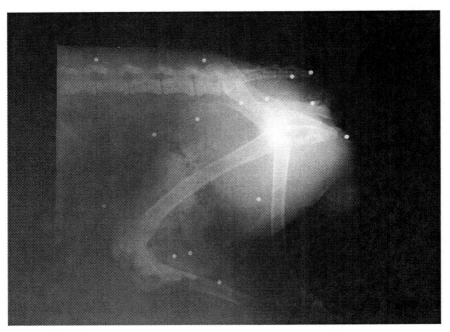

XRays taken of coyote Slot revealed multiple pellet holes in his body

I knew that no hunter with any integrity would do such a thing—and perhaps that's the key. To a person lacking integrity, each creature of the earth is viewed either as 'good' or 'bad'; the good are to be cultivated and the bad to be disposed of. Actually though, each creature has a proper place in the balance of nature and it is not man's right to determine which ones are good and bad. It's obvious that brilliant men invented weapons, which enabled everyone, even stupid ones, to use them. With this superior weaponry, an ignorant man can easily disrespect noble creatures. I think mankind will eventually be called to task for making such arrogant decisions so lightly.

Furious by these acts of indifference, I wrote a letter to the editor of the Cape Cod Times that was published soon afterward. I explained my outrage regarding these cruel, unprincipled acts. While many people sympathized with my anger that the coyotes had died both illegally and needlessly, one person who saw the letter responded to it by calling my mother.

This man identified himself as the person, along with his friends, who did the killing. He gave an apparently fictitious name that the local authorities could not identify, and he claimed that I was wrong about my claims in the letter. His excuse for leaving the carcasses was that a hunter has until the end of the season to tag a dead coyote at a check station. While he is right on that minor point (coyote pelts do not need to be tagged until the end of the season in February in Massachusetts), I simply claimed that it was illegal, and mighty unethical, to shoot an animal and not search for it to finish it off. He may have been operating from the standpoint that since he hadn't killed it outright, he would wait a few weeks for it to die, and then simply forgot about it.

The caller went on to inform my mother, in true redneck fashion, that he specifically targeted collared coyotes if he saw them. Most rednecks do not care for coyotes and scoff at research, especially if its aim is to preserve life not destroy it. And I define a redneck as an uninformed person who does not appreciate or understand the complex web of nature but just likes to kill things (contrary to a true sportsman's ethics).

Similarly, I do not care for people who relate with weapons instead of their brains and see all wildlife as bulls-eyes. These people would like to see most coyotes go by the wayside just because they are predators.

True sportsmen are ethical people who abhor sloppy hunters as much as most non-hunters and nature-lovers do, and sloppy hunters are neither sportsmen nor ethical. Sloppy hunters were never taught right, or maybe they just aren't teachable, because no person of integrity would wound something, target animal or otherwise, and not follow-up and kill it to prevent its suffering. Leaving it to languish is a sign of a lack of empathy that extends beyond animals to other humans. They should be required to hang up their weapons before their deficient mentality tempts them to use their weapons on people.

After writing the editorial, I turned to the task of writing a second letter, this one to the town of Barnstable trying to give them reasons to cancel coyote hunting on Sandy Neck and in adjacent areas. I wrote, "The amount of unethical hunting within this area is alarming and makes me angry. We are trying to conduct a long-term study of coyote ecology in Barnstable, and the Sandy Neck region is a core part of our study area. Our long-term study is only one of two or three focused on coyotes in the entire United States. Certainly our research benefits a much larger segment of the population than the miniscule hunting license fees paid for by the people committing these random acts of unnecessary violence. Your assistance in making coyote hunting illegal would be greatly appreciated. This request should not affect other sports peoples' interests but will hopefully end the needless illegal coyote killings."

My pleas went for not. The governing board informed me that it was not possible or in their interests to accommodate my requests but that I should 'continue to inform hunters' of my research. Why, I wondered, so hunters can find the coyotes more easily? Instead I simply quit conducting research there, realizing that there was no incentive to continue, despite the incredible beauty of that part of my study area. After all, why would I spend three months trying to capture an animal, only to be rewarded with the frustration of retrieving its carcass and collar? This would be especially true if people were indeed keeping tabs on where I track coyotes in order to use the information to kill the very animals I was studying.

A Case for Non-Consumptive Users

Fortunately for the coyotes, there are considerably more non-hunters than hunters in that area. And of the total population of hunters, there appear to be more ethical hunters than rednecks. Sadly though, this small unethical fraction of the population that gives hunters a bad reputation is given the leeway to do virtually anything, except obey a regulated deer-hunting season. I'm convinced that if just a few people have the moral conviction and integrity to do the right thing, progress could be made and maybe one day I, and the many residents who support our wildlife research may get to enjoy this beautiful area free from coyote hunting.

Even people who are not crazy about coyotes usually realize that well-conducted research on the top predator in an ecosystem benefits not only all the other wildlife in that system, but all the residents and observers who love and appreciate that wildlife. A balanced ecosystem, free from human interference and 'control', is the best and most successful for wildlife and for man.

Agency mismanagement of so-called protected lands and resources has resulted in nearly wiping out many unique species over our nation's history, and also in power plays that have wasted untold millions of taxpayer dollars unnecessarily. For example, bison in Montana aren't allowed to leave Yellowstone National Park for a supposed disease (brucellosis) that they have never been documented to pass on to cattle. Instead of paying the remaining cattle ranchers a lump sum of a couple million dollars to permanently stop grazing near the park, which would protect bison and ecotourism interests for 50 miles outside the park, taxpayers wastefully spend millions of dollars annually having bureaucrats round up and cull the national park service's symbol when they leave the artificial boundaries of Yellowstone. Non-commonsense decisions like that make me downright angry.

Businessmen are taught that everything is about business and profit, and businessmen run all our government departments and agencies. As I found when I tried to get hired into one such state agency hoping to protect and study wildlife, they are not about that. My interactions with bureaucracy at all levels in my advocacy efforts for wildlife, predators in particular, and specifically coyotes, has proven this out over and over.

So over time, as additional marked coyotes were taken legally during the hunting season (we lost three more coyotes to hunters in February 2005), it was more fitting to put the blame on the state fish and wildlife agencies, whose laws allow and even encourage these needless killings. One quick glance at any agency's web page will find proud postings of 'harvest records' for species within their state.

'Harvest' is a word that is easier on the non-hunting public than 'killings'. "A record deer year," for example, refers not to a time where deer are more plentiful or more commonly sighted or where great research took place on the species, but to the hunting season where the highest number of harvests (deaths) of the species occurred.

Is it too much to ask for government agencies to close less than 100 square miles (i.e., the town of Barnstable) out of an entire state that is open to coyote hunting, especially with the long-term study we are conducting? It is ironic that the large conservation areas in a matrix of urbanization are probably the least safe place to be for a coyote (and sometimes for any other form of wildlife including humans) during hunting season. This is particularly the case when a coyote has played by the rules by avoiding humans, and has successfully learned to steer clear of speeding cars in the cobweb of roads associated with "progress." Further, a coyote who avoids sleeping in the wooded parts of its territory (something contrary to coyote instinct) probably has a better survival rate during fall and winter.

What is a Wildlife Preserve?

One of the most contradictory things about state hunting regulations is that the people who enjoy watching wildlife greatly outnumber the hunters, especially in urban areas. Wildlife watchers make up about 31% of the country, while only 6% are hunters. In an urban state such as Massachusetts, about 31% percent of the population watches wildlife, while only 1.5% hunts.

Despite this staggering difference, state fish and game agencies, who make most of their revenue from hunting and fishing licenses, have a strong incentive to cater to this destructive segment of the population. Their agenda is at least partly to keep the agencies operating so the officials can keep their jobs. With hunting declining nationwide, managers are increasing hunting seasons and bag limits in an effort to increase the number of birds and animals killed. It is little more than a marketing ploy to increase sales to 'keep the company open'.

Massachusetts currently allows deer hunting for about two and a half months, likely the lengthiest hunting season since colonial days. While the state's biologists view the activity as needed because of lack of hunter participation and the so-called need to control wildlife (especially deer) numbers, others (like myself) view this 'management strategy' as giving a minority of people the opportunity to reduce the majority's chances to view and enjoy wildlife. For instance, why don't state agencies cater to the non-hunter by having fee-for-entry contests of the best photographs of wildlife in their jurisdictions or of the largest group size of a species, such as deer or coyotes? That should bring in a little revenue.

The Consumptive User

If you don't believe how pro-consumptive state wildlife departments are in encouraging hunting and trapping, then try interviewing for a position with them like I did. In March 2005 I met with their departmental select staff to interview for the 'Furbearing Biologist' job for the state. Furbearers are typically defined as any of the many species of mammals whose fur is of commercial value, including beavers, skunks, minks, weasels, otters, raccoons, and canids.

I thought I was a perfect candidate as I explained that I strongly believed that sustained research and education should be part of the job. The conversation very quickly turned to trapping, which is a major portion of the job for most furbearing biologists within a state agency. When I made my point that trapping wasn't the long-term answer to succeed in controlling wildlife in this position, I was repeatedly questioned, then lectured, about the recreational value of the activity.

The interviewer also did not seem too impressed when I pointed out that only a small minority (about 300 people in Massachusetts) actively participates in trapping, and that fur values are very low these days. The truth is that most states view trappers as a free public service. The trapper pays a nominal annual fee of around $30 and gets to trap for a specified amount of time during the established season. (That means that Massachusetts might make all of about $10,000 from its trapping program.) In doing so, they reduce predator numbers to a temporary "acceptable" level, whatever that may be.

I was probably too vocal about my views that a growing number of people are now realizing that hunters and trappers, whether they do the job ethically or not, reduce the numbers of animals people can enjoy watching, tracking, or photographing. I was not offered the job.

Is Hunting Still a Sport?

A mountain bike trip I took in late-fall 2005 solidified in my mind how the consumptive user is given precedence. I was in a state forest and greeted a couple of cordial deer hunters. After talking about deer sightings in the area (they had not yet killed one at that point), they warned me to take off my white helmet because other hunters, not as familiar with the land as they, might take a shot at me thinking that I am a deer's rump, flagging through the woods. I left shaking my head realizing how ridiculous it was that I would have to worry about my safety while mountain biking for most of the fall, my favorite time of year. In addition, should someone really be allowed to take a gun in the woods if they are shooting at anything white?

I thought, surely my head with my ugly white helmet affixed, could not look like a deer. But the man's recommendations were not ridiculous and I biked with helmet in hand the rest of the way. After all, three people were shot in separate incidents in nearby Vermont during the 2005 hunting season. One was a farmer working on his tractor. Maybe the hunter thought he was shooting at a wild elephant?

Besides worrying about staying safe from rednecks out hunting while I non-consumptively recreate, I was struck by the discrepancy between the ease of their obtaining a hunting license compared to the difficulties a mild-mannered researcher faced in obtaining a permit for scientific purposes. It is a striking example of the dichotomy that exists between some of the various stakeholders associated with wildlife.

For example, a hunter can spend a modest amount of money, about $30 in Massachusetts, to purchase an annual 'general big game' hunting license and kill or wound multiple species, sometimes with no limits, as is the case with coyotes and foxes, four months a year. Yet a legitimate scientist going about his business needs to fill out a mountain of paperwork and obtain multiple permits or protocols, including university animal care, state permits, and town land use permits (which often take up to a year), to conduct research on these same species. What's wrong with this picture?

Even if hunting or trapping are restricted in certain locales, obeying and upholding the laws are as important as the paperwork itself. I'm clearly reminded of two related instances of this. The first situation occurred when a lady showed me a picture of a coyote whom she thought was radio-collared. It was in central Massachusetts and at the time (2001) I only had collared coyotes on Cape Cod. I was very excited and was jogging my memory to think of potential coyotes it could have been. When I saw the pictures, which the women kindly emailed to me, I discovered that the coyote was not a collared disperser, but rather, it was obvious it had a broken wire-snare wrapped around its neck.

The woman, on my advice, contacted the appropriate wildlife personnel. The officials disagreed with me and did not think it was a snare, since they are illegal in Massachusetts. Obviously, had they agreed, it might have opened a can of worms. I then recommended to this concerned citizen that she should go public in order to draw attention to this illicit activity, but state wildlife personnel understandably disagreed, not wanting any more heat on the hot topic of coyote [mis]management. Thus, as far as I know, the issue slowly died out, probably in a very similar way that the poor skinny coyote in the photograph eventually succumbed.

The second circumstance actually involved a police officer from our north Boston study site. On the night of 13 February 2003, a police officer claimed to have shot a coyote within what is now Jet and Maeve's territory, because it was limping. "An obvious injury," the police report indicated. Anyone with a bit of outdoor experience, however, upon reading the police report would be suspicious.

The officer claimed to have seen the animal from approximately 200 yards away in a cemetery in the middle of the night, then simply approached and killed the animal. Now unless the officer had a night vision scope on a sniper rifle it's unlikely he could have seen that far into an area that I have trouble seeing 50 yards into during the daytime. The possibility of killing it from that far away is also not a plausible story. While there was a small chance that this occurred as described, I and many others in the area, doubted the accuracy of the report.

An investigation was requested, but because the officer had followed proper protocol, including writing a police report and calling the environmental police to dispose of the carcass, the issue was slowly put to rest. It was another six months before we had solid coyote activity back at that site, no doubt aided by the probable difficulty of dispersing coyotes reaching that extremely fragmented location, and possibly because the resident coyotes maintained a low profile after that incident.

The Coyote Slaughter

While Massachusetts has a fairly protective coyote-hunting season compared to other states, coyotes can still be legally hunted for four months a year with no bag limits. Camilla Fox and Christopher Papouchis, in *Coyotes in Our Midst*, report that in 42 of 49 (85.7%) U.S. states where coyotes live (Hawaii excluded) there are unlimited seasons on coyotes.

Legal killing methods, depending on state, include hunting, poisoning, hound-hunting, aerial gunning, calling and shooting, and trapping then killing coyotes by a club, strangulation, or gun. Taking into account all of the ways that coyotes die, and many are not reported, a conservative estimate of a half-million coyotes dying cruelly per year in this country is a reasonable guess, with too many killed using taxpayer dollars.

Coyotes are an important resource, and recreational hunting of them is a valid pastime in certain locales. Yet there are some members of the community that always wish more were done to control their numbers. Sportspeople who are legitimately interested in coyotes, even if they hunt them for their pelts and the challenge, are a source of interesting conversation, as well as debate. But it is baffling that there are people who feel it is acceptable to simply shoot to kill any coyote that they see behaving in an incomprehensible way. Most people would not call these sportsmen. Even many hunters share these feelings.

Especially disturbing are the people who gut-shoot animals and leave them to die. In addition to being illegal in Massachusetts, this is unnecessary and cruel, but it happens so frequently that it's obvious many are flagrantly disregarding the rules. The statutes require people to check in or tag each coyote killed by the end of the season. Several hundred coyotes are killed per year and legally reported in Massachusetts. Many more are killed in the northern New England states where both shooting and trapping are legal. Still, untold numbers are mortally wounded, to wander off and die later, or are killed outright year round, and these are never reported as hunting kills.

Hunters may have negative feelings toward coyotes because they compete with these predators for similar prey. What many people do not realize is that deer and many other prey animals that hunters seek are thought to be at their all time highs in Massachusetts and there is currently the most liberal hunting season allowed on deer in the last several hundred years. Wouldn't we then assume the survival of the deer's second-most effective predator, the eastern coyote, would be important to help control deer numbers.

The state of Massachusetts estimates that there are about 100,000 deer in the state and probably 2,000–4,000 coyotes. While the latter figure is reasonable based on habitat availability and territory sizes, the deer estimate is suspect and potentially inflated to allow more hunting. I rarely see deer in the territories of many of the coyote packs that I monitor; a surprising thing considering that there are an estimated 20–30 deer per square mile on the Cape. These estimates are published in local papers every fall before hunting season, no doubt to justify the need for a hunt. However, there is a slim chance that deer numbers are near that level in our study areas, except maybe in a few small locales.

Ecological Benefits

Coyotes provide obvious ecological benefits, some of which were described in Chapter 5. Research has shown that coyotes can have a positive effect on the populations of some game birds by limiting the numbers of their major predators such as foxes, raccoons, and possums. Thus, the ignorant stance that killing coyotes saves game species is a simplistic, narrow, and inaccurate viewpoint.

It's not difficult to respect the views of those who specifically hunt animals such as coyotes for sport and use the fur and meat of the animals that they harvest. However, it is disturbing to see our natural resources abused on public lands when hunting is both allowed and encouraged on nearly all large conservation areas.

It isn't uncommon that many coyotes are shot there and then not retrieved by the hunter. It's a good bet that more coyotes are "shot to rot" while hunters are pursuing other game (such as rabbit, deer, and birds) than are actually claimed by sportsmen for legitimate kills. If more hunters recognize and improve on this statistic, the sport of hunting could become more socially acceptable to the public at large. I would encourage true sportsmen to speak up and turn in people who shoot coyotes for pleasure and out of season.

Wildlife agency managers should impose fines, or at least regulate or cancel hunting in certain areas until people confess to and stop committing these illegal and objectionable offenses. In this way, sportsmen can continue their traditions in select locations while non-consumptive users, such as wildlife lovers and bird watchers, will be able to continue their pastimes unhindered as well.

My Vision

In places that are popular with nature watchers or where long-term research projects are taking place, I believe it is prudent to set these areas aside as core wildlife areas and protect them from consumptive uses such as hunting and trapping. These locations might be a section of a town or county, an entire town or county, or an important natural area within a state or federal park. They could include suburban and other developed areas within their boundaries (i.e., they don't just have to be large conservation areas).

To be effective, research such as ours is designed to be long-term. Protecting our study sites from hunting and trapping could potentially draw ecotourists and local observers of flora and fauna and at the same time allow scientists to study how predators influence an urban ecosystem. Areas that are established within human-dominated areas could be called National (or state or local) Wildlife Watching Areas (WWA) and could function much like national forests, parks, or wildlife refuges except that wildlife and not preservation (i.e., national parks) or conservation (i.e., national forests) would be the focus for a theme such as this. In these areas, common wildlife species would be part of the reason for establishing these preserves as opposed to national wildlife refuges (NWR) with the goal of protecting rare and endangered species but, on most NWR, allowing hunting and trapping of other more widespread species, like coyotes and deer.

I suggest the town of Barnstable be named an official State WWA. User fees to park and use these sites could support jobs to promote the area's mission of wildlife watching. Many state parks incorporate a wildlife watching logo into the park description. I argue that they could expand on that idea and incorporate my vision.

These wildlife locations could also serve as important refuges for all types of wildlife and the local abundance of these animals might also increase hunting opportunities outside these reserves where hunting or trapping is allowed. This is a win-win situation for all users where certain landscapes are managed for specific purposes.

In this model, future research topics at study sites could include scientific ones such as canid effects on urban community structures, canid interactions with other species (such as coyotes with fox and white-tailed deer), in-depth research into demographic changes that take place over time in canid populations, and examining human interest, understanding, and involvement in learning and caring about local resources around them.

Some places are blessed with large National Parks dedicated to animals. Other places, such as New England, do not have large numbers of wildlife reserves. Existing reserves tend to be small and most allow hunting. Therefore, certain species are often not protected by the boundaries of those landscapes. Additionally, a hypothetical landscape of five square miles set aside for non-consumptive uses to support scientific research on eastern coyotes would do little to examine coyotes in an undisturbed population since pack territories are typically twice that size. Most coyotes would therefore likely leave such a small, protected area at some point. However, a larger area (such as a town) that protects a sizeable portion of its land for such uses as wildlife watching and scientific study would be more sufficient to protect and study far-ranging species such as multiple coyote packs.

Chapter 11

Coyotes Fear Humans

We Know You!

It's a cool wet spring day at 7:20 AM on 7 April 2000 when I locate Mizz, a radio-collared female coyote. Judging by the multiple weak signals that I triangulate, she is in her den on a golf course in Hyannisport. I decide to get a more commanding view by going to the highest point of the golf course, which is right in the middle of this beautiful playing field.

As I come up the bend I notice a brown coyote—definitely not Mizz—lying down on a large rock at the edge of the marsh. Using binoculars, I watch this animal from approximately 300 meters away out in the open, but near brush. He casually watches as golfers and golf carts come within 15–20 meters of him. During this observation, a northeast breeze gusts by, signaling that Mother Nature has not yet completely given up on winter.

The moment the wind shifts directions, my scent blows toward him. Alerted, he immediately stands up and barks at me. And barks, and barks, and barks some more. I don't approach him nor even move, yet this goes on for more than 15 minutes. Bewildered, two maintenance workers drive up in their respective vehicles, one in a golf cart, the other on a riding lawn mower, from near the animal over to me. The man who arrives first asks me, "Why is that coyote barking directly at you when the golfers and I were just as close to it?"

Coyote on alert

"There's a good chance that he knows me," I reply, a bit embarrassed. "I'm a biologist studying coyotes in this area, and this coyote—and probably most collared groups in our study, could recognize my scent above and beyond the normal human scent and associate it with danger."

It only made sense that the coyotes were wary of me because my research colleagues and I were probably the only humans who ever disturbed them by following them into their bedding areas during the day. We also found their dens and pups and probably left our scent everywhere as we patrolled about in their wooded areas.

"Oh, that makes sense. Do you want to jump in one of our vehicles and get a better view?" the gentleman in the golf cart asks me.

"Sure, thanks! I'd appreciate it," I said.

I hopped into the golf cart with the greens keeper and he drove to within 20 meters of the animal. This coyote was in a regal position and I took remarkable, up-close video of it sitting alertly on top of a mini-boulder. But then it realized that I was in the cart, and it stood up and barked some more. After about 30 seconds, it sat back down and resumed its scanning of the area. I couldn't believe how close I'd gotten to this coyote and I was also elated to know that there were other sane individuals who realized that this seemingly bold canid was no threat to anyone.

The greens keeper gave me a ride back to the central part of the golf course where I resumed my watch with binoculars. Perhaps this coyote was a sentinel for Mizz's den, because about 20 minutes later he moved from his original spot and walked warily about 40 meters west-southwest of his original sighting location. There he bedded down on a large rock underneath an osprey pole within meters of

Mizz's den site. It was almost as if he wanted to concede his nervousness and get closer to the woods just in case I got any closer. But he needn't have worried because I had to get back to my truck to summarize my notes before trying to locate other collared coyotes. The first thing that I scribbled into my journal was, "*Unbelievable!*"

The incident on the golf course occurred during the denning season. Mizz was in the woods at the den site, and the coyote who barked at me seemed to be guarding the area. He was uncollared but had been sighted several times with Mizz and appeared to be either the breeding male or possibly a helper coyote, likely one of Mizz's previous offspring.

No Aggression

I never realized how timid coyotes are normally, before I began tracking them. In over 90% of our captures, the coyotes cowered in the trap and gave the most submissive posture imaginable—lying flat on the bottom of the trap and being completely still except for the movement in their ever-aware eyes.

When we captured Snix, our first adult coyote, I actually climbed into the cage and put my leather-gloved hand on top her head, while Pete Auger injected her with a dose of sedative from outside the trap. We did this in order to make sure that we did not harm her with a poor needle injection. After those first few captures, we made a decision to sedate others from outside the cage. This was primarily because of the danger of rabies that began spreading throughout eastern Massachusetts around that time (2002–2003).

Nevertheless, only a few coyotes have shown any aggressiveness, and it was obviously fear-motivated. That is, except for Casper, our huge 55-lb older female, who growled at us in a deep low-rumble during all four captures. Yet, all these coyotes were quick to hightail it out of the cage and far away as soon as they were released. Watching the actual behavior of over four dozen of these trapped coyotes leads me to believe the historical accounts of how trappers walked right up to steel-jawed trapped wolves and coyotes and simply clubbed the terrified canids to death.

All of my encounters with coyotes, including when I disturbed denning sites with multiple adults present, have ended in the same way, with the coyotes bolting away from me like lightning. These coyotes avoided me whenever possible and seemed to disappear into thin air when they became aware of my presence.

At the beginning of the study, I really suspected that coyotes would associate my scent with a free meal via baiting and conditioning them to trap sites, and they would rapidly become accustomed to my scent and comfortable around me. After several years of baiting at a single trap, one would expect the coyotes to follow bucket-bearing researchers walking along well-worn paths. But that has never been the case.

In fact, the very opposite was the norm, because we trapped, handled, collared, and tracked them. They were smart enough to realize the now-familiar scents of a select group of humans that followed them disproportionately more than was normal or safe. They were aware of enough of the process before being sedated and when recovering before release, that they found it frightening.

I often wonder if an effective management technique for bold coyotes who do not reside in my team's study areas (as we would surely try to catch and collar those) might be to trap and hold coyotes in a cage for half a day, then release it where captured. This simple, adverse non-lethal conditioning technique might quickly negatively associate a coyote from having any desire to be around people.

To illustrate further, the actual threat level of a bold coyote needs to be put into perspective with this example. An observation of Fog on 13 May 2005 in Dartmouth characterized the typical behavior that she displayed at night. Some people might construe this behavior as bold:

> 10:57 PM—Fog is in Gary Clabaugh's backyard as I stop the car. I turn my lights off and she immediately runs into the nearby park with something in her mouth. It looks like a piece of bread.

> 10:59 PM—She comes back from the park and sniffs around Gary's yard. She seems to always sniff the ground under Gary's birdfeeder.

> 11:01 PM—She sits down at the end of Gary's yard near the beginning of the park. She looks around as I watch her with binoculars. She and her collar look great. The collar box is under her chin and looks like it fits perfectly.

> 11:05–11:26 PM—Gary comes out to talk with me after spotting my parked car. Incredibly, Fog goes into the park and watches us from 25 meters away. She stays there for 8–10 minutes and is very curious as evidenced by her not running away. It seems pretty obvious she is waiting for Gary to go back inside so she can resume her backyard foraging. In the meantime, she keeps her distance but remains vigilant.

> 11:15 PM—As Gary and I continue to talk, Fog circles in the woods behind Gary's three penned-in dogs and probably goes over into the next yard. It is amazing how bold but non-aggressive Fog is. I believe that is how she was able to cross so many roads on her more than 60-mile journey from her Revere capture-site to Dartmouth. Typically, she calmly watches traffic then crosses roads when there are no cars around; as opposed to blindly running across a road. The ones that use the latter technique rarely live very long.

> 11:54 PM–12:00 AM—After Gary goes in Fog reappears and continues to forage and sniff around Gary's yard. She then crosses 30 feet from my car through Gary's yard and heads down Mary Crapo Street. This behavior is not typical of coyotes during the daytime, especially when humans are present.

Another radio-tracking experience involved Kett and his collared son Sill. They were with another coyote whom I presumed was Kett's uncollared mate (probably Gash before we collared her). The three were sleeping on top of a den that had at least four pups nearby in the midst of a forest of many towering white pine trees near Mashpee High School.

Because of the thick pine needle cover around where their year-2000 den-site was located, I was able to tread quietly to within about 30 feet of the den while the pack slept. When they detected me, they bolted and ran off howling loudly, causing chills to go down my spine. The howling and barking is the most "aggressive" a coyote pack has been around me. It obviously spooked the pups, who were out playing, to dive into their den. I happened to be in between the den and the pups and fortuitously witnessed an amazing sighting as the pups ran within four to five feet of me en route to safety. *"Dangerous beasts, aren't they?"* I sarcastically wrote in my field notes upon returning to my vehicle.

Many people today live in neighborhoods where they feel separated from nature. However, a predator like the coyote brings the spectacle of nature directly into backyards and demonstrates that urban areas are ecosystems that also have intact food webs. Sightings may occur during any season and in many locations due to the large home range of coyotes and their apt ability to roam.

It is up to us to protect our pets by leaving them inside, especially at night, and to secure our garbage in order to avoid potential encounters. I am surprised that there are not more human-coyote conflicts, considering that coyotes are year-round residents of their home ranges and that people continue to leave their pets and garbage outside. No doubt, the coyote's shy and generally evasive nature keeps them out of sight of most people most of the time.

Chapter 12

Raising a Captive Litter of Eastern Coyotes

A Dream Comes True

10 April 2002. "Are you sure that there is a den under their shed?" I questioned Trina Moruzzi of the Massachusetts Division of Fisheries and Wildlife.

Trina had called me at my office at Boston College to tell me that MassWildlife officials had confirmed a denning female coyote right near downtown Falmouth. A coyote pair that had raised litters in the same area for several years in a row, had now apparently become very comfortable around people, she told me, and now it seems they had felt free to actually take up residence under a shed of someone's empty summer home. There are usually few problems in these instances until the owners return to their cottages in the summer and find a coyote family there.

The next part of my doctoral study was opening up. I had arranged a collaboration with the Stone Zoo in Stoneham and obtained a permit from the state to bring in up to ten wild coyote pups to socialize them for a captive project. The grown animals would then become a permanent part of the Stone Zoo's exhibits. I would be able to collect data on them throughout their growing period and continue to monitor them for years as part of an ongoing study of coyote behavior.

When I heard from MassWildlife about this litter of coyote pups located so close to a heavily populated vacation area in Falmouth, it seemed like a door had opened to obtain some young coyote pups. The denning coyotes now had all the neighbors nervous and their proximity to several homes meant that wildlife personnel might have to intervene anyway. This phone call would prove to be good for the study program, the neighbors, and even the coyotes, who would likely never den so close to humans again if we could carefully nab some of their pups. Trina advised me to call the wildlife officials in Falmouth and see if we could work something out.

On 11 April 2002, I called Jason Arthurs, an officer from the Falmouth Natural Resources Department, and introduced myself. I explained I had spoken with the Mass Division of Fisheries and Wildlife and that I was interested in the litter that they had found. I said I had heard that the den was under someone's shed and it was causing some stir, but that I would be glad to help them assess the situation and, if feasible, even remove some of the pups for my Stone Zoo study.

Jason seemed glad to hear from me and to have an option for dealing with this awkward situation that would placate the neighbors. He went on to say that they had been watching the pack in that location and had seen the same mated pair in the vicinity for the past few years. The female was very brazen, he volunteered, and that she 'allows you to approach within a few feet'. He described the den as being under a shed between two main roads in a residential neighborhood. There was a main chamber entering the den and a couple of small lookout holes where they could see out to scan for danger.

I was admittedly suspicious of the initial claim by both the town and state officials that there was actually a coyote litter there, because to my mind this was not typical denning behavior. I thought it would turn out to be just a coyote-digging, but not a whelping chamber.

I told Jason that every radio-collared coyote we had monitored had denned in the middle of the woods, usually far from people, even in developed areas like Hyannis, and whelping rarely began before early-April. Then when I asked him how old the pups were, he told me he had seen them out of the den for about a week so they seemed to be a little over three weeks. It made no sense. I told him that it was really too early in the year for them to be that old, and this would indicate that the pups had been born in mid-March. "I know you are the expert," Jason declared," but that is what it looks like to me."

"Okay," I said, "it's worth a look. If they are older than 21 days though, I may not be able to take them, as the literature indicates that it is very difficult to socialize coyotes beyond their first three weeks." I got directions from him and we agreed to meet at the site around Noon the next day.

The rest of the day was a blur, but I seem to remember getting some sleep before starting tracking again around 11 PM. At 3:51 AM on 12 April 2002, I was making some final notes and I turned to Kelly Worley, a former employee of Mass-Wildlife who was tracking with me, and said. "What do you say we find Mole one more time then call it a night?" We were just finishing tracking Kett and Gash, a mated pair in the town of Mashpee, before we started out after Mole. Gash was at her wooded den site by the golf course and the reason we were tracking this night was to obtain multiple locations of denning females.

We found ten collared coyotes total that evening and could not find two others. Four of the coyotes we located were females who had denned. Overall, it was a successful evening because we obtained many locations on our coyotes in a five-and-a-half hour tracking period. We finished the tracking session by relocating Mole at 4:10 AM in a large cranberry bog, a spot where she was normally active. It was a good hunting ground with a dense concentration of rodents. She was at least three miles from her 12:10 AM location near exit 5 of the Mid-Cape Highway at the northern part of her range.

As I summarized my notes on Mole, a loud group howl consisting of at least three adults emanated from the bog that bordered that residential area and went on for about 30 seconds. Mole was very active that night, no doubt it was a welcome break from her duties with her pups.

"Okay, we got some good data tonight," I informed a half-awake Kelly. "We've got five to six hours to catch some sleep before getting some more locations tomorrow morning."

True to my word, we were out and about at 9:45 AM. Our first stop was to secure bait at the local supermarket that donates their meat scraps to me, then we were off to find a few coyotes on our way to the meeting. We located Gash in the same place as the night before, so there was a good chance it was her den site. I barely stopped for 20 seconds to confirm that en route to Falmouth, but it told me what I needed to know. A week later, I found her den in that exact location.

I easily navigated the rest of the way to the Gus Canty Center where we were meeting Jason because it happened to be the biennial location for the annual Thanksgiving Day football game between my former high school, Barnstable, and its rival, Falmouth. We arrived ten minutes early at the large recreation building so I closed my eyes for a few minutes of a welcome nap, but I roused quickly when Jason arrived on time with Phil Lang from Falmouth Animal Control.

I couldn't imagine where the coyote den was, considering we were right in the middle of downtown. We exchanged greetings and they indicated to just follow their vehicle down the street about a half-mile. Jason must have seen the disbelief in my eyes that the coyote den was so close. Within a minute and half we took a left off Route 28 and onto a street that bisected a residential neighborhood. As we turned left just off that road, Jason stopped his vehicle at the very beginning of a short dead-end street.

"What is he doing?" I muttered out loud, as I tried to focus on parking out of the way of the cars speeding by. As I came to a stop and looked up, Jason was already out of the car and pointing to his left. Simultaneously to Jason's motion, out of the corner of my eye, I saw an adult female coyote sleeping directly on the lawn in a small backyard.

"Are you kidding me?" I said quietly, pointing the coyote out to Kelly. "I can't believe how nonchalant that animal is." Although resting, the coyote was awake and watched us get out of the car. "So where is the den?" I asked, and Jason pointed while answering me. "Right behind the female."

I was stunned. I had never seen a coyote behave like that in Barnstable. I commented to them that she certainly did not seem to be a threat, but she was rather bold.

Phil nodded, "That is exactly what we tell people around here. As long as they are not fed by people they usually stay clear of you. We're not sure what attracted her to this area."

As we approached the shed, the female stayed about 50 feet away at the other end of the backyard, barking and woofing at us. This was normal as coyotes do not bark like domestic dogs; rather, they make a woof-like sound. What I found odd, was that while all radio-collared coyotes, including entire packs of three to four adults at den sites, always ran away from me, this coyote circled and continued to woof at us while we investigated the den. Of course I wasn't in a habit of taking a group of people with me and approaching den sites with such young pups in them. This mother must have been horrified for her young and fearing the worst.

Jason pointed to the shed in the small backyard of the house. The bordering yards are just as small, leaving only a couple of shrubs for cover for the female, hardly a viable option for a non-habituated coyote. I shined my flashlight into the den and saw three pairs of reflecting eyes. "Darn!" I thought. Their eyes were wide open and their ears are vertical already.

Captive coyotes came from the den dug under this shed
(see far right side for hole)

"You're right Jason," I said. "They must be a little over three weeks of age so I'm not sure if we can take them,"

Just as I said that I noticed a little head poke out of one of the tiny three to four inch peepholes. I caught everyone by surprise as I quietly dashed over and managed to grab the pup by its shoulders and pull it right out through the small hole.

Wow, is this thing tiny," I said. "Its eyes are barely open—it might only be two weeks old. Could one of you hold this one? I'll see if I can grab the others."

I opened up the narrow entrance of the den with a shovel while the mother coyote continued to circle us. Phil kept an eye on her in case she approached too closely. The next thing I knew I was yelling "Ouch" and getting stung by hornets. I think the female purposely denned there so an intruder that tried to dig out the pups would pay the price by running afoul of a hornet's nest.

Anyway, after shoveling away the hornets, I managed to scoop up three more pups. On examination, they did seem to be older, about 3.5 weeks. Not only were their eyes open and ears erect, but all of their puppy teeth were fully erupted. They must have been born in mid-March. Looked like Jason's description on the phone was 100% accurate.

"Now what?" Jason asked.

Well, first we needed to be certain that these were all of the pups. We spent 20 minutes digging around all edges of the shed and we astoundingly found five more pups. We corralled the last few and put them with the others on a blanket in a makeshift den next to the house. After I had finished digging and came across a dead squirrel, I was pretty confident that there were no more pups remaining. I couldn't believe we had found nine pups in one litter. "This is amazing!" I remarked. "Five pups is the average-sized litter, making this one huge.

Pups in temporary cardboard den

We were all elated, but continued to be wary of the mother who was still pacing back and forth behind us. The pups were not exhibiting any fear or crying out in pain, so while their mom was clearly perturbed by our actions, she continued to keep her distance. I sat down on the grass in the backyard with the pups while Phil watched her. A quick exam determined there were three male and six female pups.

After comparing body sizes, I noticed two of the pups were grossly underweight. The one I took out of the peephole was a severely runted female and it appeared to be starving. The other was a male who was smaller than the rest of the females.

Assessing the situation, I commented to the group, which now included Mark Patton, head of the Falmouth Department of Natural Resources, "I'm not really sure what to do. They are older than I hoped for, but with a litter this large, I highly doubt that the parents would be able to take care of all of them without causing problems in this neighborhood. It would be beneficial to take at least some of them. And two of the pups are severely underweight compared to their siblings and might not survive here anyway." Mark advised me to take them if I felt it was workable. "Last year was a nightmare because of a similarly large litter near this location." he added.

After a solid 20 minutes of debating, I decide to take five of the pups. My state-issued research permit was for up to ten pups, and the Stone Zoo only needed three or four, but I decided to take an extra one for insurance. I felt this was wise in case one died, a very likely possibility given the petite size of two of them and the uncertainty of their adjusting to zoo life and being without their parents. We would place the four other pups back to be raised in the wild.

Additionally, I reasoned that we could start our captive coyote study this way and save at least one life since the runt was sure to starve to death if left there. Taking these pups also meant that I would not have to disrupt the litter of a non-problem-causing collared female from our study. The original size of this litter would have severely taxed the wild parents to provide for them all, and their wide-spread foraging for food within this residential community was already a concern to some local residents.

"So, Jon, besides the two smallest pups, which other ones will you be taking?" Jason asked, already bonded to one of the females.

Needless to say, I was concerned that one or both of the runts might not make it. Secondly, I wanted to try and prove people and the literature wrong about not being able to socialize pups over three weeks of age. Thinking out loud, I rationalized, "Obviously this type of thing is rarely, if ever, done so there is no guideline to help us determine the best candidates. I say we subjectively look at and take two of the females who show the least amount of fear toward us and do the same with one of the two males.

Using my best judgment, I picked three of the remaining pups. Both little males looked large for their age, but the one who showed a little aggression when held was a tad bigger than the one we eventually opted to take. I also chose the largest female. The final one, a female, was of average size compared to the remaining three.

Mark all but begged me to take all nine, realizing the unique situation of my having a permit to take so many. The law otherwise required that the coyotes be left there. I knew my hands would be quite full with five, so I urged them to begin resituating the ones that were staying back in their dug-up den, and replacing the dirt. Then I told them the good news: "I can almost guarantee the female will move the pups tonight."

True to my prediction, while Jason was observing them at Midnight, the mother moved the remaining four pups a few hundred yards away to a more wooded area. The new location was still within 100 meters of local housing, but it made all of the difference in the world to this community because :

1) it was not in someone's immediate backyard; and
2) the coyote parents now had only four mouths to feed.

All four pups were seen in the vicinity during the remainder of the summer, but Falmouth personnel were not able to document how long they survived past their first fall. A few sightings of four full-sized canids in the area that winter indicate that at least a few of them survived and remained with their parents.

Why Captive Data Was Important

The majority of data on the ecology of wild canines has been recovered via radio-telemetry. Most of the time we do not directly observe the animals, as data is recovered based on the monotonous beep-beep emitted from our radio-receivers. Since coyotes are difficult to observe in the wild, I knew that a companion study of captive coyotes, especially from the same general population I had been studying, would be an ideal complement to the wild radio-tracking portion of the research. It was a dream of mine from the start of this project to acquire a captive group of coyotes, and now we were into this next phase of our coyote study.

My aspiration was realized in 2002 when Zoo New England agreed to let me raise a litter at their Stone Zoo facility. To acquire the pups we initially planned on simply tracking one of our radio-collared females, finding her den, and removing pups for the study. The available literature indicates that wolf and coyote pups need to be taken before they are three weeks of age in order to socialize with or bond to people.

By tracking and locating our radio-collared females we were able to ascertain dates of localizations around a den site and to approximate whelping dates within a day or two. Thus we could pinpoint the females on a daily basis. Eighteen days after localization, we would go in and take the pups. This would give us a day or two before the end of the critical 21-day period.

But before we actually put that plan into action, we wanted to see if there were an alternate means of obtaining pups in order to avoid, in effect, stealing offspring from a female who was not causing problems. We thought the chance would be very small but we wanted to explore our options in case there might be a litter on Cape Cod that was discovered in a problem area. With the aid of MassWildlife and the Falmouth Department of Natural Resources and Animal Control officers, that's exactly what happened when we learned of the coyote litter I've just discussed. The rest is history.

Ethical Issues for a Captive Study

Because the coyotes chosen for this study would live their lives in captivity, it was important to consider the ethical aspects of a captive study. The taking of a wild-born litter and relegating it to captivity might seem inhumane to some but there were several good reasons to legitimize this research.

First, the education afforded in enabling the general public to see and learn about a creature such as the now-prevalent but elusive eastern coyote who now inhabits our environs is important for humans and coyotes alike.

Second, some scientific behavioral data simply cannot be obtained in the wild, since free-ranging coyotes are difficult to observe. For instance, most researchers cannot quantify the interactions between wild coyotes like they can in captive situations.

Third, results of studies have shown that only about 33% of all wild pups survive to adulthood; thus, transferring a litter of five wild pups to a captive setting would translate to actually removing only one or two adult animals out of the wild population. These captive pups would now bypass many of the hardships of life in the wild with growth to adulthood fairly assured. And as they lived out a reasonable life span, they would provide crucial data for our study on coyotes that could not be obtained in any other way.

Fourth, in many states, a litter such as this one would be entirely removed and destroyed for encroaching so close to people.

A fifth benign consideration is that living in the wild is not an easy proposition for most wild coyotes. Captive coyotes, on the other hand, are generally well-cared for in a zoo environment and receive a consistent and healthy diet throughout their lives. Among other considerations, this would enable us to gain data on this species that hopefully represented their optimal size, height, and weight.

Sixth, these pups were so young and inexperienced before being taken into captivity, it was a good assumption that they would neither remember nor miss their wild life. Being treated kindly in a captive environment and bonding to a keeper (and considering how fast they would grow up), they would likely soon forget their wild parents. It would be considerably different than to relegate a wild already-adult coyote to captivity in an enclosure a fraction the size of its home range. For all of these reasons, I believed that a captive coyote study was both necessary and humane.

Chapter 13

Coyotes In My House

Mr. Mom

15 April 2002. 2:30 AM. I awakened to something climbing clumsily on my face. It took me a few seconds to gain my bearings and realize my location, sleeping on the floor next to five coyote pups in my basement room of my grandparents' house. I had been operating non-stop on just snatches of sleep here and there, and after situating the pups with me in my downstairs bachelor pad the previous evening, I crashed into a deep and much-needed sleep. My basement room had been temporarily transformed to a puppy nursery and I gave myself a strong mental suggestion not to move lest I roll over on one of them. Now the pups were just becoming active after sleeping for a solid six hours.

The next morning was the second day that I had had the pups, and all of them were finally starting to venture out of the little artificial den chamber, a cardboard box placed in my newspaper-lined closet. The biggest one (whom I initially dubbed #2) and the smallest (called #5), were the boldest of the litter and the most active in exploring their surroundings. As soon as #2 was finished scratching my face, he walked off my back in lumbering puppy fashion and moved away from me toward the cardboard den.

I carefully stood up and turned on the light. On my way over, I stepped in something squishy that was not there when I went to sleep. I needed no light to recognize it as puppy poop. "*Welcome to the world of coyote parenthood,*" I said to myself as I realized it was time for the babies' two o'clock feeding.

Once the light was on I sat down near my makeshift bed, an old foam pad that I expected would be filthy and chewed up by the time the pups left my house for the zoo in a month. By 2:35 AM all the pups were out of the den box and active.

This was the first action that I had seen from #1, a very timid female whose neck had a small string collar to distinguish her from #3, a similar but smaller female.

I used their activity as a cue to quickly run upstairs and prepare some warm milk, specially formulated for puppies. I was concerned because only #2 and #5 had gained any weight even with two days of regular feedings. But I was happy that the runt, #5, at least, appeared to be out of the woods and was no longer in danger of starving. She literally sucked anything placed near her mouth, especially my fingers. Even objects like pencils and pens were of interest to her and I was diligent in keeping these objects away from her. I was observing her boldness and felt it would serve her well in the future as she developed amongst four other hungry siblings. Still, the other three had not yet fed proficiently.

Within five minutes of preparing the food, I was running back downstairs with their milk formula in one hand and some fresh puppy kibble in the other. The puppies, led by bold #2, eagerly greeted me upon my return. None were interested in the boring food items that I offered. They were more interested in their clumsy, tumbling play game of chase and wrestle. They stayed active until 3:00 AM, then within minutes, all of them tired and crashed back in their cardboard den. I decided to follow their lead and get a few more hours of rest knowing that they would soon wake me up again around dawn.

Captive coyote pups climbing on author

At 5:30 AM, just before first light, the pups became quite active again. All were moving around and testing their awkward coordination. I could not help but chuckle at their ungainly movements, realizing what amazingly graceful and athletic creatures they would eventually become. I offered them some fresh warm milk but only #5 drank a considerable amount. However, with some coaxing I got the other four to take at least a few more sips of it.

I jotted in my notes, "They all need to eat a little better except for tenacious #5."

At 6:15 AM, pup #2, spontaneously howled, followed by the others, the first such vocalization that I had heard. I recorded it on my micro-cassette.

"They are getting much more comfortable with me after only being in captivity for a couple of days," I recorded in my journal, "though, they still need to eat much better before I become comfortable with the prospects of their good health."

From 7:00 until 9:10 AM I took my third nap of the day. Living with coyote pups does not afford one much consistent rest; one hour on, two or three hours off, is the norm.

At 9:10 AM, the youngsters again woke me up according to their own internal clocks. Male #2 pawing at my face with his razor sharp puppy claws was enough impetus to get me to immediately spring to my feet. I grabbed their chow and offered the dark little male #4 some moist dog food. He accepted the invitation and had a few bites. For the past two days he had fed from my hand and seemed to be bonding with me, an important component of a study that requires frequent handling of the study subjects. Even #1 and #3 lapped up a little milk from the bowl and #3 tried the soggy dog food that #4 was eating from my hand. Little did I know that just about two hours from then would be a turning point in my brief acquaintance with these little creatures.

At 10:30 AM I rounded up some materials at my parents' house about two miles away to build a temporary outdoor enclosure for the pups behind my grandparents' house. Next I went to the store for additional supplies and then off to the most important stop, my butcher at the Osterville A&P, for a donation of meat scraps. Today, I picked up some chicken with freshly expired labels and some equally juicy slivers of red meat—perfect fare for wild canids.

I drove straight home to prepare their meal, rationalizing that wild parents would be feeding partially digested meat to their pups over three weeks old. Unwilling to bring food back to the den and regurgitate it for them, I trusted they would be able to manage to digest a raw meal chopped into small bites. Since there was little choice in what they could be offered, I hoped it would be both interesting and palatable to them.

At 11:15 AM I tested my theory. I went downstairs with two dinner plates loaded with gourmet coyote chow "a la Way", and bold little #2 immediately greeted me at the door. As I put the food down near their cardboard den, all the other pups emerged. Pups #2, #4, and #5 immediately dove in to feed.

Wolfish #2 latched onto a little meaty bone and carried it off to the other side of the room to eat in peace. Pups #1 and #3 came out of their small nest chamber after seeing that the coast was clear and within five minutes they were gorging themselves too. Katie-Jo Glover, a high school student helping me care for the pups at my house, made a video of the interaction.

The pups were ravenous. They totally let their appetites rule, and for the first time #1 and #3 were not skittish with someone else present. Ignoring Katie-

Jo, they all ate their fill of the raw meat. Then around Noon, they returned to the den box with their little round bellies, formed a puppy-pile, and went happily to sleep.

Time For a Playpen

While the pups slept, Jason Arthurs and I constructed an outdoor pen to contain them. We attached the fence to the house in a "U" shape so I could open the rear sliding glass door directly into the rectangular enclosure. This would enable the pups to move in and out of the house at will.

Pups at fence at the author's grandparent's house

At 3:00 PM I met with my advisor, Eric Strauss, and his stepdaughter Rachael, to introduce the coyote pups to them. To sidetrack the pups from being afraid of yet more unfamiliar people, I brought out some fresh chicken I got from my mother's house, and put the plate in the middle of the small outdoor area that the pups would use for the next four weeks. Eric and Rachael sat a few feet away and I went inside to wake up 'the pack'.

Led by #2, the groggy entourage followed me to the edge of the doorway that led outside. I left the door open in case they got afraid and needed to beat a retreat back to their safety zone. Who would imagine that coyotes would be more comfortable inside than out? But they were still infants and had faced a lot of changes in their little lives in the last few days, so it was all about accommodating them.

Pups #2 and #5 had already partially bonded to me. Outside they immediately greeted me and then went right for the chicken. After a minute or so #4 came out, and several minutes after that #3 stumbled outside. Clearly aware and wary of strangers, #1 watched from inside, acting as if the door were still closed and not budging to come outside. The one most at ease, #2, stuffed himself royally, then hauled a mouthful of food inside the house and cached it under the edge of the couch in the back of my bedroom.

"This instinctual behavior is interesting to observe at such a young age," I noted in my journal. *"I wonder if he will return to get it later?"*

As I came to learn, these "natural" behaviors predominated even in captivity as the pups matured into adults. (And in an interesting development that might also happen in the wild, later that evening, another pup would find and eat the "hidden" meat).

After Eric and Rachael left at 3:35 PM, I sat very still near the food and #1 came out to the bowl of chicken in the outdoor area. The other four pups were inside so she was reluctant to come outside by herself. Not surprisingly, she quickly waddled back inside to the den box after taking a couple of quick bites. I decided to try hand feeding her inside in an attempt to beef her up. She wasn't difficult to entice, and ate three palmfuls of meat from my hand, including some dog food I had mixed in. Once I knew I could give her individual attention like this, I finally felt more satisfied with her progress.

So here we were, three days into our new pack relationship and I knew the pups were starting to habituate to me. I pondered letting out a loud howl in hopes that they would respond to me and it would strengthen the developing bond. Conversely, I also feared I might scare the daylights out of them and ruin the bond that had already begun. "Ah, what the heck." I thought, "Let's give it a try."

"Aaaaaaaaaaa-ooooooohhhhhhhhhhhh," I howled, cupping my mouth with my hands. At first, I imagined that I had frightened them with my loud howl, but after a few seconds I was rewarded as all five responded as if they had been waiting for that signal, trying to howl with their tiny voices and rushing forward on their little spindly legs to climb all over me. I wasn't sure what I had said in coyote, but it was apparently the right thing, and it worked better than I ever could have expected.

Once started, they continued to howl enthusiastically for almost a minute. I jotted down in my journal, *"It seems that they have all accepted me as their parent. Yes!"* From that point on I never got anything but an excited response from them whenever I greeted them.

There's no way to explain how excited I was when this project actually got underway. It was almost surreal. I had wanted to do this project for so long but I never knew if it was actually going to happen. My sister Nicole said to me after I brought the coyote puppies home from Falmouth that day in a small box, "Jon, you sure are something. You know, we never really thought you were going to pull this off. And there you are at Gram and Papa's with five coyote pups." The pups stayed at my grandparent's house with me until they were two months old

Moments of Uncertainty

I have to confess, when I initially brought the pups home, I was nervous about the possibility that they would not socialize well or bond to me because they were supposedly past the critical age of three weeks. However, by that first night, the biggest coyote (#2, eventually named Lupe) and the smallest coyote (#5, Late) were already approaching me.

Lupe was fairly unafraid and seemed to be approaching me and a few of my colleagues purely out of curiosity. Late was approaching me because she was hungry and weak and desperately needed the warm milk that I was all too glad to give her. It took more than two full stressful days to get the middle three pups (#1 Cane; #3 Caon; and #4 Trans) to start eating any significant amount.

The three middle pups had actually lost weight up to that point and I was becoming deeply concerned because they would not eat. We even offered them Esbilac®, a specific brand of puppy milk, and puppy weaning formula, which is sort of like soggy dog food. But by the end of the third day, after I gave them that "magical" package of raw chicken, it was like the difference between night and day. It seemed they somehow needed to know that I was providing for them like a parent, because after devouring the poultry I brought them, they were all completely bonded to me.

Pups eating from plate

From that point on, the pups continued to eat meat. We initially gave them partially cooked meat scraps that I picked up from a butcher and fresh road-kills.

However, they did eat dog food and reconstituted dog milk when I was low on animal protein. Later as adults at the zoo, they ate mostly raw meat, especially ground horsemeat and frozen mice and rats. Dry dog kibble was supplied ad lib, but was not preferred.

Fortunately, both runts easily survived the transition from the wild to captivity and grew strong and healthy on a consistent diet. Late was always one of the best eaters of the group, no doubt a byproduct of her nearly fatal puppyhood. Trans, a healthy smallish male, was always nervous around humans and normally refused to feed near anyone except me.

The coyotes stayed in my basement room until they were large enough (at about eight weeks old) to be placed in a zoo setting. While living at my house they were the star attractions and 20 or more people sometimes came during a given evening to watch them interact. Most people watched them from outside the fence. The puppies clearly treated the inside of the house as their den and frequently went to the sliding door (their den entrance) and waited for me to open it for them to retreat into, becoming upset and whining piteously if I refused.

Puppy sitting comfortably inside while looking outside

The puppies were usually nervous when outside alone except for one interesting encounter. We live in a residential area and one night around 11:00 PM I was sitting down at the edge of the door with the outside light on so I could summarize my notes. Suddenly I noticed all the coyote pups move to the far edge of the fence, led by their leader, Lupe. When I looked up I saw a wild adult coyote staring at us from the edge of our property, less than 50 feet away. Possibly attracted by the coyote puppy sounds, it stayed there, staring at the pups for about 30 seconds, until I moved.

As it trotted away, I could only imagine what that wild coyote thought after seeing a litter of coyote pups with a human within its territory. If an additional coyote litter were not enough, having them at my house must surely have perplexed the wild canid. I made a second sighting of a similar looking coyote, under comparable circumstances (late at night, all pups outside), before the pups departed from my house for the zoo. That animal had the identical perplexed look on its face. If this were the cartoon Wile E. Coyote and the Roadrunner, the coyote surely would have been scratching its head while the roadrunner trumped his previous maneuver.

As the captive pups grew, I tried to only allow them free access to about half my room. I put plywood up as a barrier around my sofabed so that those times when I really needed sleep, it would be possible. Now that they were more independent, I had transitioned from sleeping on the foam pad on the floor, back to the sofa. But regardless of the best-laid plans of man and coyotes, I still often woke up to a few pups sleeping with me on my bed. Frequently they left a scat or two on the covers probably just to say hi!

And there were the times when the runts, unable to climb up on the bed to get to me and their siblings, let loose with squeaky little howls of disappointment and woke the whole household. They would not stop vocalizing until I reunited them all. This was often an endless cycle. After a few nights of that I gave up trying to sleep in my bed and resorted back to the makeshift foam bed next to their closet den box. I originally slept next to them in an attempt to bond with them, reasoning that they would become better habituated to me that way. Now, I did it to avoid their annoying late-night antics.

Sleeping with them worked well in order to get accepted into the pack, but once they were bonded to me I thought I would get decent periods of sleep in my own bed. Clearly the pups had a different idea. Now I can understand why wild mothers try to spend time away from their pups when the pups get around two months old and close to being weaned. Obviously it's part of the weaning process, but I can see the mothers' patience wearing thin about that time, and that may even influence the move to rendezvous sites.

Usually there are other adults, especially the female's mate, to help with feeding the pups solid food. Since the mother weans the pups at about eight weeks, she is now not as important to their nutritional survival. I often locate collared females tending the pups at night but sleeping away from the den during the daytime. No doubt this is partly for self-preservation so she can sleep in peace, as well as an effective weaning tool. The wild mothers usually relocate at least a mile away, making it more difficult to be found compared to my short-distance situation.

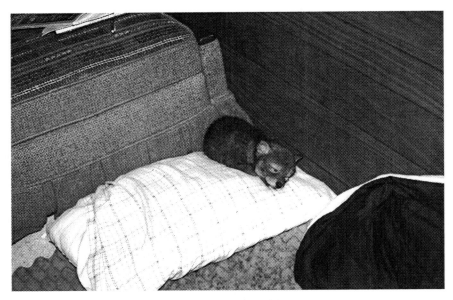

Puppy sleeping on pillow

The Captive Pack

To give the reader a better understanding of the individual personalities that surfaced in these captive animals during this early phase of the study, the remainder of this chapter is dedicated to providing a description of each of the five coyote pups. They were officially named during the evening of 15 April 2002:

Lupe (male)—a.k.a #2—was named after the Latin word for 'wolf', *Canis lupus*. The largest of the five pups taken into captivity, he weighed 3 lbs 3 oz when captured—approximately the same size as the other male pup we left behind to be raised wild. He was very bold and wolf-like in appearance and behavior and was one of the only coyotes to regularly approach people other than myself.

Still, he did maintain a wary distance from other people that he was not familiar with. I believe that his personality was the most important reason why the others bonded so quickly to me. He was always the most dominant and heaviest pup of the five, and as an adult he maxed out at an impressive 57-lbs. He averaged 50–55-lbs as a young adult. This weight is at the extreme high end of the range reported for the species. In addition to his bold behavior, he was a tall, robust, dark gray coyote—very similar to a wolf!

Cane (female)—a.k.a. #1—was named after *Canis latrans*, the coyote's scientific name. She was 2 lbs. 15 oz. when originally taken from the wild. She was the last pup to socialize to me but was probably the most closely bonded to me of all the coyotes as an adult. Despite being a 42–44-lb adult female, she commonly wanted to climb up on my lap for attention.

She looked very much like a cross between a coyote and red wolf; tawny to red in color with grizzled black-tipped fur, she was very lanky, and longer than five feet from nose to tail tip. If there were any Tyra Banks-like coyote supermodels, she would surely have been the one, as her finesse, exquisite physique, and strikingly beautiful appearance strongly distinguished her. She had always been the dominant female in the litter until she was in a serious fight with her sibling Caon and they needed to be separated in February 2005.

Caon (female)—a.k.a. #3—was named after the eastern race of the wolf, *Canis lupus* lycaon or *Canis lycaon*, depending on sources. She was 2 lbs 10 oz when taken from the wild and her weight fluctuated around 36-lbs as a mature adult. She was very independent and greeted me only on her own terms, partly because she was a low-ranking female.

She had a rather stocky appearance for a coyote and was very submissive around her group, including me. As an adult, while still being affectionate with me, she was afraid of everyone else and would not allow anyone to even approach, let alone touch her, including the zookeepers who always fed her.

Trans (male)—a.k.a. #4—was named after *Canis latrans*. He was barely 2-lbs when originally captured. His color had always been very dark, almost black, and his many black tipped hairs combined with a brownish head and lower body gave him a distinct appearance. He instigated the most play as a pup and loved to run around. He was the fastest of the five although he remained a rather small 36–37-lbs as an adult male.

Next to Caon, Trans was the most nervous around other people excluding myself. As a pup, he commonly had to be separated from the others at feeding time in order to make sure he had enough to eat. Similarly at the zoo, when a keeper was nearby he would not feed. Yet Trans was also very close to me and commonly sat or stood on my lap when not interacting with others.

Still, he was very shy and did not readily approach other people—even the zookeepers—when they entered the enclosure. Originally next to the bottom on the dominance hierarchy, by late summer of his first year (2002) he became the second-ranked coyote from the top, behind only Lupe. Trans remained in that position until being permanently separated from the group in November 2003 due to increasing episodes of intra-litter aggression.

Late (female)—a.k.a. #5—was duly named after *Canis **latrans*** and also because of her **late** development. She was 1 lb 1 oz when captured and appeared very close to death. The true runt of the litter, she made up for that in a big way and was ultimately one of the best feeders of the five.

Even though she only weighed 26–28-lbs as an adult, she could eat as much as Lupe in one sitting. She once weighed a chunky 32-lbs because of her piggish eating habits. One day, when they were all together, I kept scenting a kielbasa-like smell in the exhibit. It wasn't until Late came over to me several times that I realized that it was she, burping out the garlic-laced meat that she coyoted (not wolfed) down. (The coyotes sometimes received garlic in their diet so it would enter their bloodstream to help repel flies during the summertime).

Trans on the author's lap

Late had a red fox-like white-tipped tail and a Chihuahua-like face, a consequence of her stunted growth as a pup. No doubt her delayed development affected not only her final body size and appearance, but also her lack of social position. She had always been low-ranking and, in my opinion, was lucky the others didn't pick on her more often. She was ultimately separated from her sibling pack in fall 2003 after fighting with the female Caon. Since social positions can change naturally in the wild over time, her consistent nourishment and improved health may have motivated her to strike out to climb the social ranking ladder. In a captive situation such as in a zoo exhibit, such aggression is counter-productive to the animals' safety, and can result in injuries or even death where the loser has nowhere to flee.

Chapter 14

Bonding With The Litter

Phase 2

13 May 2002. 8:00 AM. "Get off my face," I mumbled to Lupe (like he understood me) who just woke me up frantically licking my eyes, "I just need one more hour of sleep." I moaned as I rolled over and covered my face with my arm, but it was no use. Lupe's trespassing onto my bed with his small posse was becoming an all too familiar occurrence. Despite numerous attempts to isolate my bed and a portion of my living quarters with a wall of plywood, Lupe, Cane and Caon repeatedly managed to intrude on me midway through my sleep, which due to my normal nocturnal tracking of wild coyotes, had not begun until 2:30 AM on that particular day. I was beyond exhausted.

Although I had grown to truly love the pups since the first phase of the captive coyote research began just over a month before, it was obvious that these highly intelligent and active creatures were too restricted in this relatively small area. And the tight living quarters and lack of privacy imposed on me in the process were nearly driving me crazy as well. As I pushed Lupe off my face and toward my stomach, he squatted down and urinated on the covers. It was too late to stop him as he forced out a night's worth of excretion. "This is the last straw," I groaned silently to myself. "They've got to go soon."

I dragged myself to a sitting position and rubbed my sleep-deprived coyote-saliva-coated eyes, and managed to stand up. Even letting them outside, as I finally did at 3:02 AM, required me to keep nearly a constant eye on them. Going back to sleep was out of the question until they were settled down. Still, I couldn't help but chuckle as they went rushing outside, running around with dogged determination in a full-fledged game of chase. "I wish I had that type of energy after just a few hours sleep," I thought, "especially at this time of the morning!" Finally at 3:59 AM they were back inside and settled down to go back to sleep. I immediately followed suit.

I woke up again at 9:00 AM, not too much the worse for wear, and offered the pups some meat scraps, which quickly filled their growing bellies. As I would find out, this would turn out to be a stupid move, for they were soon to be loaded into a dog carrier in the back of my truck—with unexpected consequences. Today was their last day at my house.

Phase 2 of the captive coyote study plan was for the pups to be placed into quarantine for 30 days at the Franklin Park Zoo hospital before being transported to their ultimate destination at the Stone Zoo. My grandmother came downstairs around noontime to videotape them, and then I began the 'loading process'.

I put the dog carrier in a vertical position and placed the pups inside, one by one. Keeping the dog carrier upright ensured that they would not be able to get out of this temporary confinement. I envisioned an endless cycle of placing coyote puppies back inside the box over and over again if done in the cage's normal position. After five minutes I had all five youngsters safely secured in the crate. I placed them inside the cap in the back of my pickup truck. Then I spent about an hour and a half cleaning up my room the best I could so the next time I came home it would be semi-livable. I left with the pups at 1:30 PM in a torrential downpour.

"Goodbye Gram and Papa," I said. "Thank you for helping me make a dream come true with these captive coyotes. I promise I will get the room back in shape," I said, my last words echoing as I backed out of the driveway. Chances are they never believed the second part of my claim for a moment, since the coyotes had pretty much trashed the area.

New Digs

It was more than an hour's drive to the Franklin Park Zoo in Mattapan in a steady rain. And it was slow going due to the bad weather and the precious cargo locked in the back of my truck. But when I arrived at the zoo, the coyotes looked anything but precious. They had gotten carsick, just like I did when I rode in the backseat of a vehicle. I jotted down in my notes, *"This is scary; they are too much like their adopted father!"*

I brought the pups into the small, approximately 16-square-meter holding cell under the watchful eyes of the veterinarians, veterinary technicians, and some of the management staff. The enclosure was divided into two equal-sized shiftable cages that we would all call home for the next month.

The pups were disgustingly dirty when I released them from the carrier, and I felt embarrassed claiming responsibility for the condition of such smelly, ratty-looking creatures. They were soggy with vomit and reeked, while still drooling heavily from their ordeal. Trans, especially, had strings of mucous all over his dark, pointy little face.

"We had a rough trip with the rain and them getting carsick," I assured the staff. "I swear they don't usually look like this."

"Sure," an unidentified smart-aleck quipped.

Once inside, we used clean towels to dry off the pups. One of the veterinarians commented that they now looked good enough to go to their 'room'. We put them back in the cramped kennel and transported them to their temporary living quarters.

I opened the dog carrier and released them into their quarantine living space, and sat down at one end of their small stall, while the five staff members positioned themselves on the other end. Lupe immediately ran over to me and that prompted the others to join in our greeting. Although the pups were used to many people from their days at my grandparents' house, they were clearly nervous being in another strange place. The excited and amused staff watched as the pups climbed all over me, needing to be reassured by my presence.

Within five minutes the pups slowly felt free to walk over toward the others but still used me as a base of operations. Lupe, in particular, acted weird and climbed on my shoulders and stayed up there. "That is strange behavior for a bold, dominant coyote like Lupe," I thought. After about 15 minutes, I stood up and left the cage. All the puppies grew visibly nervous as I departed. When I returned, bringing their food for the night, I managed to get all but Lupe to loosen up. He was in the area of the pen without the dog kennel, which they ended up using as a den box for the night. There he stayed, hiding in the corner in an almost catatonic possum-like state. Possibly something happened in his little wild head when I left him alone. I wrote,

> "I have no idea why he looks this petrified. He is visibly shivering. All the others were relatively nervous but not nearly this bad. He is the last one that I would expect this type of behavior from. This is a perfect example of individual variation in effect."

Eventually all of the Zoo New England staff temporarily left the quarantine area, and it suddenly became quiet in their kennel. Lupe then took the opportunity to stand up and walk toward me and the other pups. But when a veterinary technician walked by, the motion frightened him and he fled back into the crevice of the wall nearest him. A worried management staffer asked me if he were all right. I was also surprised at his behavior, but said I thought he would be OK. Now I had to pull out my ace-in-the-hole.

To prove my point that the coyote pups would adapt well to their new home, I decided to give a howl and see how they responded. With any luck, it would have a calming effect on them. The zoo staff already thought I was crazy for living with coyotes, but the pups needed to hear from me. I took a deep breath and let out a loud, "Aaaaaaaaaaahhhhhhh-oooooooooooooo," which resonated even more loudly off the old concrete walls of the hospital facility. Before I finished my howl, the suddenly-unified pack all joined in, even nervous Lupe.

I sighed with relief. The group howl had reminded them they weren't alone in this strange place. We were all together so everything must be all right. Now I knew they should make a good transition to their new living quarters. After all, *'they have only been here for a few hours and they are already making great strides,"* I wrote in my notes.

The author with the pups in quarantine

Indeed, the coyotes did remarkably well in their new environs, and while taking medication for kennel cough and salmonella, they easily made it through the 30 days in quarantine, all while growing into leggy three-month-old mini-adolescents. I still cringe at the thought that they greeted me multiple times per day by licking my mouth while carrying the rod-shaped bacterium that can cause food poisoning.

The coyotes also transitioned in a similar fashion when moved to their Stone Zoo exhibit. The larger size of the over 400-square-meter exhibit buffered some of their nervousness because they now had multiple hiding places and secure resting sites in the more natural exhibit. Aided by my nearly constant presence, the young pups developed into five beautiful and nearly perfectly socialized adult coyotes.

Socialization, Rank, and Bonding

The socialization process, which can vary depending upon the circumstances, in this case was aimed at habituating the coyotes to myself. This would also impact how they would interact with each other. The captive coyote study would not be practical if the coyotes I was researching were afraid of me. As one would imagine, recording them running away from me, a scenario I normally observed in wild radio-collared coyotes, would have little scientific value. It was necessary not that I 'domesticate' them, but that I bond with them.

Bonding with the coyote pups involved playing a parental role so that they would see me as their alpha. The alphas of a coyote pack do much of the hunting and decision-making about when and where to hunt. Since captive coyotes would not be hunting, I would be providing for them by giving them dead mice, chicks, and rats. Hand-feeding them further enabled them to associate me as their parent/provider. Also within this realm was affirming them with lots of petting and individual attention. From my detailed journal notes, I gleaned the following information:

Between 12 April 2002 until September 2003, I spent 1651.5 hours with the coyotes;

I averaged 2.3—14.5 hours per day depending on the month;

I interacted with them on 77% of 524 available days within that time frame;

I was with them on the 90°F days with oppressive humidity and on bone-numbing −5°F mornings, as well.

In short, I literally spent more time with these coyotes than I did with other humans during their first year of their life. Torrential rainstorms were really the only conditions where it was hard to collect data because of the difficulty of writing and using audio-equipment. On these days, I interacted with the coyotes but waited to write in my notebooks until I reached a dry place, usually the nearby bathroom.

Through all of these interactions, I came to understand their individual personalities, and I could identify all five coyotes in the dark just from their movements and mannerisms. Cane often growled under her breath when other coyotes interrupted her getting patted by me. Caon often sulked around in a submissive posture with her body low to the ground. Late had an unmistakable hyper personality and was constantly moving around, while Trans was often pestering one of the other four. Laid-back Lupe, meanwhile, preferred to relax and sit next to me while his littermates were causing havoc.

I was even able to differentiate between them purely by smell. Late always smelled pretty bad, apparently because of the way she reacted to eating garlic-laced food, smelling like human sausage-burps. Some of the others smelled of saliva from scrapping with each other. Lupe's fur was usually fresh and clean as the others rarely bothered or challenged his dominance.

Initiating group howling turned out to be an important part of the socialization and family-bonding process. Sleeping next to them as a coyote parent, to familiarize them with my scent, was also important no matter how often I woke up to a pup, usually Lupe, peeing or pooping near my face. There is little doubt that wild puppies establish bonds with the providers who spend the most time with them. Throughout this process, I was positively and subconsciously conditioning them with my presence that I was there to protect them, feed them, and parent them.

At the same time, I had to simply let coyotes be coyotes. I had to accept and respect the fact that I might get bitten, scratched and clawed when I was with them. I also signed a waiver for the zoo, not holding them liable for any damages (to me) that occurred as a result of these activities. I still have three small scars remaining to show for it.

One is on the palm of my hand from a bite delivered by Cane as I was trying to prevent her from attacking Late.

The second is on the triceps muscle of my right arm that happened accidentally when Caon went to nip at Late's rear end while I was holding her for a routine weighing. Luckily for Late, but not for me, the bite missed her derrière (a common region where coyotes bite other coyotes) and instead tore open my shirt and a one-inch section of my arm.

The third one was inflicted on my left index finger by an unidentifiable assailant. It probably hit a vein because it never healed properly. It happened when I got in the middle of the pack trying to break up a group mob on Caon. Although a small wound, that one hurt the most and seemed to take forever and many paper towels to stop the bleeding. These events were very rare and were a willing sacrifice I made in order to live with and raise the coyotes.

Although my little pack was clearly loyal to me, coyotes as a species are also very rough, even during positive interactions. One of their forms of play involves pinning each other to the ground and biting each other's necks. Sounds like fun, huh? That also explains their thick ruffs of neck fur, which not only protects them from genuine fighting injuries, but from family squabbles and continuous hierarchical disciplining.

Despite their normal species aggressiveness around me, they were much tougher with each other. They never showed me any direct aggression except a complaining growl here or there, almost always when I was too close and they had a food item such as a prized rat carcass in possession. Even though I gave them those items, once they had them in custody they clearly did not want me to bother them.

It is important to stress here that taming coyotes to people is much different than domesticating them. When they were at my house during their first two months, they never grasped the bad manners of chewing and climbing on my bed (and on me), or urinating and defecating on the rug despite having outside access. I found out very quickly why coyotes, even those 'tamed' or socialized to people, needed to be in a naturalistic setting like a zoo. Apart from being illegal, it would be much too expensive and probably even fruitless to raise a group of coyotes in an appropriate setting at a private home.

Don't Try This At Home

Before continuing on with the captive coyote story, it is critical to emphasize that I purposely treated the captive pups much differently than wild coyotes. This situation was a once-in-a-lifetime opportunity where a group of coyotes could intentionally be conditioned to people, and it could only happen because the coyotes were intended to remain in a zoo for their lifetimes.

In order to conduct the study, we needed to receive three separate protocols or permits: one each from Boston College, from Zoo New England, and from the state of Massachusetts, that, in total, took two years to procure. This was not an easy process and was for a specific and unique purpose. I want to stress that under ordinary conditions, people should never attempt to raise wild coyotes like I described here.

In the wild-coyote portion of our research study, things are completely different. We give all our free-ranging coyotes plenty of distance and make an effort not to disturb them. Wild coyotes should never be fed or approached by people. They do not make good pets and will potentially cause problems if accustomed to human company and/or feeding. Remember this adage: *A fed coyote can be a dead coyote!*

Many people have asked me if my study results would end up being severely biased because the animals are in captivity and bonded to a human rather than their natural parents. Their concern seemed to suggest that a human raising coyotes could not possibly replicate what would occur in the wild for those animals. While this may be partially true, canids, such as wolves, coyotes, and foxes, show many species-specific behaviors even in captivity.

The goal of my captive project was to research the interactions of a coyote litter amongst siblings. Wild pups spend most of their time with litter mates and much less time with the parents who come and go amid hunting forays and periods of rest. My observations found that the coyotes actually behaved very naturally, even in a zoo setting.

For one thing, they had a normal strict hierarchy and also did a lot of successful hunting within the exhibit by catching birds and rodents on a regular (about once per week) basis. As you will see in the next section, even the problems encountered as a result of their pack interactions as they matured, proved instructional to extrapolate to wild circumstances. The considerable amount of data that I obtained during this project was priceless to the body of knowledge about eastern coyotes, and maybe canids in general, and one of the first studies of captive eastern coyotes that I am aware of.

Phase 3

Once the quarantine period was completed and the captive coyotes were permanently situated in their new habitat enclosure at the Stone Zoo, Phase 3 of the captive coyote study began. During this phase, which started on 13 June 2002, I made it part of my schedule to see the coyotes in their exhibit area on a daily basis. My visit normally began with my entering the exhibit and going over to a large low boulder and being seated. This boulder was actually a 'fake rock' that was 'wired for heat' in the event that the exhibit inhabitants required it during cold weather. In my case, it was a welcome heat source during the many cold winter days and it made it possible to be with them for long time periods of time under adverse conditions. This rock became our rendezvous point—the place where the coyotes greeted me when I showed up.

The captive pack was so strongly bonded to me that, upon my initial entrance into their exhibit each day, they would follow me around and nearly mob me with their happy greeting when I sat down. This is similar to routine behavior I have observed of pups greeting their parents in the wild. They also howled with me just about anytime that I initiated it, unlike habituated wolves who are said to choose at their pleasure whether they will participate in that show of bonding with humans.

Pups playing around the author on the 'Fake Rock'

The bonding process worked so well with the coyote litter that they literally played and fought on my lap. This gave me an up-close and first-hand account of developing sibling interactions. Documenting their behavior during the socialization process between the coyotes and myself was an unexpected and scientifically rewarding aspect of this study that I did not predict at the beginning.

Many researchers studying captive canids, mainly wolves, have been asked how humans fit into the social dynamics of the animals they raise. Quite a few people feel that a companion wild animal does not regard the person as part of the animal's pack but rather as a welcome visitor. I have to disagree with them from my own experience, as the coyotes definitely treated me as part of their group. After all, I did hand-raise them from little puppies. However, I do doubt that they considered me part of their canid hierarchy.

For example, the dominant male, Lupe, frequently licked my mouth when I entered the exhibit, which is a sign of active submission. He never challenged me, most likely because I was much bigger than he. It is doubtful the coyotes instinctively measured my 6'0" tall and 170–175 pounds as compared to their 2'0" height at the shoulders, (or 5'0" on hindlegs), and approximate 35–55 pounds. Yet Lupe frequently socialized with me just as he did with the other coyotes.

Interestingly, Lupe did distinguish (and did not like) unfamiliar, tall skinny males, or sometimes tall, thin females with short hair. He aggressively woofed at them through the enclosure. It might seem odd to think they might have judged humans visually this way, but many keepers, and I also, believed he was treating such individuals as a threat because the person was so similar in appearance to one from his own pack—me!

As another example of treating me as part of the group, if I urinated in the back of the exhibit (before the zoo opened when no one was around), Cane would make a deliberate show of urinating over it. This turned out to be an interesting behavioral component of the study. Double marking is a common activity for pair-bonded wild canids. It occurs when one gender, usually the female, scent-marks over the other's mark. While I am sure that Cane realized that I was not a potential suitor for her (well, at least I hope so!), instinctual behaviors like this are probably ingrained in dominant females and instinct must guide their actions.

Lupe also sometimes raise-leg urinated (RLU) over my mark, as many dominant males do, but not as doggedly (no pun intended) as Cane made her flex-legged urinations (FLUs). It was obvious that these actions of theirs related to the dominance hierarchy, because the other more submissive coyotes, notably Caon, rarely paid attention to my markings, or they did so with a wary eye toward the more dominant coyotes. Apparently such marking was a privilege for the 'upper class' only. The lower ranking coyotes, like Caon, often squat-urinated (SQU) and expelled most of their urine in one sitting as opposed to dousing it in strategic areas. (Researchers have found that non-territorial dispersing canids often urinate in rivers and other such areas to hide their presence from resident packs).

When I arrived at the coyote exhibit each day, only the more dominant coyotes typically approached me at the initial greeting ceremony even though all were visibly anxious and excited, with tails and bodies wagging. The lower ranking coyotes simply were chased away. I have seen similar circumstances in the wild during greeting ceremonies. For example, Cane, the dominant female, was very attached to me and stayed as close to me as possible as long as I greeted her. This typically lasted 15–20 minutes when I first arrived but could last up to three-quarters of an hour.

While this behavior may seem more like a domestic dog, Cane quickly turned into a wild coyote when prey entered the exhibit. She was by far the best hunter of the group and although she would happily throw herself onto my lap with wild abandon, she routinely left my lap to hunt starlings, house sparrows, and even rats and chipmunks who tried to steal their dog food. It was amazing how frequently she succeeded in catching prey despite the sparsely vegetated habitat enclosure, which provided scant hunting cover. These unparalleled, up-close captive interactions gave me a detailed portrait of individual coyote behavior and how it might equate to wild situations.

Cane with her catch of the day—a starling

It was apparent that the dominant coyotes who obtained greater access to me, the provider, in a wild setting would probably obtain more food in their natal pack and also develop closer bonds with their parents. This instinctive behavior would be reinforced through their regular interactions with them. These two factors might cause higher-ranking juveniles to remain longer with their parents while other lower-ranking ones might disperse from the group.

Chapter 15

The Daily Routine

The Great Escape

26 October 2002. 1:02 AM. A phone call came in from John, a member of the Stone Zoo security staff. Nervous as to why he was calling me at such a late hour, I found out that I had a right to be. He informed me that some of the coyotes had escaped from their quarters. My heart suddenly felt like it was beating 1,000 times a minute. I questioned him if he were sure it was the zoo coyotes and not wild coyotes who might have entered the zoo grounds. John confirmed he had seen only three in the exhibit on his evening patrol and then spotted the others running around on the public paths. He asked me to come over quickly.

Things like this never happen at a good time. They knew that I was sick at home recovering from mononucleosis, so the thought of me rushing over to the zoo to help the coyotes was a concern for them, but nothing would have prevented me from responding to such a call for help. I made it in record time from Arlington to Stoneham and arrived at the zoo about 15 minutes later at 1:24 AM. After the Franklin Park Zoo Head of Security arrived, we headed into the zoo grounds.

"I don't want to sound bossy guys, but can you let me go in alone? The coyotes will be very afraid and might be impossible for me to grab if they see you," I pleaded to the three staff members. They were consummate professionals who understood the situation and immediately backed off.

I verified my suspicions that it was Late and Caon, the two smallest coyotes, running around on the public pathway near their exhibit. Caon was currently at the most unsocialized point of her life, probably because of her low status within the group and the constant tormenting she sustained from the others in that position. Late, although low-ranking, loved me dearly, no doubt because she instinctively associated me with those life-saving drops of warm bottled milk she received as a starving infant.

I walked to the public path and sat down. "Come here, Latey," I said quietly, hoping that my quiet voice would sooth her into realizing that I was there to help her. I knew that being out of their enclosure put them in uncharted territory, and they must both be nervous and frightened. Ten seconds later I heard her next to me and she dove into my lap. I petted her for a few seconds to comfort her, then maintaining a firm grip, I stood up with her in my arms and brought her safely into the holding area.

"Guys, I've got one of them," I said softly as I brought her in, but I was apprehensive now, because the next one could be a little more difficult. Caon had become wild and almost unhandleable, even for me.

I went back to the same location where I retrieved Late and waited for Caon. "Come here, Kie," I spoke out into the dark, using her nickname. It was completely silent all around me and I grew concerned wondering if she were still in the area or had she managed to pull a further escape from the zoo grounds. I waited a tense five minutes and then I suddenly saw her. Caon did approach me, but then withdrew, clearly torn between reuniting with her adopted father or making a run for it while she had the chance. She may have been so fearful as to not actually be sure it was really me.

Another five minutes went by while she hid and tried to make up her mind. I decided that I had to do something differently, so I resorted to my fallback plan, which was howling to her. I'm sure that as good as I might think my howls were, they were also distinctive by my humanity. She couldn't help but recognize them and know that it was her Dad calling her and it might have been as close to an order as a coyote would understand.

On my second howl, Caon emerged from the shadows of a bush wagging her tail, and approached to within two feet of me. She never liked being restrained so I grabbed one of her paws with a lightning-like movement. She bit my arm, which was moot at that point because I already had control of her, but she relaxed her grip on my arm as I renegotiated for a more secure hold. I picked her up and securely held her in my arms, then walked directly back to the holding area and reunited her with the group.

At 1:40 AM I recorded in my notes, *"Thank goodness the situation is resolved. I got both pups!"*

I was excited that I had just avoided a potentially disastrous circumstance involving an entire zoo staff trying to track down a couple of habituated coyotes with unknown consequences such as possible harm to the coyotes or the people as a result. As sick as I felt, I was hosting so much adrenaline from the gravity of the situation, it wasn't until it was all over that I suddenly got a little weak-kneed. I had to sit down, but I was satisfied knowing that the coyotes were safe and that likely no one else could have done this, at least with these five coyotes.

The security guards and I located the escape route, which was a hole the pups dug underneath an entrance door. It was large enough for only the smallest of the coyotes to fit through, making Late and Caon perfect candidates for becoming zoo fugitives. We promptly blocked it up with large rocks, knowing that the zoo maintenance staff would soon make a permanent repair to prevent further escapes. I informed the staffers that I would stay around for another half hour or so. After all, I went all the way over there, I might as well enjoy some time with the pack.

As a mini-celebration, I relaxed with the coyotes for about half an hour. I greeted them at the usual rendezvous rock, grateful that it was heated; it was perfect for the 39°F weather of that early morning. While on the fake rock, which was just turned on for the season, I even petted Caon, normally one to avoid me during her adolescence. Late was all over me, also happy to be home. Lupe greeted and then slept next to me, clearly not used to being active during this time of night. I could tell by their grogginess that they were usually asleep now, but instead a couple of them had planned a 'great escape' tonight. I jotted down some brief notes on our latest adventure, sleepy myself. I left shortly thereafter, returning to visit them again at 8:22 AM.

Standard Behavioral Sessions

Life with the coyotes was usually much more predictable than the previous anecdote. Normally after greeting the coyotes for 15–20 minutes, I conducted one or two 30-minute behavioral sequences or studies per block of time I spent with them. A block of time typically consisted of two to three hours in the morning five to seven days per week, and two to three hours in the evening one to three days per week once they were on exhibit at the zoo.

Earlier in their lives, when they were at my house and also during their quarantine at Franklin Park, I was able to spend even more time with them. Each behavioral session involved selecting a focal animal and recording what it did every 15 seconds. It was tedious at best, but provided many interesting observations. Because the coyotes were habituated to me, I was able to follow them around the exhibit without them altering their behavior dramatically from how they would have behaved if they were alone.

Jane Goodall, with her "follows" of wild chimpanzees in Gombe, Tanzania, used a similar strategy to collect data on her study subjects. I found this method to be a major advantage of studying hand-raised coyotes in that they were not afraid of me and I was able to document their "natural" (within a zoo habitat) behavioral interactions without my presence influencing them. By conducting these behavioral studies, I created an inventory of their different action patterns (called an ethogram). My team discerned 540 different acts, grouped into 16 major categories, ranging from sleeping to group play, and from exploring and investigating to greeting each other.

Not surprisingly, coyotes are usually more active in the cooler winter months than during the hot summer. From my observances of the captive pack, I also found out that they were more aggressive with each other during the winter months, as this is their breeding season. Lupe, who was vasectomized, bred with

Cane and Caon in late January and early February, respectively, of their second year. This is typical of wild coyotes and wolves but deviates from dogs and coyote-dog hybrids which have different breeding seasons. The notion that the eastern coyote is a hybrid 'coy-dog' is probably inaccurate because the coy-dog normally breeds during the fall, when wild canids aren't even thinking about breeding.

Coyotes wrestling, which is an important form of play

Lupe breeding his sisters was another interesting observation. In the wild, scientists have discovered through DNA research that canids generally avoid inbreeding. That is not surprising given their long-range movement potentials and ability to reach unrelated mates with relative ease. In captivity, of course, that is different. With nowhere else to go and raging hormone levels in mid-winter, they must abandon the strategy employed by their wild kin and breed whomever they can while they have chance, because female coyotes come into heat only once or twice a year and male coyotes are only fertile for a couple of months a year.

Besides conducting frequent behavioral studies, other activities involved separating and weighing them several times per week. Body measurements were taken about once per month. This data was relatively easy to obtain because they acted tame toward me and followed me around the exhibit. Whenever I wished to, I simply walked them into the holding area before data collection time to keep them confined. The coyotes became so used to the routine that I often just brought out the bathroom scale and picked up each coyote to do the weighing. I then gave them a treat for their participation, usually consisting of a frozen mouse or a guinea pig.

Lupe, being dominant, did not like to be controlled. He was the only coyote to ever offer resistance, which at most was just avoiding me so I could not pick him up. (Lupe's behavior was intriguing given that he was the only coyote to approach most people that entered the exhibit.) None of them ever bit me during weighing, except as little puppies.

Once I was ready to do a weighing, I simply weighed myself on a bathroom scale holding the target coyote. I obtained their weight by subtracting my weight from the total value. I weighed each coyote three times to ensure that the measurements were accurate. I was able to collect significant data on morphology, enabling me to track when they maximized their growth as three-month-old pups, when they approached full size around nine months of age, and how their weight continued to fluctuate by a few pounds every so often despite having a very consistent diet.

After weighing and rewarding them, I did mundane tasks like cleaning their exhibit and feeding them their daily chow and meat diet. The zookeepers did this on the days that I was absent from the exhibit. All the coyotes except Lupe generally avoided the zookeepers and anyone else who entered their exhibit, such as curators and veterinarians. On days when I was not with the coyotes, the zookeepers typically cleaned their exhibit as quickly as possible, placed their food trays in holding, and then left the area to ensure that all the coyotes had an equal opportunity to feed.

The fact that the coyotes were generally nervous around people other than myself was particularly intriguing. The zookeepers said that this was a very common trait for hand-raised animals. I initially thought that these animals would show heavily-reliant behavior toward humans, being in a zoo, and would do poorly in the wild. But after having actually raised coyotes in captivity, I had second thoughts about their prospects in the wild.

One of the first things that began to change my mind was observing Cane's hunting prowess. I now believe that if they were suddenly wild again, they would be able to adjust and survive without causing significant "problems" around human dwellings. And I bet they would quickly become self-sufficient. My biggest worry would be that they might not learn to avoid speeding cars. Of course, this experiment will never take place as these coyotes will remain captive for life. A similar scenario has been under scrutiny on the Alligator River National Wildlife Refuge in eastern North Carolina, with the monitoring of a successful reintroduction of captive-bred red wolves (*Canis rufus*) that began in the mid-1980s. These animals, formerly believed to be extinct in the wild, were not socialized to humans and so they quickly adapted to wild living.

During my time with the coyotes, I regularly took 35-mm and digital pictures, as well as videos of them to document their development. Their tractability around me enabled me to take the high quality photo images of them seen in this book. These multi-media images have been viewed as an integral part of scientific and educational presentations for numerous high school and college students, and for the general public and scientific community alike. Video of coyote behavior has provided a great learning opportunity for students in the classroom, as well as for lay audiences at my regular speaking engagements.

Study Benefits of Hand-Rearing

In summary, hand-rearing these coyotes and the conducting of a captive study resulted in many benefits. The major one was being able to record a detailed history of a group of wild-born creatures without causing trauma to them. It is the considered opinion of our research team that the lives of these five animals were legitimately enriched by their selection for this project. Besides giving them typical zoo-available items such as frozen rats and mice, other zoo animal scat and urination, balls and toys, and boxes and phonebooks to tear up, my physical presence with them appeared to visibly enhance their lives.

The author with coyotes Trans (left) and Cane

Throughout the study period, the coyotes were easy to handle during routine veterinary exams from which data was procured, and appeared totally unstressed by their contributions. In fact, the only time any of them had to be sedated was when the two males had vasectomies (11 August 2002), and when Late had a canine tooth stuck in her lip that required surgical repair (11 February 2003). I was also able to record on film and video many of their species-specific behaviors, which later were studied, analyzed, and used for educational and scientific purposes.

Finally, I was able to give educational talks to a number of school groups while interacting with the coyotes in their exhibit. In my presentations, I always stressed that these coyotes reacted uniquely around me because I hand-raised them, making it clear that they were not pets. The learning experience derived from directly observing the natural display of coyote behavior in the zoo exhibit afforded students a truly unique opportunity regarding both coyotes specifically, and wild canids in general, that would have been impossible to obtain in the wild.

Chapter 16

Captive Coyote Social Behavior

Hierarchical Behavior

13 December 2002. 8:20 AM. I entered the exhibit and walked directly to the centrally-located heated rock. This was our meeting location and the coyotes knew it. Lupe, Cane, and Trans immediately came over and greeted me. Caon, one of the lowest ranking member of the pack, also came over, moving skillfully in and out of the mass of active coyotes but the more aggressive and dominant coyotes claimed the area as I petted and massaged them.

Poor little Late, still the runt, stayed on the periphery, afraid that she might get disciplined if she approached me. Coyote discipline entails being growled at, and for a wrongdoing, forcefully pinned to the ground in a passive submission posture. It is clear when this occurs that the dominant coyote is saying, "I am boss—do not mess with me."

At 8:35 AM I stood up and walked to the entrance of the exhibit. "Come here, girl," I said to Late, as I sat down by the entrance doors. Lupe, Cane, and Trans usually were not as possessive of me when I was not at the greeting area, though they still spent a significant amount of time near or on me. For the moment, I petted Caon who now could get a little more attention away from the rendezvous rock.

Late, always excited to see me, ran over and literally dove onto my lap to beat any other group member from reaching the prized location. The plump little 31-pounder was calm while she sat on my lap, clearly loving the attention that I gave her. To the average person, she might look confident in her maneuvers but I could tell from her low-slinking body posture and her ears displayed backward, that she was nervous. The other coyotes were nearby, so she was taking a risk.

However, the moment she reached my lap I knew there was going to be trouble. I almost literally saw fire in Cane's amber-brown eyes from across the exhibit.

The juveniles were now nine months old and just about full-grown. That means that they had a well-developed and rigidly enforced hierarchy. Cane was the dominant female and did not like the low-ranking omega to do anything that could be interpreted as gaining ground—or the provider's attention. In a heartbeat, Cane took a few swift strides and was by my side.

For the next three to four minutes she sidled this way and that around me trying to attack Late to drive her from my lap. To protect Late, I fended Cane off with one arm, which kept Late very contently on my lap. In fact, my defense of Late gave her a burst of confidence and she growled and bit back at Cane every time she approached.

To the average observer this would probably appear comical. But to a coyote biologist, this was a very touchy situation that needed to be resolved safely. In nature, a dominant coyote would not tolerate a subordinate stealing such precious resources. In captivity, where food was regularly provided, I was the more important commodity.

After a little over four minutes, I became furious that Cane stubbornly would not retreat. I knew she would never behave like that around another human and I had had enough of her taking nips at Late, which more times than not ended up being a poke of her snout into my own arm or rib. But with her position threatened, Cane was extremely agitated and would not back down.

"Gee, do you think that Cane regards me as part of the group?" I later recorded sarcastically in my journal.

I decided to be more forceful in my attempts to calm Cane, so I put Late down on the opposite side of Cane and grabbed Cane's hackles and pinned her to the ground. I held her for over 30 seconds. She continually growled at me while I kept her pinned to the ground. Late had read the writing on the wall and ran to the other side of the exhibit and hid in a cluster of pine trees. All three of us knew that if I released my grip on Cane she would immediately search for and discipline Late.

As I watched Late, I accidentally lost my leverage on Cane and she managed to squirm around and bite my left hand to get out from under my control. Blood immediately gushed from my palm near the large muscle that controls the thumb; Cane's action had the desired result. Released, she immediately ran over and forcefully pinned Late to the ground. Because my hand was bleeding so profusely, I quickly made my way to the nearby bathroom and held it under cold running water for about five minutes. I put a healthy dose of antibiotic ointment on the wound but continued to lose blood until I wrapped it tightly in a paper towel and electrical tape—a good makeshift bandage.

I returned to the exhibit enclosure at 8:50 AM. The coyotes all greeted me again by the rendezvous rock as they did when I first showed up earlier. When I sat on the fake rock, Cane was the first to greet me by sitting on my lap. Judging from her behavior, it was like nothing had occurred. A painful experience for me was just 'business as usual' for coyotes. Humans could learn a thing or two from them about not holding grudges. *"Tough love"* was the first thing that I wrote in my notes. *"Cane obviously gets very jealous and aggressive when the other two females approach me, but quickly forgets about it afterwards."* That flesh wound ended up resulting in a small one centimeter-long scar running laterally across the palm of my hand.

Cane on the author's lap with Trans (right) and Lupe nearby

As per zoo policy, from that point on I was very careful to not interrupt disputes unless they became serious. The definition of 'serious' was deemed to be if one or more of the coyotes might be injured. I had read that adult coyotes remained calm and uninvolved when their full-grown pups squabbled and never meddled in sibling quarrels. That day I quickly discovered at least one reason why. Indeed, particularly in winter when food is generally at its lowest point, it is every coyote for themself unless a wild pack inhabits an area that has numerous winter-weakened deer, elk, or moose. One thing is clear, and that is that rank within the pack is never guaranteed.

A dramatic example of an individual behavioral change involved Caon, the middle-ranked and mid-sized female of the captive group. During fall 2003, when the coyotes were 18 months old, Late and Caon started to fight quite often. It was clear that they had grown competitive and they constantly tested each other. While the group treated Caon as the omega or scapegoat, as similarly described in wolves, Caon was dominant over Late in dyadic (paired) interactions.

Late's delayed or stunted development left Caon, the most naturally behaving coyote, as the object of the other coyotes' bullying. Their paired interactions became more and more aggressive until they eventually started fighting seriously. (I could never figure out why Caon, and not Late, was the omega of the group at the time. Perhaps Caon seemed more fitting for omega as she was more timid than bold little Late.)

In the wild, omegas and runts can protect themselves by running off or dispersing and take their chances at becoming a loner to avoid these sibling squabbles. This was not an option for the captive pups as they grew up. They were all restricted to whatever happened within the walls of their exhibit enclosure, and in this respect, the data that I gathered on their interactions was both enlightening and biased by their enforced closed situation. The enmity that was growing between Late and Caon was compounded by Trans, the second-ranking male, joining in their disagreements and picking on Caon.

In wolves, it is common for beta males to pick on the lowest-ranking pack member. When this draws down the entire pack against the omegas, these scuffles are called 'group mobbings'. In this case, Caon had not always been the omega. She was formerly dominant over Trans until they were three-and-a-half months old. Even though that changed when they were still relatively young pups, it appeared that Trans still had it in for Caon.

Sibling Rivalry Splits the Pack

In November 2003 we had to permanently remove Late and Trans from the exhibit due to this intra-litter aggression. After splitting the now-grown litter, the frequency of fighting went down sharply. Caon, who remained in the original exhibit, was now no longer being mobbed by the group and instantly sought attention from me when I arrived at the exhibit. She was generally calmer and noticeably friendlier toward me. She repeatedly greeted me when I was in with them, despite the jealous rebuffs by her bigger sister Cane, and occasionally from mild-mannered Lupe, too. But it was obvious Caon recognized that one attacker was better than many, and Cane's disciplining her was nothing compared to the violence of the group trouncings she previously experienced when all five coyotes lived together. Had that gone on, and with her having nowhere to flee, she might eventually have been severely injured or even killed.

Extrapolating Caon's behavior to a wild situation might go something like this: if she were constantly being picked on by her siblings and about to disperse from the group, what if her biggest intra-pack rival suddenly got killed? After a traumatic event like that within the coyote pack (regardless of whether they were aware of the fate of the missing member), tensions among the rest of the group would normally subside. It is at this point that Caon would be free to decide, either consciously or not (which is another issue in itself), to be philopatric and remain to help raise the next year's litter of young without objection. Gleaning these little tidbits of information, with analysis on my part, could only be obtained from a captive coyote study.

Late and Trans were moved to the same exhibit in the Franklin Park Zoo in December 2003, at which point I was no longer able to see them. The zoo directors decided that they needed to retrain them to be obedient around keepers in general, not just to me. They reasoned that since they could not be returned to their pack, they might eventually be transferred to a different zoo.

While the coyotes admittedly were not very tractable around other people due to the nature of my study, I strongly disagreed with the zoo's decision of preventing my access to them cold turkey. Through some collaborative decision-making, I was more than amenable to altering my schedule to accommodate the zoo's needs if they would have permitted me to still see them. That did not happen, however, and the fact remains that I have not seen them since they left the Stone Zoo.

In the zoo's defense, I do not think that they could possibly have realized just how strong a bond I had with them, and certainly if they had, it still would not have made any difference, since their considerations were purely aimed at maintaining the smoothest logistics of zoo and exhibit operations. I confess to having stronger emotions regarding the objects of this study than I anticipated, and I have missed Late and Trans dearly. I still sometimes experience periods of intense anger and disappointment and I may suddenly get in a bad mood just thinking about the situation. I will never forget the circumstances of obtaining them and knowing that it was solely my decision that probably saved their lives as malnourished little pups.

Even though the Captive Coyote Project was always a scientific study from the beginning, and the subjects involved grew up to behave like the wild coyotes that they are, it was impossible to not get attached to these animals whom I quite literally lived and bonded with while documenting their development from puppies to full grown adults. On the flip side, it was clear from her behavior that Caon did not miss them. She was like a different animal after they left. This separation turned out to be very advantageous for her, while being Strike One in the downturn of my relationship with all the captive coyotes I had grown to love as one loves their own dog.

Chapter 17

The Fight That Ends It All

The Fight

On 7 February 2005, Caon, in heat, got into a fight with Cane. This was similar to the first situation that caused the group to permanently split in November 2003 when Caon and Late were constantly fighting. Caon, formerly submissive to Cane, would not back down to her bigger sister on this day. Caon latched onto the scruff of Cane's neck, and Lupe joined in to pester Cane.

Seeing Cane's predicament, I jumped on top of Caon and literally pried her jaws off Cane. In the process, my index finger was cut open by Caon's shearing carnassial teeth. I managed to separate the two females before tending to my bloody but minor wound. Caon and Lupe were then housed in the exhibit and Cane was kept in the holding area.

Zoo staff reported the incident and officials notified me that they wanted to reunite the coyotes before I went back in with them with the stipulation that I would not interfere in any more fights. Not breaking up fights was a concession that I was willing to grant, for although I was clearly part of their group, they were also wild animals, and I was not. But I didn't see what my separation from them would accomplish.

I remember that day very clearly and mentioned to zoo staff that Caon might get more confidence with Cane removed from the trio. I thought that Cane and Lupe should have been put together, and Caon separated because Caon was, in essence, the dominant female as she was housed with the alpha male of the small pack.

Dealing With Separation

On 15 February 2005 I visited the coyotes. Cane was still separated from the group and she and Caon growled at each other through the chain-link fence that separated them. I remember thinking that they could never be reunited. With Caon's new bold and aggressive demeanor, I knew then and there that she would not back down to her heavier and formerly dominant sister Cane. My observation session ended on 9:08 AM on that day, after a brief 42 minutes. They were all howling wildly and somberly.

As I prepared to leave, I noted that it was a very distinct howl and was noticeably different from the ones that I initiated when I was in the cage with them. Researchers studying wolves have also documented this mourningful-sounding howl, which often occurs following the death of a pack-mate. I had no doubt that the captive coyotes were howling like that because I was not able to be in the pen with them.

They may also have sensed my anxiety while they were already in a state of unrest with the separation of the remaining three of them and thus were subject to compounded pack instability. Perhaps they even knew instinctively what I was later to find out. For the moment, it probably would have seemed pretty obvious to even the novice coyote-watcher, as the coyotes did not stop howling even as I left the zoo area and returned to my car.

I felt almost overcome with grief not being able to join my coyote group-mates. After all, I had spent the better part of the past three years with them, which was more time than I spent with anyone, including family and friends. I knew their moods and I thought that I could help the situation by giving them a timely distraction in the form of my attention and the body massages they loved so much. It is safe to say I recognized every subtle gesture of these canids in the same way that a parent sees hurt or joy in the eyes of their children, or how couples communicate without words. Nonetheless, that turned out to be the last time I saw the captive coyotes.

About a month later in mid-March 2005, zoo staff unsuccessfully tried to reunite them. Apparently Cane went after Caon and Caon retaliated and bit Cane in the face. I was later e-mailed and told that I would have to wait some time longer to see them. In the back of my mind I began to understand that meant I would never get to be with them again, because I could not envision Caon ever again surrendering her dominant position within the captive group.

Although I will never know if things would have been different if Cane were initially housed with Lupe, rather than alone during the separation, I can't help but think that things might have worked out. I remember sending an email to zoo staff indicating that, and noting that if I were consulted or involved in the reuniting process it might have turned out more positively. That was my mild and controlled way of saying how frustrated I was by that turn of events and the fact that the coyotes themselves were not making it easy.

Throughout the next several months, consisting of summer and fall 2005, and into winter of 2006, my feelings vacillated from anxiety that stemmed from needing to be with my canine family again to bouts of time filled with raging anger. Up to that point in my studies, I was constantly on the move with a burning desire to know as much about coyotes as I could. Now the separation from them caused that same inferno to boil inside me like a hot tea kettle on a lit stove.

Perhaps I had let myself in for this, not guessing the possible difficulties that could arise as these creatures grew into mature animals and appropriately began to vie for their places in the pack. These were the very types of things a researcher would have great difficulty discovering with a wild population. But without anyone else who understood the gravity of what was happening with the coyotes at this time, it was the worst possible time for me to lose contact with them. I'm certain I understood the inner workings of the captive pack's social structure, yet I was not able to do what I could to resolve things. It not only would have been in the coyotes' best interests, but in the zoo's as well. Yet the entire situation was controlled by people whose stake in it was so different than mine. At times, I thought I was going to explode.

I underestimated the bond that both man and canines are capable of developing for each other and I needed to be with the coyotes that I raised from infants. I didn't want to deal with the people or the politics of the zoo. I just wanted to be able to sit on the heated rock in 20-degree weather with Cane on my lap, and have Lupe greet me when I walked into the exhibit. I longed to see Caon testing her boundaries with Cane and greeting me whenever her bigger sister wasn't near me.

But I knew that that was never going to happen again. I realized, but didn't want to accept, that my time with these beautiful creatures was over. I struggled with why people had to make life so difficult. In the movies, the hero would have pulled up to the zoo in the middle of the night with a big truck, kidnapped his beloved canines, and driven off with them, never to be heard from again. But I had to go about my business, try to stay interested in my research, and deal with my grief the best I could. It wasn't easy.

War of Words

During late-summer 2005, having never received a callback from the zoo after their unsuccessful attempt to reunite the coyotes in mid-March, I wrote a strongly-worded letter explaining my utter frustration with what had happened. A return letter in early September indicated the zoo staff's 'collective surprise' to my reaction as they stated they understood my project to be ending in 2007 or whenever I received my doctorate, whichever came first."

A once collaborative project then came down to a war of words. I responded by noting that was not the agreement. Rather, I planned all along, and always understood the agreement to be, that I would permanently be part of the coyotes' lives and that the graduate process was only a stepping stone toward my long-term study of these misunderstood creatures. I felt I had made that abundantly clear during the several years that I practically lived with my captive subjects. Anyone working at Stone Zoo knew that I didn't plan on abandoning either the study or the coyotes upon receiving my doctoral degree.

The wording of the proposal, of "the project ending in 2007, with potential future work," seemed to prove my claim, but because I didn't own the coyotes and they were housed at the zoo, made it a moot point. Technically, I didn't have a leg to stand on.

Dr. Eric Strauss and I met with the zoo staff, after our written communication. This meeting on 29 September 2005 at the Franklin Park Zoo, not surprisingly, formally restricted my direct access to the coyotes. It seemed to have been predetermined by desk-bound zoo personnel that when I completed my degree, my access to the coyotes would be terminated. The coyote bite incident just accelerated that.

In the zoo's defense as an accredited facility, they felt they could not accept the chance of injury to staff or researchers. That often means death to the animals involved, in order to test for rabies, for example, if someone gets bitten. So this was their position despite my having signed a waiver absolving the zoo of any liability should I sustain injuries associated with the captive pack during the study.

At that point, I knew that I made a huge mistake forging the relationship for this effort with the zoo back in 2001, the year before I got the captive coyotes. It was never supposed to be about me and how much I might care for the animals I was studying. But I never expected it to disadvantage the coyotes because I was just about the only one who knew what they needed. But as often happens with contracts where details are not accurately spelled out, bureaucracy reigns supreme, and those in control can change the rules at any time.

During that meeting, I realized that a non-research institution like the zoo would not weigh in the fact that my up-close observations and the bond that I formed with the coyotes was an unparalleled way to learn about coyote behavior. I often wondered throughout this agonizing process if this were an example of a systemic attitude that has historically prevented certain zoos from joining the ranks of the nationally known educational facilities such as the Bronx or San Diego Zoos.

The end result of the meeting was that I could write a new proposal and, if accepted, I would have permission to continue to observe the coyotes, but only from outside their cage. During the meeting, Eric could see that I was deeply disappointed by the outcome. I felt insulted and rationalized that it would be like visiting family members in jail for the rest of their lives. Zoo staff countered by noting that other species, notably elephants, can be observed from a distance, without direct interaction or danger to the observers, and behavioral changes can still be detected. They felt I could do the same with the coyotes.

My counter argument, that since the coyotes had never attacked me, such dramatic changes to our established protocols was an unnecessary over-reaction, and dealt a severely negative blow to our research and to me, was not well received. Zoo officials proceeded to state unequivocally that they now thought it was in the 'coyotes best interest to be weaned away from me'. From my research perspective, I always considered that the unique bond that I built with them was what made the project work. Even the zookeepers knew that without my personal bond with the coyotes, I would never have been unable to take even the basic physical measurements on the coyotes that I routinely took unless each animal was sedated each time. If the coyotes could talk I knew they would agree with me. Not only did the coyotes never object to being weighed, measured and observed only by me, but their wagging tails and excitement whenever I arrived at their exhibit showed unequivocally that I was a major positive factor in their lives.

I left the meeting feeling more dejected than at any time during the past seven months of my separation from the coyotes. In effect, it was a reluctant closure to a wonderful two years and ten months that I was able to spend with these ambassador coyotes. To add insult to injury, after the meeting I briefly spotted Late and Trans, who were housed together right near the building headquarters. They also saw Eric and me as we were leaving. My heart sank into my stomach as I had to walk off, agonized by the reality I might never be with or possibly ever see them again.

At that point, I had been upset for too long to fight the frustration of my helplessness anymore. If I were a child I probably would have broken down and cried. Inside I felt the raging contradiction between grief and anger; and being caught between them in the hands of an unfeeling bureaucratic system that insisted on determining my fate with these animals that I had saved and then put my heart and soul into. I just wanted to forget all about it and move on, realizing it was a fruitless battle.

Be Thankful For What You Had

Some say 'it is better to have loved and lost, than never to have loved at all'. Although this was coined in reference to people, it is probably true in my relationship with these coyotes as well. I had spent almost three years interacting with these creatures. I learned tremendously from being up-close with them and now a third-party-enforced gulf between us made me miss them with the sorrow that one feels when they lose a cherished one.

During the past three years with the coyotes, I had constantly gathered data on them, yet I was now in this powerless position. They did not belong to me, except in their hearts. Eric and I knew there was no way that we could get legal authority and possession of the coyotes, especially since the state once again disappeared when we needed their help. Even if I were somehow able to demand ownership, I did not have an acceptable place to move them to, nor did I even have a full time job and paycheck, since this was right after I finished my Ph.D.

We met with the state fish and game authorities in July 2005 and pleaded for their assistance, yet received no response until they randomly copied Eric on a letter they sent to the zoo nearly three months later giving them ownership of the animals. I guess they believed that someone who had earned both a Master's and a Doctoral degree in conjunction with these subjects, was not sufficiently qualified to take care of them. If that weren't enough, receiving the news second-hand from my advisor, rather than directly, was insulting.

At the time I laughed sarcastically and shook my head, like an athlete who chuckles at the perception of unfairness on the part of a referee in order to displace his anger and not get penalized. It made me ponder the relevance of Canadian wolf biologist John Theberge's comment that bureaucratic workplaces are tainted by 'issue avoiders', rather than 'issue solvers'. Clearly, the state was not supporting its scientists. To them, our research was just another pile of papers attached to a permit, regardless of the sound science being conducted or the value of the education we were disseminating to the public.

All of the decision-makers Eric and I approached about the situation knew the unique relationship that I had forged with the captive coyotes and how greatly it had played into our extensive database of study material, yet none of them made any attempt to challenge this impulsive decision to try to work out a solution appropriate for both parties. Perhaps my mistake was that I had 'betrayed my weakness in front of the enemy' by disclosing my emotions. Showing emotion in a bureaucratic environment about a technically-controlled issue is a definite no-no. It seemed as if the fact that I cared so much for the coyotes was being played up as detrimental to their welfare. After all, they were just zoo animals. But it may actually have been seen as detrimental to the zoo's image. The coyotes' perceived wildness may actually have been an ace-in-the-hole for the zoo—something that was missing as long as I was in the picture.

For me, it was worse than a Disney animal movie where the worst possible scenarios of helpless animals and powerful villains are hatched and thrown at the quivering audience, leaving parents and children in tears, when suddenly the hero bursts forth to set things right in last few moments of the film. But this was reality and there was no heroic antidote. Being banned from interacting with my canine family of three years with permission to just watch them from outside their cage like the general public was not a good enough alternative for me.

Moving On

The zoo staff was, in all fairness, attempting to look out for what they thought were the 'best interests of their collection'. The personalized research that I was doing was beyond their range of acceptability and probably their liability as well. When negotiations began, I was an eager young graduate student and thought that everyone would love to be involved in such a project. Now I wish that I had been wise enough to conduct this project elsewhere. It's clear that my intended collaboration with the zoo to benefit both of us was naïve and misguided.

The professional contacts that I forged and the permit that I pursued to enable me to obtain wild baby animals for the zoo (on the condition that I would raise them and have them available to me for indefinite observation) proved decidedly in the zoo's favor. Once I did the work, the zoo got a new animal exhibit. And a few years down the road my research project was instantly terminated at the whim of zoo managers and a few state desk-jockeys. When push came to shove my advisor Eric Strauss was the only one who supported me, aside from my family and friends.

Environmental groups, eager to use my data on wild coyotes to support their anti-hunting agenda, disappeared as well. Many people feel that it is inhumane to keep wild animals in captivity, so some of the same organizations that collaborated with me on other aspects of my work realized that these captive coyotes would be a political taboo if their organization got involved in helping me.

Boston College, too interested in molecular biology to care, was also blatantly silent at this time, despite Eric's influence and position as a very popular faculty member. Other environmental or animal advocacy groups and colleagues who might have sympathized, were in no position to help. Things did not work out as I planned and the drama of the zoo situation will probably affect me the rest of my life.

Jennie Sheldon, a wildlife biologist at Yellowstone National Park, once also raised captive coyotes before moving to the Yellowstone area. She told me she still has not fully recovered from a similar experience of losing a hand-raised litter despite it being over 20 years ago. There is a little bit of the fairy tale in the wildlife studies of biologists, but it only works when the researchers truly care for the species and the individual animals they are studying, and remain well out of the reach of their bureaucratic 'supporters'. Today the whole world knows the outcome of Jane Goodall's long-term studies and can see her list of recognitions and awards to prove it. Many who could have supported her work but scoffed at her in the early days wish they were in the limelight with her now.

This situation with the captive coyotes at the Stone Zoo had pitted bureaucracy against layman, and science against monetary and regulatory interests. I was on the wrong end of the dispute and never had a chance, and am now battle-scarred as the unlikely end result of scholarly pursuits. Wildlife protection issues, and coyotes in particular, bring out passionate feelings in many people. Lots of people hate them while others see them as God's creatures and so important for the ecosystem they should never be harmed. Few, however, ever get the chance to know the creatures themselves as I did.

The bond I forged with the captive coyotes caused me to experience some of my highest and lowest professional experiences. Not a day goes by that I do not miss them, like a parent who suddenly lost custody of a child they had raised. Yet, one positive outcome of the captive experience was my realizing that they are only animals and are probably neither as good nor as bad as people think they are. Still, it's obvious that as a society, we need to reach some middle ground in order to coexist with them.

Cane sitting alert with Caon in background

Cane 'standing over' Caon

Profile of Caon

Caon covered in snow

Cane standing alert

Caon standing alert

Cane and Caon on guard

Note the size difference of the three females:
Late (left), Cane (middle), and Caon

Lupe and Cane play-wrestling

Late standing alert

Lupe alert

Lupe howling

Trans in snow

Coyotes greeting the author

Adolescent coyotes howling around the author

Lupe greeting the author

Coyotes in snow

Coyotes interacting

The last day the author saw Late and Trans

The last day the author saw Caon, Cane, and Lupe

Chapter 18

The Education Mission

An Educational Experience

28 October 2004. I began giving instructions for an in-class assignment to 14 students in Dave Eatough's Advanced Placement Environmental Studies class at Revere High School. "Okay class, today you are going to take on the role of a wildlife biologist. You will gain knowledge of important terminology and skill in actual operations. Once you have completed your 'training,' you will actually be going into the field to track real coyotes with us.

"To begin, there are five different sets of index cards with ten cards per group. Each cluster of cards contains ten locations for a real coyote that we have tracked in the field. Your job is to find all the cards for one coyote and graph them on the map that I created of Mr. Eatough's room. The classroom is a hypothetical 150 square miles, which is a typical study area size for a species like the coyote. Any questions? Okay, go find the coyote that I assigned to you."

"Jon, I am finding the cards for Glope, and his are spread throughout the room. What does that mean?" Alana asks me.

"Think about it," I reply. "If that animal's locations are distributed throughout the room, does that indicate a large or a small range?"

"Large. Oh, so he must be a nomadic coyote," group member Janelle responds.

"Very good guys. Now you are watching a video of this coyote and the four others, so I don't want to give away too much of the activity, but you are certainly on the right track," I tell them.

"Jon, I have a quick question also," Laura asks. "I am tracking Kash, and all of the cards are in the same place. Could this be correct?"

"Well, if all the five different social classes have to be represented and one probably has a smaller range than the others, it will soon be obvious, if it isn't already," I respond.

"Oh that makes sense now." Ryan answers. "I think I know what it is, a pup!"

"Very good! You guys are getting the point of the exercise."

After I notice all the students in groups of two and three pick up their cards and begin mapping their respective coyotes' ranges on the chalkboard, I ask them some questions about the activity.

"Remember, the home range is the area that an animal regularly uses. You have just mapped out these ranges. You see how large Glope's range is and how small Kash's is. That is for a reason. Can someone estimate how large their coyote's range is?"

Anton responds, "I had Kett, and his range was about 15."

"Fifteen what?" I ask him.

"Fifteen miles," he answers.

"Now remember guys, we are talking about area, so that..."

"Square miles. Fifteen square miles," Alana responds, interrupting me, but correctly answering the question.

"Good, so Kett's range is an average-sized home range for eastern coyotes. Remember, you already read the scientific paper that I published with my colleagues. It said that average territories on the Cape are about 12 square miles. Well, 15 is pretty close to that. How many don't understand this?" I ask.

A couple of hands go up. "Okay," I began to explain, "you see the shape created around the home range? That is called a polygon. To calculate the home range we need to figure out the area of the polygon. Well, the length of Kett's range is about five miles long, and the width of the range is three. Thus, the home range has to be around 15 square miles."

"Yes, that makes sense now," Dan says out loud.

"Good. I'm glad that you are all getting it," I went on. "That is an important concept to understand in wildlife ecology. Why don't we look at the videos now and see if each of you can identify the social class of your coyote. To make that guess, you need to watch video-clips on that specific coyote. The actual video might not be a dead give-away, so you will also need to use information on your coyote's home range size and the clues that I give out loud."

"You really only need to pay attention to the coyote whom you tracked," I continued, "but theoretically, by process of elimination, if you know the coyotes that match with the other four social classes you could probably guess yours. That is because there are five social classes of coyotes and there is only one of each in this exercise." At this point the instructor, and my colleague Dave Eatough, always one to try and embarrass me when he can, interrupted with "Jon, could you move over a bit. You're blocking my field of view."

"Okay," I said, stepping back from the screen, "Here is film clip number one:

"My name is Mizz. Although I am a weird looking coyote. I regularly attend my pups, but I also have to travel throughout my home range to obtain enough food such as rabbits, squirrels, mice, and possibly cats. However, I regularly have to return to and nurse my pups." I dictated the description to them, repeating it twice.

"That's easy." Amanda answers. "If she has pups, she must be a breeding female. Plus her range is about eight square miles which is within the range of a breeding female."

"Good job. I need to show these clips quickly, before the class period ends so here is clue number two:

"My name is Kett. I have lived here for over three years. My boundaries are well established. I regularly patrol them while my mate nurses the pups."

"Resident associate," James says.

"Now think again, guys. If this coyote is patrolling its boundaries (I deliberately avoid referencing the gender to try and make the simple example a little more difficult for them) and has been there for a few years, do you think that is the correct answer?"

"I know—breeding male," Anton says.

"Very good. Does this make sense to everybody?" No hands go up so I continue. Okay, let's move on to the next one. Here is segment three:

"My name is Glope. Formerly I used to roam the study area, but I recently joined the group you are watching. I can be seen in the back watching two of my packmates interact. Then you can see me traveling alone on a golf course. What was my social status before joining this group?"

Dan puts his hand up. "Glope must have been a transient before being accepted into a pack."

"Good work, Dan. See, I told you this was pretty easy. Here is the fourth clip:

"My name is Sill. Although not a dad yet, I still bring food to my younger packmates (siblings). I live mostly on my natal home range, but occasionally leave it to explore surrounding areas."

Alana shouts during the clip, "Resident associate. If he is living with his parents he has to be a helper coyote."

"Good job, smart aleck," I say smiling, "however, he is currently a breeding male. Sill left his father Kett in 2001 and settled at the eastern edge of Kett's range. He is still alive and is now the breeding male in Marstons Mills. He often goes into my parent's backyard as their house is within his pack's territory." I added, "And I have a trap in their back yard."

"Okay, here is the final clip. I am sure you can guess the answer ahead of time, but to be thorough, I will play it anyway:

"My name is Kash. I am impatient and howl with my siblings when I want food. I wait around the den and play with my siblings for most of my waking hours. I don't explore much—yet! I was captured when I was four months old."

Class, can you guess Kash's social status?"

"Pup. Juvenile," the class yells in unison. Juvenile was the correct terminology.

"Good job, guys!" I tell them just as the bell rings for their next class.

By completing this in-class project, these high school students learned:

1) techniques to estimate home range and population sizes of coyotes;
2) characteristics of five actual coyotes being studied in the wild on Cape Cod, Massachusetts; and
3) the different social classes of coyotes and how to correlate social status to home range use.

Activities like this enabled us to teach students about our research during a normal school schedule. This curriculum unit and others serve as a foundation for urban science education throughout the Boston Public School system and could be modified for use at the undergraduate level.

My eight-year ecological and behavioral study of wild and captive eastern coyotes was expanded upon in my doctoral studies and involved assessing student learning and interest in coyotes. Generally, there is a paucity of data on student learning of animal behavior because there is so little associated curriculum units taught on the subject. For that reason, one of the objectives of the educational component of my research was to provide some concrete information relating to student understanding of coyotes.

To accomplish this, I developed a broad curriculum of study for high school students relating to coyote natural history and research in human-dominated areas. This curriculum piece included an assessment and analysis of how students learned, formed opinions, and created perceptions about coyotes. The purpose of the education part of my research was to understand the relationship between an ecological concept and student learning. Thus, I examined student understanding and perceptions of coyotes, which as predators, often elicit strong emotions. An overarching purpose of these curriculum interventions was to validate my professional work, which was to attempt to bridge the gap between the educational and scientific community.

I co-developed and co-taught (with participating teachers) a several-week technology-enhanced curriculum unit that used multi-media tools such as Powerpoint© slides, Windows Media-Player© videos of coyotes in action, classroom activities simulating a coyote biologist (the activity at the beginning of this chapter), posters of coyotes in the classroom, handouts/readings, web-based resources such as my web site, and a visit to see the live captive coyote exhibit. The curriculum unit focused on the research conducted at our three study sites (two wild, one captive). Topics included capture techniques, handling and radio-collaring procedures, coyote ecology in the wild, behavior in captivity, behavior around people, and societal perceptions (for example, showing a video of Wile E. Coyote and the Roadrunner).

My main purpose was to craft a partnership with high schools, with the specific mission of working side-by-side with students and teachers in designing wildlife studies, and specifically, projects on eastern coyotes. The research question that served as the focus of this study was: How does a curriculum intervention comprised of an ecologically-based concept on coyote behavior affect student learning and perceptions of coyotes? I examined these sub-questions related to the above inquiry:

- In what ways do students' knowledge of coyotes change after participating in this curriculum?
- In what ways do students become engaged in and empowered by science issues after being introduced to our place-based intervention?

After conducting a pilot study in a suburban classroom on Cape Cod, I focused on classes in two Boston-based schools; one north Boston school that was urban in nature, and the other school in South Boston which was located in the inner-city. The participants in this study were the students of the two high school science teachers who taught environmentally-based courses at their respective schools.

Student Involvement in Authentic Research

The education portion of the eastern coyote study was largely a naturalistic, qualitative study with some quantitative components. I used interviews, journals and field notes (classroom observations), and pre/post/post-delayed tests to obtain data. The active, hands-on involvement of students allowed to participate in an authentic study near where they lived was unparalleled. In fact, as the next chapter depicts, some of the students felt so strongly about coyotes after taking the class that they literally agonized over learning of the poisoning deaths of the collared pack they had been studying.

The study of one's local environment is known as placed-based education, and has been described in depth by David Sobel in his book *Place-based Education: Connecting Classrooms and Communities*. Place-based education is renowned for empowering students to care about their local environment ranging from inner city gardens to caring for endangered species in rural areas.

Providing students with an opportunity to see me interacting with the captive pack of coyotes at the Stone Zoo was a very important component for student appreciation of the coyote curriculum, as attested to by this student's comment after visiting the zoo:

"Now that we studied them, everything about coyotes interests me. They are just like... I had no idea what they were like. It was amazing seeing them at the zoo in real life. You see them in pictures and don't get that much of an idea about them until you see them in real life. Their actions, the way they are. I wish the unit was longer. I even told Mr. Eatough, 'Hey, can we go to the zoo again?' "

Seeing live coyotes was so important, in fact, that one of the major complaints about the curriculum unit, aside from its brevity, was made by a student who did not visit the zoo:

> "I want to see them in more than on videos. It would be kind of interesting. I could study them better if I could see them face to face."

After students visited the zoo, they clearly became more interested and involved in the study as this quote demonstrates. Here the student used specific examples in his response:

> "Well, since I've seen them now...I mean, you can show us as many pictures of the coyotes as you want, but it is so hard to distinguish the coyotes—but when I was at the zoo, by the end of the field trip I could easily distinguish them even with their backs toward me. I saw their different behaviors, like when Lupe wanted your attention and how he got it."

These quotations, and much other feedback that we received from the students, demonstrated that the curriculum impacted them because they lived near the creatures they studied. Authentic science activities such as these provide an opportunity for the students to learn how scientists conduct their research. This could include students directly participating with scientists, or by the use of simulations such as videos (indirect participation).

Simulating an authentic experience provides the possibility for students to engage nature like scientists do, even when it is not feasible to take students into the scientists' domains for monetary or logistic reasons. The students in the classes that I taught were often hyperactive until the video came on, then most viewers became quiet and watched the film intently. Another student's comment sums up how the personalized nature of the field videos was very important and meaningful to them:

> "I liked the videos because we were there. We did it. It was us doing it."

The interesting thing about this comment was that this student never did any field research with us. It appeared that she gained her perspective purely by participating in the class activities presented to the students by the scientist/researcher in collaboration with their normal teacher. Videos could be used in many diverse settings in order to make the curriculum unit more real for the consumers/students. For instance, someone in the Midwest could obtain video-footage of coyotes in an agricultural region near them and bring it into the classroom.

This research demonstrated that students need both real-world experiences, like viewing coyotes at a zoo, and simulation, in order to fully appreciate and understand such wildlife. While the simulation concept seems to be effective and more transferable to other settings, the trip to the zoo gave the unit added meaning.

Researchers and instructors working together, designing place-based authentic experiences for students, give meaning to science education that is critically important to their learning. This means it doesn't have to exclusively occur outside, but when properly done, it can occur in classrooms as well. In essence, that was my job as a scientist-instructor, as I spent many long hours in the field to obtain the data and video coverage that became the database for my work and could later be shown to the students in my teaching exercises.

This simulated way of learning allowed the students in the classroom to understand important concepts relating to wildlife/coyotes without having to do anything but sit and listen. While the ultimate way to eventually learn about any wildlife such as coyotes would be to perform field studies on wild or captive animals, this is not a teaching tool that could be used under broad circumstances; however, video or Powerpoint© slides are tools that can be used in most any classroom.

A great deal of research has documented the importance of hands-on, inquiry-based curriculum that is conducted outdoors and related to the environment. I summarized much of that research in my dissertation entitled *Assessing Student Learning and Interest in Eastern Coyotes*. Providing students with experiences and examples from the real world is crucial to their understanding of science. The students in my educational study expressed that they felt a richer connection to the curriculum unit when they visited the zoo and were able to observe real coyotes who were named and part of an actual study.

Student Interest and Preference in Coyote Research

The value of understanding students' interests and preferences in learning about coyotes, and science in general, was a significant component of the educational study. While it is important to assess student performance and their understanding of science concepts, instructors also have to understand how they prefer to learn and what interests them in the science issues under study.

For example, because students today, most especially urban students, obtain much of their environmental information from television, the videos used in my curriculum unit proved to be a highly effective teaching tool. Observing animals, whether in the wild or on video, is an activity most students can manage effectively. Thus, observing media presentations of animal behavior affords an easy and captivating entry into the world of scientific inquiry.

Richard Louv, in his new book *Last Child in the Woods*, noted that TV and video games now keep children inside rather than actively exploring and learning about nature on their own. I think the job of educators is to encourage students to explore the outdoors, like studying coyotes in just about any landscape, as well as teaching them about nature through media like television that they are used to.

Combining outdoors and simulation learning is a mechanism that effectively increases students' knowledge and interest in science.

The need for scientists and schools to form partnerships is potentially beneficial for all, especially when engaging in an authentic scientific project. In the partnership described in this study, students were afforded the opportunity to learn from a scientist while participating in legitimate scholarly, school-based activities. This partnership introduced students to a socio-scientific issue and a person who worked in that field (me). The students all responded very positively regarding the unit, and that potentially might increase student interest in science. In addition, students were able to grasp how scientists investigated a novel topic, which might inspire future scientists.

Another major benefit of the developed curriculum, and one which whetted the intellectual appetite of even the least excitable student, was having the involved scientist deliver field updates on the coyote research project, to the students. Thus the unit was successful because it was designed from a local, place-based arena in the students' eyes. In essence, it was real to them. Further, it was taught using a diverse array of teaching tools to maintain student interest and to encourage further learning about the topics presented.

Students Embrace Their Research Targets

It became apparent in the delivery of information in my curriculum unit on coyotes that the students appreciated having an involved scientist presenting the teaching material. At the beginning of the unit, students were essentially completely ignorant about the ecology and behavior of wild coyotes. For example, many of them had been led to believe that coyotes were not only unwanted neighbors, but that they could be easily removed from an area.

Linguistics within any field of science includes both buzzwords and ordinary scientific terms. Urban students, being unfamiliar with both wildlife and related ecology jargon, often used inappropriate terminology to discuss the coyotes. For example, one student used the word 'terminate', when instead he meant 'extirpate'.

"If we really wanted to target and terminate them, yeah, we could do it. It would take a lot of power, a lot of resources to do it."

It was unclear as to what kind of power he was referring to (no follow-up question attempted to clarify this), but we suspect he meant man-power and effort to literally eradicate coyotes. Other students agreed that it was possible to eliminate coyotes, but were vocal that they just did not think it was the right thing to do. Their overall positive view toward coyotes was apparent, but they clearly did not understand coyote ecology, as demonstrated by this student's comment to explain why coyotes could not be eliminated:

"I think the coyote species is limited enough in heavily populated areas that they could be eliminated, but I just think that it would be wrong."

In general, student understanding of coyote ecology increased dramatically after the curriculum units. Some had a complete understanding of coyote ecology by the end of the unit and thus explained their results in an accurate and complete way during the post interviews. This student's response was particularly notable among the interviewees:

Interviewer: "Do you believe that it is possible to completely eliminate coyotes?"
Student: "No, because of what you told us in class. If you eliminate a certain pack then other packs are going to come in. So, no I don't think that you can eliminate them all."
Interviewer: "So you can get rid of individuals, but not coyotes in general?"
Student: "Correct."

During the intervention, we noticed that some students were grasping some of the important concepts of the course, and thus we were not surprised that students better understood the futility of killing coyotes. For example, on 22 October 2004, one student asked an important question when we were talking about coyote home ranges and territoriality. My response was somewhat similar to many of their answers from the interview session:

Student: "If coyotes are killed, won't others just move in?"
Researcher: "Yes, that is exactly why control efforts are useless unless specific animals are causing unacceptable damage or are a threat to people. A basic ecological concept like that is usually misunderstood. The scientific paper that I will be presenting on Home Range and Territoriality of Cape Cod Coyotes, although technically written, states that precisely."

The quotations in this chapter are just a few examples of some of our educational findings. The major findings of our education research were:

- Because coyotes were objects of local interest, students loved to learn about them in the classroom.
- Using coyotes as a teaching tool in science class facilitated student learning and promoted interest in socio-scientific issues.
- Using place-based local settings for teaching topics such as the coyote project were important because it was authentic and meaningful to the students.
- Using technology-enhanced presentations (videos, slides) to illustrate concepts gave students a sense of hands-on experience even when not physically working in the field.

- Seeing live subjects (the captive coyotes at the zoo) who were part of an authentic study and who were interacting with the instructor, enhanced student appreciation of the curriculum topic and made the unit more personal.

The public often views large carnivores like wolves and tigers as flagship or charismatic species because they are familiar to many people and are icons for exotic places far away. Conservationists often use these popular species to raise public awareness about the plight of endangered species. Coyotes, on the other hand, are not only not endangered, they are sufficiently prolific that they might be seen by just about anyone with the right information about how to locate them. And because they are relatively large, local, wild canines closely related to dogs, they naturally invoke interest in the students. Our data seems to support that.

Dave Eatough holding coyote Maeve with Revere High students and the author (second from right) and Steve Cifuni (right)

Due to the predatory habits of coyotes and their presence in urban areas, the public is very aware of them. This makes them an ideal subject for science education. Their continent-wide range and broad interest appeal makes them an exciting potential study topic for science educators in quite diverse settings. Coyotes could serve as a flagship species for engaging students in science education and ecology-related issues and to empower students' to become active in caring about their local environment, especially in urbanized settings.

Suburban residents need programs like this to raise awareness of coyotes as common sights in residential areas, and to value, instead of despise, these experiences. Coyote ecology such as large home ranges and territories demands that they be true to their instincts and routine species behavior, like travel near and through residential areas. Once the public understands that concept, trapping and removing coyotes, which is normally only a short-term solution, will be seen for what it is, an unneeded option in most cases.

In conclusion, this curriculum unit was important and useable in multiple contexts because:

1) Learning about a predator like a coyote naturally seemed to capture the interest of the students.

2) Coyotes were familiar to many people because they are local and closely related to domestic dogs. Thus, it took little effort to engage students in the subject.

3) The diverse instructional techniques were exciting to students and produced significant student learning in a relatively short period of time.

4) A scientist was involved in the curriculum development and used current, high-technology teaching tools to assist in student learning of animal behavior.

5) Using a curriculum unit that was locally relevant motivated students to care about protecting, conserving, and learning about the environment around them. The unit may also be effective in teaching people how to learn to coexist with other species.

6) Because of the coyote's adaptability and distribution across the North American continent, this unit is potentially transferable to numerous and varied scholastic settings from rural to urban environments.

Chapter 19

A Stressful Struggle

The Difficult Discovery

Easter Sunday, 27 March 2005. I was down on the Cape for a couple days of rest during the holiday after a busy week of research in north Boston and academics at Boston College. I was on the phone with Dave Eatough at my parent's house in Marstons Mills. After he spoke, I found myself stunned with shock and disbelief. The words tumbled out of my mouth. "What do you mean…Maeve is dead?"

It was a conference call with Dave and Steve Cifuni, my colleagues in the coyote project. It started out normally enough until I heard him say something I simply couldn't process. "I just tracked her two days ago and she seemed fine," I said helplessly. "She looked like she was ready to have a litter of pups in barely a week or two."

"I know…but we found her dead in the middle of the Jewish Cemetery," Steve quietly informed me. It was obvious he hadn't gotten over finding her himself, but was trying to explain it clinically, something we all do to try to keep our emotions from going crazy when something happens to one of the coyotes we call our "study subjects".

"She was horribly skinny, weighing only 28 lbs. Her ribs were very pronounced," Steve went on. He explained that he had met Dave in the cemetery to make a quick inspection of the carcass.

"Hard to believe…" my voice trailed off. "What else could go wrong with this study?" I demanded to no one in particular. "It seems like every coyote from the north Boston study, except for Fog who beat it out of town, has died soon after being collared!" I couldn't express how devastated I was to hear about it.

"I'll give Bob a call and see if we can come by his clinic tomorrow morning," I told Dave, referring to Dr. Bob Binder of Saugus Animal Hospital. Dave knew that we would have to bring Maeve over there so we could conduct a necropsy while her body was still fresh.

The Examination

28 March 2005. Steve and I retrieved Maeve's carcass from a shallow snow bank at Steve's house and brought it to the Saugus Animal Hospital at 11:45 AM. Dr. Bob met us there with some of his staff. When he first saw me, I was just standing outside his clinic with Maeve in my arms.

"What is it with this study? They seem to be dropping like flies," Dr. Binder said to me, as he opened the door for me to bring her in. I just shook my head in response.

I started out by doing a quick inspection of Maeve's external condition. She was indeed skinny. I found I could easily get my hand between her neck and the collar. I remembered originally putting the collar on fairly tight.

"The circumference of her collar is only 31.7 centimeters and it's very loose on her. Normally we have collars set at 32 or 33 centimeters and they fit relatively snugly," I remarked to Dr. Binder and Steve.

"Bring her inside and let's have a look at her," Bob said.

From there, we went straight to the operating room. Bob began by making a ventral incision on Maeve's underside, from the neck to the pubic region because we needed to see the internal condition of her body. We quickly saw an unusual amount of bleeding in her uterus and that she was actually not pregnant. What I may have perceived when I saw her was likely abdominal swelling unrelated to pregnancy. No fetuses were visible and her stomach contained no digestive content, just dark blood and grass. There was more bleeding throughout the GI track. Bob took some blood samples to send to a laboratory for analysis.

I questioned him as to the cause of her death. He indicated it seemed apparent that she had bled to death, but the cause of the bleeding wasn't immediately clear. If it were some type of anti-coagulant like rat poison, it still would not explain why she was not pregnant. He explained that traditional rat poisons are "anticoagulant rodenticides" and cause death to rats and mice by deactivating the ability of Vitamin K to motivate normal blood clotting. When any bleeding begins, it becomes necessary to form a clot, which requires Vitamin K. As the clotting factors are activated, Vitamin K is inactivated but later recycled by certain enzymes to motivate clotting later whenever needed.

As long as there is plenty of Vitamin K in the body, blood clotting can proceed normally. Anticoagulant rodenticides act by abolishing Vitamin K recycling, so as soon as active Vitamin K reserves are depleted, there can be no meaningful blood clotting. In cases of poisoning, one might expect symptoms to be nearly immediate, but in actuality, it takes several days to deplete Vitamin K. In domestic pets, this can often delay treatment if symptoms are not immediately apparent.

After that, even the smallest of jostles and traumas can lead to life-threatening bleeds. Since these are the most commonly available poisons, sometimes pets accidentally eat such products left out for rats. If it is clear that poisoning is a result of a rodenticide and treatment is begun in time, there is a readily available antidote (Vitamin K) for ingesting these poisons.

Bob promised to let us know the lab results as soon as he had them and the rest of us left to scout out the cemetery for the other coyotes. Our spirits sinking, none of us wanted to think about what could have happened if Maeve's death had been due to deliberate poisoning.

We had tracked her for nearly the past 11 months and knew everything about her. We knew where she denned (right next to the artificial canal of Town Line Brook), and that she gave birth to five pups, that one of her pups, Jem, weighed in that early fall at 22-lbs, and another one, Cour, weighed 27-lbs. I knew her mate was Jet, and I knew where the pack slept, in a small cluster of bushes in a field just south of a large hill that blocked the northeast wind during bad weather.

I knew they had a very small territory of about a square mile, and how they restricted their movements during extreme snow depths to minimize energy expenditure. And now, of course, I knew where she died—uncharacteristically out in the open, in the middle of her small range.

The Search Continues

Later that day and evening, I tracked her mate Jet, and full-grown pup Cour. They were all that remained of the four coyotes we had collared the previous fall. Jem dispersed 11 December 2004 before the winter began. We had not found her again since she left the area. In addition to the father-son combination, there seemed to be one more remaining coyote who was uncollared. It was a beautiful pale yellow with black markings on the top of its coat and a very white belly. I guessed it to be one of the remaining pups who, like Cour, stayed with family and did not disperse during the deep-snow winter of 2004/2005.

Jet was locally active in the cattails, a strip of woods that contained a small 50-foot diameter wetland that bisected their range between the two major cemeteries. This was a favorite location where the coyotes rendezvoused, and also where they rested for the day. Human activity in this immediate area was limited, despite people being active in the cemeteries less than 50 meters away on either side.

Cour was more widely active in their small range. At 8:55 PM I got a strong signal from both, but Cour's was in the middle of Holy Cross Cemetery, the second largest of the four cemeteries that comprised the bulk of their territory. *"Why can't I see him?"* I asked myself, as the melting snow and the bright crescent-shaped moon provided enough illumination for me that I should notice at least the shadow of his body. *"He is like a ghost,"* I thought.

At 9:20 PM I finally saw Cour as he walked slowly in the west-central part of Holy Cross. He was on open grass in between graves and he was in no hurry. He eyed my car, which was parked and turned off, then casually walked off. Somehow it didn't strike me as odd that right then this normally energetic creature was walking. *"At least these two seem to be doing okay,"* I wrote in my notes. Finally after nearly an hour more of tracking that night, I left the coyotes at 10:15 PM, with both males still active in the core region of their range.

On 30 March 2005 I was once again out tracking both males, and this would be the last time. I arrived at the site at 2:35 AM, delighted that it was a balmy 40°F, a tropical paradise compared to the past couple of months of cold weather. The snow had just about melted, making it more difficult to see their phantom-like bodies shifting from one place to the other in their nocturnal activities.

I noted that Jet was right in the cattails again and was not terribly active. I then drove to the south-central part of their range at the southern boundary of Woodlawn, the largest cemetery in their small range. Cour was active in that area. He stayed down there, probably poking around for rats, mice, and potentially some garbage left by cemetery visitors, until 4:05 AM. He then walked east, then north while looping around their southern and eastern range boundaries.

I knew he would not go further south or east because the area is packed tight with high density housing lots. In the city of Everett, aside from these cemeteries, there is not much open space in this region just a few miles north of downtown Boston. I thought back to Fog, the transient coyote who traveled through their range, and the only other coyote we knew that had the nerve to traverse this urban jungle.

Realizing that Cour was going to move north since he was at the southeast part of their range, I parked on Washington Street, one of the area's main north-to-south thoroughfares. At 4:22 AM I watched him in the eastern part of Woodlawn, immediately west of Washington Street. He initially looked at my car through the cemetery fence from about 50 feet away, but seemed more focused on the traffic on Route 1 just to our east. He looked around for two minutes, then loped casually off with a noticeable limp in his right hind leg.

I proceeded to drive north to Glenwood Cemetery and parked right at the entrance near a narrow opening in the fence that they commonly used to move from one cemetery to the next. In fact, before I found this seven-inch-wide opening, coyotes appeared to vanish from my view as they ran through it from Glenwood into Woodlawn.

As I pulled into Glenwood at 4:28 AM, a police car was leaving the cemetery. They knew that I tracked coyotes in the area and rarely bothered me. I tried to do likewise with them. I turned off my car and remained motionless in my vehicle with the windows rolled up so Cour wouldn't be able to scent me. Cour's signal was very strong to my south, so I grabbed my binoculars and scanned for him in Woodlawn. Within seconds I found him looking around through the gap in the fence before he stepped through it over a low horizontal bar.

He entered Glenwood and casually walked by my car about 30 feet away. He looked normal, aside from the limp in his right rear leg. However, I sensed that something was wrong. He walked north with an uncharacteristic lethargy, whereas

Micro-corridors connecting two cemeteries

coyotes almost always moved in an active trot. He was headed back to the most wooded part of their range. I saw him two more times as he moved toward the east about half a mile from where his father Jet was bedded.

I called Dave just as I was about to finish up tracking. I reported that I saw Cour a bunch of times during the early-morning throughout their range, and that he was alone and walking slowly. Jet didn't move much but I said I didn't want to bother him. I asked Dave to track him that night or the next day and see what he was up to. It was 6:52 AM, so I was carefully making the call eight minutes before I started getting charged minutes to use my cell phone and before Dave began his academic duties at Revere High School.

Meave's death had upset us all and Dave was nervous about Jet. Unsurprisingly, he confessed to having 'an insanely busy next couple of days at school', but promised to see what he could do. I knew his crazy schedule and told him I understood.

31 March 2005, 8:30 PM. Dave called me just after I got home from a long day at Boston College working on my dissertation. I needed to ask him how things went, but I wasn't prepared for his matter-of-fact answer.

"Not too good. Jet is dead." Dave said, his distress mirrored in his voice. A few more comments were exchanged, most of it inappropriate to mention in this text. Both of us were now barely able to talk coherently. Then I asked Dave where he was, and his answer struck me.

"In the same place where you located him yesterday," he responded.

My stomach got queasy and I felt sick. I knew I should have walked in on Jet yesterday and seen if he were okay. I also knew this was going to bother me for weeks to come—and it did, because I knew I didn't help him when I should have. Dave was also sick about it, fairly certain now that they had both been poisoned.

There was a long moment of silence on the phone when neither of us could say anything. The anger we felt was palpable. We were ready to explode, knowing that someone had perpetrated this overt act of cruelty and we couldn't do anything about it. After a moment, when I was able to speak again, I told Dave weakly that I would call Steve and we would bring Jet's body over to Dr. Bob's and see if it were in the same condition as Maeve's. Then, we had to end the conversation. Both of us were out of things to say.

01 April 2005. Steve and I transported Jet to the Saugus Animal Hospital. Dr. Bob, like Dr. Larry Venezia down on the Cape, was always ready to donate his veterinary services to our project. We weighed Jet and he was an emaciated 31.5-lbs with very pronouncedly protruding bones, especially from his hip. Blood was discharging from his penis onto his fur. Before even conducting the necropsy, I knew that Jet too had bled to death.

As expected, we found the same results as with Maeve's autopsy: massive internal bleeding. Bob Binder again collected samples to send to the laboratory, specifically to test for poisoning this time.

We thanked Dr. Bob for his help once again. We were devastated by what had happened during the past week, but the worst part was knowing how these poor animals must have suffered. I could only imagine how much pain they must have been in as they died. Given their exclusively urban range, they rarely came in contact with humans and so it was unlikely they were targeted for causing any problems with people. Sometimes, however, the problem is just their mere presence in areas where people perceive them to be a danger. It would have been some small comfort if I had been able to think that it was an accident—that they had somehow ingested something accidentally that was really meant for rats. But the evidence didn't seem to point in that direction as there was just too much poison used to kill two large animals so close together.

Dr. Bob was a comfort, as well as a colleague. He constantly reminded us why we were doing this kind of work to observe and document how these urban creatures lived, or aptly in this case, how they died. Even though we needed to hear it, we didn't want to. He then made a practical suggestion, and suggested that we take some Vitamin K and put it in bait outside the trap and hope that Cour and others would eat it. If reached in time, it would help counter any potential poisons in their systems. I couldn't believe that we had to resort to doing this to try and save our study animals. Still brooding, I took the Vitamin K and slunk out of the clinic.

As Steve and I were finishing Jet's necropsy at the Saugus Animal Hospital, Dave had the unhappy task of telling his students that the study animals that were the objects of their curriculum were dead. As he recounted his experience of picking up Jet's motionless body from the edge of the cemetery, he noticed one of the students crying in the back of the room. Hardly able to control his own emotions after spending three years capturing, collaring, and tracking these coyotes, he quickly changed the subject. This dramatic outcome had struck at the hearts of everyone involved, from the study collaborators to the numerous students who were involved in the curriculum unit. No one could have foreseen this turn of events.

Dave was a consummate professional, and he now deliberately focused his attention elsewhere in the class, knowing he might lose it if he continued to look at the weeping student. Nonetheless, his voice had become heavy and subdued, an unnatural tone for a normally enthusiastic teacher. He told me afterward that delivering the news of Jet's death was one of the worst and most difficult things he had ever had to do in front of a class. There were tears on the faces of half of the students. He recalled it felt like giving an unprepared eulogy, saying whatever first came to mind. I was grateful not to have been the one to handle that aspect of it.

There Was Still Hope

Later that night I tracked Cour and found him semi-active in his range. *"At least he is still moving!"* I wrote in my notes. The next day Dave got a spot location on him and put more bait at the site, but noted that the bait that I had put out had not been touched.

03 April 2005. I was out tracking with my girlfriend, Nadia. It was 43°F with just a slight wind. Dave just finished tracking Cour for a couple of hours and thought that he was slightly active by the canal that separates the two main cemeteries. At 9:30 PM I got him just east of the cattails between the Jewish (JC) and Holy Cross Cemeteries. It seemed like he was further away at first but that might just have been because his collar is naturally weak (like Sill's transmitter on the Cape, Cour had an ATS collar).

After 30 minutes of waiting at the north-central part of the Jewish Cemetery, I decided this time to walk in on him. The signal was peculiar as I couldn't seem to get a strong fix anywhere despite circling around that small area, less than 200 meters across. I told Nadia to stay in the car until I got back, and she was naturally nervous to be left alone near not just one, but four cemeteries. She is a slender woman originally from Sao Paulo, Brazil, an urban area equivalent to New York City in the states. The coyotes' cemetery stomping grounds, although surrounded by cities, appeared completely rural in her eyes. And to tell the truth, it is an eerie location, even though it is surrounded by the municipalities of Malden, Everett, and Revere.

The area where we were was very dark and quiet. Many shady people tended to hang out in this locale, as it is one of the few places that they can get away with illicit behavior unseen. Under normal conditions, we mostly ignored these types and they usually did likewise, as the tracking antenna pointing out of our cars might have been interpreted as some form of authoritative activity. Only during the daytime did we ever get questions from people who were unfamiliar with our research. Nadia begged me to hurry up, knowing by now that I would not obey her wishes and stay with her. I heard the door locks snapping down as I walked away from the truck.

Hope Was Gone

At 10:10 PM I walked along the Town Line Brook, the artificial canal that served as the boundary between Malden and Everett. I was suddenly caught up short when I came across Cour, belly-up in the creek. "No wonder I couldn't get a strong signal," I thought as that same nauseous feeling began to creep over me again. While he was in the creek, the cement on both sides had been bouncing the signal around. Since he was about five feet below surface level, the signal was weaker. He had probably been dead for some time. I surmised that the tidal flow must have tossed his body around, thereby giving Dave a variable signal when he took a location fix. And that would have indicated that Cour was still alive.

After calling Dave and Steve to join me, we retrieved Cour's body from the water. Dave cautiously navigated down the steep and slippery canal wall, then stepped into the murky water and fished Cour out of the shallow two-foot deep creek. He gave the carcass to me and I dragged it up the slope onto level ground. It was low tide so we had to negotiate quite a bit more of the bank than normal to get to him.

The dead weight of a waterlogged 40-lb coyote was surprisingly heavy. All I could think of was how easily he used to navigate this canal. What a horrible seven days this had been. I found myself angry beyond reason, wanting to scream, wanting to get back at the people who did this.

"What cowards!" I yelled, both emotionally drained, yet still enraged over the week's events. Dave and Steve felt the same way and couldn't even speak. We all departed the area knowing that this would be yet one more miserable night, our stomachs tied in knots and wrenched with agony. I knew I was supposed to be a detached scientist, but instead I felt like I had just lost three friends. We found them thousands of times in the past nine months and knew everything that they did; when they became active, where they slept, where they gave birth, what they ate, and where they scent-marked the borders of their small territory.

"I am so sorry," Nadia said to me helplessly with her distinct Portuguese accent when I returned to the car. But I couldn't answer her. I was so angry and frustrated, I couldn't say anything. Afterwards, we drove home in silence and it took me hours to fall asleep. I just couldn't stop thinking about everything that happened.

The Evidence

I heard from Dr. Bob a week later that the laboratories verified our worst fears—that all three coyotes were killed by a very toxic type of poison called Brodificoum, the active ingredient in potent rodenticides such as d-Con®. We now knew that it likely took the poor animals a week or so to die from the internal hemorrhaging associated with this slow and cruel death. For weeks we all felt like we were the ones who had been poisoned.

It was difficult to describe the horrible feelings that encompassed me, my colleagues, and the students involved in the coyote research project. Research was supposed to be enlightening, rewarding, and educational, not gut-wrenching and painful. We were all overwhelmed with sadness, especially after Jet died, realizing that Cour and any other coyotes who still lived there were going to die and there was nothing we could do about it.

We constantly questioned our own actions, thinking that if only Cour ate some of the Vitamin K, maybe his body would have been able to generate the normal clotting response to blood vessel damage. Practically, though, we would have needed to be in the field 24 hours a day to prevent his death. Dave sent me almost daily e-mails reiterating his anger. We all communicated with each other frequently. It was the only way we could deal with it, trying to flush away the horrible events of the past week, trying to find someone to blame, talk about punishing them, wanting to punish ourselves for letting it happen, and then always coming up empty.

My nearly daily phone conversations with Dave and Steve calmed us all, but only to a degree. And still, even weeks after the incident, my stomach felt nauseated as the anger continued to simmer inside me. And in the midst of the anger, we found ourselves deeply grieving in a way we found difficult to understand.

Discovering and Responding to the Poisonings

After a few weeks of inactivity I decided that something had to be done. I carefully wrote and posted an account of these horrible incidents on my web page. Before long I began to receive responses and a very sympathetic general reaction from the local residents. That in itself was comforting, but aside from accepting my detailed report given to an Environmental Police Officer, the state did nothing to assist us, either in locating the perpetrator (which would have been a formidable task) or covering the expenses associated with the findings.

We ultimately solicited donations and there was another outpouring of response, both from those expressing sympathy and from those that wished to help. We collected just over $600 to pay for nearly all the laboratory expenses. Boston College picked up the remaining tab. A few supporters of our project even gave $100 each, but the $15 donation that a Medford lady gave to me from her daughter's Mother's Day gift to her was the most memorable. These may seem like little things, but we all felt so wounded by the acts of possibly just one person, that it took the empathy that many expressed to help us begin to get past our pain.

To bring increased attention to this urgent matter, we went public with the details once the laboratory confirmed the cause of the deaths. The story of the poisonings made it to a few of the major Boston news networks. Almost everyone, except for a couple of anti-coyote locals (who almost certainly didn't poison them), were furious about these cruel acts.

Nevertheless, the poisoner(s) is still at large. And just like in some of the places on the Cape where people deliberately shot our collared coyotes, we ceased our research in that area due to both frustration and a recognition of the potential waste of our time and resources. The necessity of avoiding the mental anguish and disgust of dealing with people who are not disciplined in their actions prevents me from returning to these areas.

Dave completely stopped his two-year routine of visiting that area which is only a mile and a half from where he teaches at Revere High School. He confessed that the anger that is evoked in him when he thinks of the incidents is so strong, that he can no longer go there. (Dave did end up rebaiting the site six months later as new coyotes colonized the area and Dave's anger had somewhat abated.)

What is most disappointing to me is that the killings of our collared coyotes are supported by current state law, which allows for the killing of an unlimited number of coyotes during four months of the year in Massachusetts. While it is certainly illegal to use poison to kill wild animals outside of one's home, a pack of coyotes in a more rural area could just as easily have been shot and killed by a 'predator' hunter.

Just from a monetary perspective, it seems both contradictory and unproductive that a couple of guys that pay well under a $100 combined for their state hunting permits, have the right to bring a complete halt to a broadly organized, long-term research project also authorized and licensed by the state, supported by educational institutions, the public, and long, usually uncompensated hours by numerous professionals in the scientific and educational communities.

But this is possible because collared coyotes are not exempt from being hunted, and in fact may even be more targeted than non-collared animals. Many people knew about the coyotes that we tracked in the cemeteries and it just takes one bad apple to illegally poison them (or to shoot them in other areas).

With the dispersal ability of coyotes, new ones always seem to recolonize sink habitats, which are areas that have low survival rates compared to the surrounding landscape. The coyotes we collared in north Boston have not lived long and it is probably not what would be considered quality coyote habitat because of the high densities of humans and the sprawl associated with the area. However, coyotes will likely always show up in these types of areas due to dispersal from other regions, as was the case in summer 2005, just a few months after the poisonings in the cemeteries. There, locals reported to us that at least two new coyotes showed up in the cemeteries, which confirms that whatever we do to these beautiful creatures their population levels will always bounce back.

To add to our frustrations, in May 2006 Dave captured a coyote inside the old box-trap that originally captured Maeve, Jem, and Cour, but it managed to escape by literally breaking apart the trap. Two months later, in early July, cemetery workers saw two adults and at least four pups together eerily close to where Maeve died. They swore that one of the adults was the beautiful yellow coyote that was observed with the three collared coyotes before the poisonings claimed their lives.

Chapter 20

Politics and Frustrations

Permit Issues

People may think, aside from some of the low points we experienced such as the poisoning account, that I am leading the golden life doing all of these cool and interesting projects on coyotes, some of which involve research in the area where I grew up. However, I have barely touched upon all the hard work that was necessary to get to this point. Before we ever got to begin the research discussed in this book, we were required to obtain nine separate protocols or permits, as well as numerous permission forms for conducting research in each of the separate cities or towns within our study sites.

My dealings with the state have been rocky and permits associated with the coyote study have taken forever to get at all levels. Although we now have a working relationship with state officials, there was noticeable unwillingness among some of their staff to allow "outsiders," or people not affiliated with their division, to start a study on coyotes. Luckily some leaders in the wildlife department, like Jim Cardoza, Dr. Rob Deblinger, and Tom O'Shea, recognized the importance of our conducting such a project.

As a 22-year-old biologist back in 1998, this reluctance was difficult for me to comprehend. "How is it," I thought, "that anyone with a hunting and a gun license can legally blow away as many of these creatures as they want one-third of the year in Massachusetts (and in many other states hunting is allowed year-round), but individuals or organizations who wish to study them without taking their lives have to jump through hoops to radio-collar them?"

There was initially an overt political resistance to this research taking place. The reasons were not clear at first, but it seems that the state fish and game department may have realized that we, not they, would then be the experts on urbanized coyotes. When we published on them, it became obvious that fact alone was a pretty powerful reason to keep the status quo.

In short, information on coyotes like that found in this book, could not have been obtained without a valid permit, and those who control the permits, control the flow of information. So to implement a research project on coyotes such as we were proposing, was perceived as a challenge to the authority of state wildlife personages, even though we were simply trying to obtain and disseminate accurate information on the local coyote population to the Massachusetts public. We were ultimately trying to help the coyotes as well, by giving people a valid picture of their actual ecology.

This type of suspicion, and even antagonism, of municipal authorities toward outside (non-government) researchers is well-documented in scientific circles. John Theberge, in his book *Wolf Country*, recounts his experience with his mentor, who informed him that, "They will throw endless barriers in your way," as he tried to study and protect the wolves in Algonquin Park, Ontario.

Government interests in wildlife management are usually diametrically opposed to those of the scientific communities, being far more concerned with the income from killing them, than the value to individuals of their beauty and contributions as integral segments of the environment. While this viewpoint is changing somewhat and even predators are being looked at in a more positive light by some of the more progressive state fish and game departments like Massachusetts', we too experienced this anti-research bias as we waited every year for permit renewals, or even simply to get the permits initially. So now I understand all too well the bitterness that characterizes many researchers' feelings toward state and federal governments.

Funding Problems

The operating budget for the coyote project was yet another issue. After waiting for months to obtain permission to simply study the animals, we also had to deal with funding issues. The study operated on a shoe-string budget since its inception. This minute amount of funding would be laughable to government-employed biologists doing similar work with state or federal funding. We have had to use piecemeal purchases, such as obtaining just one trap or collar here and there, in order to make ends meet.

It is ironic that coyotes are a hot wildlife issue in Massachusetts, yet no agency wants to step up to the plate to foot the bills to study them. The Massachusetts Division of Fisheries and Wildlife, a likely candidate for funding the study, barely received enough funding for their own staff in the year 2000. Despite the fact that proportionately few people hunt in Massachusetts, the wildlife division is still only funded primarily by hunters, not by tax-payers.

Considerably more money is generated from wildlife watching than consumptive uses, but state agencies do not receive that income because it is bureaucratically ear-marked for the general economy. This lopsided funding scheme is what enables hunters to brag that they are the ones supporting governmental wildlife agencies and the upkeep of most wildlife reservations. This is something that should be changed, for the good of the wildlife as well as for the good of our state's wildlife-appreciating citizens.

Politicians were even trying to take the hunting license proceeds and use them elsewhere, not within the Division of Fisheries and Wildlife. In that bureaucratic situation, funding coyote research would certainly be out of the question since most hunters don't want to pay to study them. This traditional system of hunting fees paying for most of wildlife management, if not changed, will likely prevent us from appropriately coexisting with wildlife, especially in areas where hunting is not an option. If tax dollars were used for wildlife management, we might have received funding that would have resulted in more robust science and a stronger education component that would have benefited a far greater number of people than the traditional mode of catering to the decreasing hunting industry.

A case in point about the disparity between the current ideology of most fish and game departments and my vision for successful wildlife management occurred in 2005 when legislation was again being pushed to legalize leg-hold traps. The usual pro-hunting arguments concerning coyotes were made, emphasizing the notion that they need to be controlled because they are overabundant. Even the average non-hunting suburban folks advocated that the "coyote problem" had to be addressed. As far as I know, no one requested a scientific perspective of the situation during the legislative hearing. (I did not attend the hearing because I had academic duties at Boston College.)

In September 2005, I wrote to Massachusetts' legislators explaining my frustration with their stance on potentially making the traps legal again when other methods such as research and education had been proven to work. I noted:

> "I believe that our precious public resources would be much better spent by providing our citizens with objective research and education about coyotes. The state of New York recently granted Cornell University over $400,000 of public support to study coyotes. The research program is designed to be similar to the studies that our Massachusetts team has completed and published."

> "We invest a great deal of our time and emotions in this research and are convinced that support for our project could go a long way toward improving the coyote's image. I have proposed the creation of an Eastern Coyote Discovery Center, including a museum and educational center devoted to coyote research and management. Although I am working closely with local municipalities and private entities, funding from the state would be an important and appropriate way to achieve this goal. From my perspective, the Commonwealth has focused too narrowly on limited strategies and is ceding the leadership role on coyote research and management to New York State."

Leg-hold traps notoriously serve a minority of the public who participate in the activity, but their use does nothing to actually regulate coyote numbers. As of this writing, the state has provided no help/support for our research team, public education, or the coyote. I am still waiting for a response to my letter. The hidden fact behind this controversy is that trapping does exactly the opposite of decreasing coyote numbers, since it actually stimulates the surviving coyotes to reproduce more prolifically.

Most of our day-to-day radio-tracking expeditions, the very activities that allow the pieces of the coyote puzzle to be put together, were usually funded out of our own pockets. If they were not coming from our own pocket they usually came from sources unrelated to wildlife. For instance, one of my advisors, Eric Strauss, generously donated some of his general travel funds at Boston College to me for the study. Pete Auger also more than compensated me for travel expenses whenever I helped him with research related projects.

Environmental groups have donated to the project at important times. However, my graduate program, originally intended to compensate for the lack of funding associated with wildlife studies, was anything but well-funded. While Eric Strauss and Charlie Lord have thoughtfully and repeatedly allotted some of their Environmental Studies and Urban Ecology Institute budgets, respectfully, for equipment (mostly radio-collars), I never received any funding for the coyote research from the Lynch School of Education, the school that I was enrolled in at Boston College. I had over $500 in publication costs associated with coyote articles and manuscripts in peer-reviewed journals, but was not able to pay them promptly because the Lynch School said that they do not pay for scientific publications (education journals generally do not have page costs) and the Biology Department disavowed that I was a graduate student there; a typical Catch 22 scenario!

So instead of enjoying the best of both worlds by being affiliated with two schools within a university during the five years of my coyote research, the project struggled to stay afloat because I was caught in the middle. Making my efforts more daunting was that I essentially wrote two dissertations, one for each school, while at Boston College.

The ecology-based research was in the form of peer-reviewed manuscripts while the education portion was my official doctoral dissertation for Boston College. The Biology Department did graciously employ me as a teaching assistant in their department, which helped to partially fund me during my graduate work and they were the ones (through Eric Strauss's Environmental Studies Program budget) that bought the majority of the traps and radio-collars for our study. Such is the life of a graduate student, which constituted much of the time that I spent on this research.

Coyotes Being Coyotes

While we waited to hear results from this legislative session, coyotes did what they do best, with a lot of help from the media; wreak havoc with people's pets. A small dog was killed in Jamaica Plain, an urban area on the south side of Boston. The dog owner was angered and said that something had to be done about the "coyote problem."

The little dog was left out alone in the dark, albeit near the house, in a wooded corridor of woods. The man said he saw the coyote drag the little pooch away through a spotlight that illuminated his backyard. The next week, the pet owner and I were pitted against each other on New England Cable Network News. The program host spent most of his time interviewing the dog owner about his emotional investment in his pet, but not on the real problem which involved responsible pet ownership.

I was allowed to speak briefly about the need to educate people about coyotes and the relative lack of risk they present, and to provide as many facts about them as I could with the limited time that I was allocated. I stressed that it was completely natural to have coyotes in these urban locations. In the end, I left the news network shaking my head and reflecting on the fact that our society does not understand how science and research can shed light on such situations to the benefit of average residents. The widowed dog owner happened to have a Ph.D. in an unrelated field, which surprised me given his illogical, unrelenting stance that the coyote problem must be addressed.

If the city of Boston had the foresight to hire an urban biologist, part of that person's job could be to inform residents about where coyotes were distributed and how they are able to live in a highly developed setting. These residents would then be able to make informed decisions about their pets because they would understand more about their wild neighbors.

Peaks and Valleys

In addition to the coyote research project funding and permit issues that plague many wildlife studies, there were also the emotional fluctuations that resulted from constant exposure to the research targets, the coyotes themselves. Life as a biologist who studies a persecuted species such as the coyote can be characterized by many emotional ups and down, both in attitude and state of mind.

There were many highs associated with our research, such as receiving permits, getting funding for more traps or collars, our first capture, amazing sightings, capturing two coyotes in separate box-traps a few miles apart on the same day, and obtaining the pups for the captive coyote study. During events such as these, my enthusiasm for the project was naturally quite high.

As far as my professional life was concerned, nothing will ever beat March to April 2002, during which time I captured six new coyotes. There was one two-day period when I captured two coyotes on the same day, had over ten coyotes to radio-track on Cape Cod, started a new study of coyotes in north Boston, and obtained the captive coyote pups. I was so busy and elated that I barely slept. But then again, who could sleep with a bunch of coyote puppies running around and barfing on their bed?

During this busy and pleasant stretch, I remember thinking that, despite being young in my scholarly and professional pursuits, it would be difficult to top these experiences. In the back of my mind, I also sensed that because I had experienced an apex early in my career as a coyote biologist, a string of bad events might be difficult to cope with. And that is exactly what happened starting in winter 2005. Ironically, it was just as I was finishing my doctoral research, a time that I thought would be one of the proudest and happiest of my life.

While the good moments in a career are noteworthy and make for great stories, the low points can be some of the most traumatic events to occur in one's life. Bad breaks in a research career are inevitable. Some of mine occurred when what I thought was a great manuscript was rejected by the editor of a journal, or when one of our collared coyotes was shot or hit by a car, or when a trap was sprung and nothing was inside and I feared a coyote escaped and would never come back. On the other hand, positive events such as funding actually coming through or a new coyote capture, quickly caused me to move forward with renewed passion for my research.

In January 2005, I lost my 85-year-old grandmother to cancer. Nana succumbed from a lifetime of smoking cigarettes that continued right until her death. She was the one with whom I frequently stayed when in the Boston area, sleeping on her old couch in her one bedroom apartment in a senior citizen's project in Lynn. Her place was my second home while I was conducting the north Boston research and was frequently going to the Stone Zoo.

That loss was followed by a coyote-laden set of catastrophes that started when three of our Cape Cod coyotes were shot by hunters in separate incidents within a couple of weeks. Each time I heard that one of them was dead, it was a new blow. That winter of 2005 was a record year for snowfall on the Cape too, with over ten feet deposited. It seemed as if every storm intensified when it hit this coastal area. This made tracking coyotes super-easy, especially for hunters. Using vehicles, they could simply drive to a fresh set of tracks and then attract the fleet-footed, long-distance traveling canids with predator calls. No doubt the coyotes were hungry, and thinking that they were near an easy meal of an injured, squealing rabbit, they paid for it with their lives. By the end of February 2005, I had to retrieve the collars from the dead bodies of Gash, Snour, and Carm.

But Things Change

During that same time in February 2005, there was the break-up of the captive coyote pack at the zoo, and my forced separation from them. Shortly afterward, the death of our entire collared pack of coyotes in north Boston was agonizing, as related in the previous chapter.

In early February 2005 I was part of three great studies, a mere couple of months later all of them were only smoldering like a recently extinguished fire. I knew that the studies were going nowhere. It was at this time that Eric Strauss, my science advisor and friend at Boston College, encouraged me to see a therapist to help me deal with internalizing all the trauma we had been exposed to. As one of the youngest of the team, I knew I was taking everything the hardest. And on top of the coyote-related issues, I was also trying to finish and defend my doctoral dissertation, which happened during summer 2005.

The next thing I knew I was in an endless search for a full-time job that might allow me to stay in the area and continue this research. Although I never followed up and saw a therapist, partially because I doubted that my mediocre graduate school insurance policy would cover it, over time I slowly managed to become less depressed.

I spent some time camping in favorite places, looking for wolves and grizzly bears in Yellowstone National Park, and for moose, deer, and beaver in the White Mountain National Forest. I watched many movies, like an ordinary person who has free time, and regularly played basketball with my buddies to get some exercise. I also did a good amount of writing to occupy my time, working on about ten professional manuscripts, along with my dissertation and this book. After all, having been so busy for so many years previously, I needed to stay occupied or I really would have gone crazy.

During this time, we also started a new coyote study in the Newton area, which in some sections is immediately adjacent to and on the Boston College campus. Our study began formally on 27 June 2005, with the capture and collaring of Chestnut (or Ches), a small 14-lb pup we tracked through the winter of 2005/2006. Despite these small gains on the positive side of my research, I still had not been able to fully recover from what had transpired just the few months prior. (As of fall 2006, Ches is still alive and living within his natal territory.)

One of the disadvantages that I faced at that time was that I was not collaborating with any other scientists on my research. This restriction, however, did not prevent me from bringing the details of our situation to the public. I began writing letters to the editors of the local and regional newspapers, especially the Cape Cod Times, in order to promote the image of coyotes. I started speaking out on their behalf, giving numerous public lectures on coyotes and informing as many as possible of our research.

At the same time I was dealing with the people who shot the collared coyotes that were part of our study on the Cape, living with the poisoning nightmare of our study subjects in north Boston, and, of course, dealing with the zoo personnel and the clash between our vastly different viewpoints. I felt like the proverbial dog chasing his tail. I was doing a lot, but not really getting anywhere. I had no real job and limited funding to pursue my scientific and academic interests.

During the hard times, I often asked myself why I continued with this work. Lots of grief and little money characterize the life of many field biologists even after they obtain multiple advanced degrees. On the other hand, the end product of making a difference and trying to make the world a better place for my study subjects is why I persevered. This book is an attempt to highlight the eastern coyote in all its positive aspects. After reading this book, I hope you agree and share a similar fascination and respect for these amazing creatures.

After the discouraging events I just related, I often discussed with friends and colleagues if I should attempt to continue the study or move elsewhere and try to start a new project in a different area. Eric Strauss was always quick to point out that the work I am doing on coyotes in an urbanized area like Massachusetts is unique; so distinctive in fact, that it is currently very hard to find a job in this relatively new field we call 'urban ecology'.

The traditional model of science had always been to go to the most pristine area and only then could you observe what was "really happening" in a system. This might be the case for a wilderness ecosystem, and might have been the case for coyotes when they only existed 'elsewhere', but this book provides a new ideology which stresses that the urban landscape is an ecosystem in its own right and coyotes, as predators, define that. Now that many species of wildlife, and coyotes in particular, have expanded their range throughout the country and carved out a niche for themselves in the middle of our suburbs and even live and breed within large cities like Los Angeles, New York City, and Boston, it's obvious that urban ecology has become an entirely new field of research that must be addressed. Eric is convinced that I would make a much greater contribution to this field if I stuck it out and stayed here, despite the tough times. While I agree with him, I am still not sure that, given the choice, if making that contribution is more important than living a sane, peaceful life. One always hopes for both.

Hopefully I might be successful in opening a discovery center on coyotes and obtaining captive coyotes again, but that certainly is a long way off as of this writing. How cool would it be, I have thought, to team up with colleagues in Yellowstone and carry out research in a place where people do not bother (or blatantly kill) one's study subjects? And then I hear Eric interrupting my thoughts by saying, "The eastern coyotes in Massachusetts need you a lot more than the many people already researching predators out in Yellowstone."

Chapter 21

Recommendations for Conservation

A New Look At Coyote Management

The focus is on Massachusetts, a state with an already reasonable and relatively protective statute on coyotes compared to other states. Recommendations, ranging from general to more specific management activities, are necessary in satisfying the conservation interests of coyotes while providing recreational activities for consumptive users of wildlife. These suggestions should be heeded by other states for proper management of the species where they are afforded less protection than in Massachusetts.

The rationale for a year-round hunting season supported by the claim that coyotes can compensate for a large annual die-off, is a poor excuse and not justified by available data and current societal motivation to provide humane management policies that avoid animal suffering. For careless hunters, it is just an excuse to kill for the sake of killing. For desk-bound wildlife bureaucrats, decisions like these are made out of ignorance, for the sake of convenience, and for filling the department's coffers with hunting permit fees. We can do better for a social animal remarkably similar to the domestic canid who sleeps at the foot of our beds.

I offer the following management suggestions based on known coyote facts that have been further confirmed by my ten years of active research on them in Massachusetts.

Make Poison Illegal

The discovery of the how the Cemetery Pack all bled to death was devastating to our research group. There is no reason that people should be able to go to a hardware or grocery store and buy such a dangerous, harmful product. These poisons, intended for rodents, can even kill people.

Poison is terrible for the ecosystem. Even if rats are killed by rodenticides, predators can still suffer. Seth Riley and his colleagues in southern California have found bobcats, coyotes, and mountain lions that have died from eating other animals killed from anticoagulant poisoning. The toxin in the deceased animal's tissues is transferred to the animal eating it through a process called biomagnification. The predator, who is high up in the food chain, eventually dies from an accumulation of toxic material in its own tissues. This is the very same way that ospreys, hawks, and eagles were affected by DDT back in the 1970s.

I offer that rodenticides should be illegal to use by private homeowners. Rather, a professional animal removal specialist should be required to dispense them. But the average homeowner needn't go that far. My best advice is to get a loving cat, keep it indoors, and watch it take care of your indoor rodent problem for free. You will save many non-rodent lives in the process.

Revise the Months of Hunting Season

Because we have documented coyotes giving birth in mid-March, the coyote hunting season in Massachusetts should end in early to mid-February at the latest, instead of the end of February as is current law. In this way, hunting would end before pregnant females are too far along in their short two-month gestation process.

Further, since concerns regarding humane treatment of animals are now a major issue when we set up management practices, this first piece of the management puzzle is important to reduce stress on pregnant females and encourage that the young are not aborted or stillborn. Thus, revising the Massachusetts coyote hunting season to extend from November to January would be appropriate.

I remember looking at the carcass of Gash, Kett's longtime mate, shot by hunters using a predator call at night in mid-February 2005. She was an eight-year-old animal in magnificent condition. After skinning her 36-lb body with the hunters, I determined that she was carrying eight little fetuses. I can imagine the sense of loss that Kett, probably mated to her for at least five years, felt after his mate's sudden disappearance. There is no doubt in my mind that a social animal like a canid mourns a missing member of their pack.

The mournful howls of the captive coyotes when I visited them after being away from them for a time seemed to convey their anxiety at being separated from me. To this day, fish and game departments overlook the intense social bonds that coyotes and many other animals have. After watching how the captive coyotes behaved in my presence, it's more than conjecture that coyotes form intense personal bonds and endure a great deal of grief after the loss of a pack member or a long-time mate. I don't believe there is any research possible that can determine how long it takes for them to recover. Extrapolating from humans, experts who do grief counseling testify that the loss of a loved one can be carried for a lifetime.

Cognitive animals like coyotes no doubt have similar abilities to remember during the course of their shorter lifetimes.

Biologically, wild animals may be adapted to recover from tragic or unexplainable events occurring, whether naturally or artificially induced, and usually these animals re-establish social bonds again, if purely for reasons of survival. However, the opposite sometimes occurs and there are many instances in the literature, especially of wolves, of entire packs or family units breaking up and dispersing following the death of a breeding canid in that clan.

We are no longer a civilization that depends on fur as we once did, and with comparable and lighter-weight synthetics available, at least half the incentive we once had for killing furbearing animals is gone. We are a changing civilization, and many individuals within it have the intellect to recognize the value of rapidly diminishing wild spaces around us and want to preserve them and their inhabitants intact. Aside from national parks, there should be many other places where animals can live out their existence without constant "management," that is, being killed by humans.

Institute a Bag Limit

There should be a bag limit of no more than two or three coyotes per year for an individual hunter in Massachusetts. Although a relatively arbitrary number, it does amount to a typical-sized social group of coyotes, certainly a significant number for a local group to absorb the deaths of and still survive. Destroying multiple breeding groups virtually assures in increase in the settling transients and higher birth rates for the following year. This limit would still ensure numerous recreational opportunities for the fraction of people who wish to "control" or hunt coyotes, yet would also provide wildlife watchers with plenty of observation opportunities as well.

There are areas, including the Cape, where individual hunters take many more than that in this very limited region. For example, one hunter routinely claims to bait in and bag over 20 coyotes a year for just their presence on private property. With the current management regulations in place, other people may not have the opportunity to enjoy coyotes in those areas of localized control, and the coyotes killed may not serve out their full ecological service to the broader ecosystems they belong to.

These hunted-out locales act like sinks where resident coyotes don't exist and there is a nearly constant influx of dispersing transient coyotes. Having a bait pile in ones' backyard and picking off everything (including Mizz) that comes by is an astonishingly unsportsmen-like and very unethical way to kill a large number of coyotes in an area. It's true that baiting for coyotes is legal in most states, but these areas of intense persecution will persistently have coyotes around anyway, due to the colonizing ability of the species, so what is the point? Are actions like these acceptable in our society today?

It's the opinion of many that state fish and game agencies should take the lead in encouraging non-lethal alternatives to wildlife management, rather than perpetuate the annual slayings. Far more effective coyote population control exists, ranging from leaving food and pets inside (and leashing dogs) to aversive conditioning, such as behaving aggressively to coyotes that are repeatedly sighted in urban areas, to applying lithium chloride to livestock carcasses in farming communities. Having photography contests might also appeal to the non-hunter and make the coyote as valuable on photo paper as the carcass is at a state game checking station.

Ban Baiting and Hounding

Baiting or using dogs to hunt coyotes should be banned. In 1996, Massachusetts voters made these practices illegal for bobcats and bears; and the same guidelines should apply for all predators.

Hounding is when hunters attempt to run coyotes to exhaustion using dogs, then shoot them when they circle back to the hunters. A case in point occurred in 1998 when a hunter actually tried this from one of my trap sites in a watershed in Cotuit on the Cape. He was near a main road and one of my friends working for the water department asked him what he was doing waiting by one of my traps. The man responded with something like, "I am hunting coyotes and currently my dogs are on a fresh trail."

Fortunately, they never got one, and I and the man from the water department (who also hunts) knew that the dogs had a greater chance of getting killed by a passing vehicle than the coyote did to get killed by the dogs. Nonetheless, it is an appalling practice still commonly used by many hunters. Massachusetts will be better by changing the legality of that practice.

Non-Lethal Alternatives First

The centuries-old law that allows anyone to kill a predator near their livestock should be changed to a statute that is more balanced and in keeping with current times. For instance, livestock owners should be required to maintain proper husbandry techniques. In collaboration with organizations like the Massachusetts Society for the Prevention of Cruelty to Animals' (MSPCA) Living with Wildlife program, non-lethal alternatives should be tried before lethal options are considered. An animal in the act of killing livestock could still be legally culled, or "managed," from the population. Efforts should focus on identifying individual "problem" predators and ways to resolve conflicts when or even before they occur.

This same strategy should also apply to coyote management situations. For example, there are some areas on the Cape and elsewhere where population levels of coyotes and other predators are managed to protect breeding birds or game species. Before control actions occur, research should be conducted that documents the effectiveness of a particular culling strategy. The strategy of 'kill first and ask questions later' is no longer acceptable in a civilized nation.

Federal agents in April 2004 reportedly killed 11 adult coyotes and three pups on four-and-a-half square mile Monomoy Island within a two week period to protect a nesting bird colony. Based on easily verifiable data, if there were actually that many adult coyotes resident on the island's small land mass they would be living at a record density for the species. More likely, there were numerous transients searching for available territories and possibly neighboring resident coyote groups from the mainland that immediately, maybe within days or hours, explored the wildlife refuge following the death of resident coyotes from there whose territorial presence previously kept them away.

A much more humane, ethical, and logical strategy would be to study the location first to determine if there were a resident group of coyotes. It is possible, but doubtful, that there was more than one, given the small land area. Having done that, it would then be possible to utilize non-lethal techniques to adversely condition specific individuals to the nesting bird colony, which comprises only a fraction of the island. Handling the situation in this manner would be more effective because the presence of the resident pack themselves would tend to keep transient coyotes at bay and leave only the negatively conditioned pack members on the island.

In many circumstances, not just on Monomoy, the excuse has been used that there is no solid data explaining the effectiveness of non-lethal techniques, leaving 'lethal actions' as the only option. This is a cop-out and should not be accepted by the public, since taxpayer monies are used for most of these operations.

The state of Maine, often noted for its high quality wildlife management programs, formerly snared coyotes in winter deer yards in northern and Downeast Maine. Instead of making common sense management decisions such as improving winter habitat so deer had more food and protection, the coyotes were targeted as an easy answer to the problem.

It is inexcusable that this form of slaughter is still called 'wildlife management' in this day and age. Roughly 500 coyotes per year were strangled to death, with a third of those called 'bobble-heads' because the coyotes' eyes literally popped out of their heads during a violent, yet slow, struggle after being strangled by the snare. What a horrible way to die.

Environmental groups sued and managed to stop the activity, but they did not win the battle because of humane concerns, despite repeated public protests against the program (even in rural Maine, the majority of people statewide do not hunt). The lawsuit succeeded on a technicality because the federal government required a permit that the state had not yet obtained. This permit would exonerate the state of any penalty if a trapper killed a federally protected species such as a wolf, lynx, or bald eagle. The fact that State of Maine Fish and Game department had conducted no research to document the effectiveness, or lack thereof, of this coyote control program, is mind-boggling. And the snaring issue is anything but a closed case, with potential reinstatement of the practice imminent in the future.

Citizens, and farmers in particular, should realize the ecological benefits that coyotes can provide. Volumes of research besides our own indicates that coyotes regularly consume large numbers of moles, rats, mice and voles. They are very effective at limiting rodent populations in croplands and could indirectly save farmers and non-sheep-raising ranchers hundreds or thousands of dollars presently spent on rodent traps, poisons, and specialized pest control. Good husbandry techniques utilizing proper containment for livestock protected by dogs and fences, could exploit the coyote's ecological benefit by integrating it when designing management plans.

Prioritize Integration of Transportation Safety

Wildlife needs should be incorporated into transportation projects since road-kill is an increasing problem both for wildlife and automobile drivers. Experimenting with and providing wildlife with safe street crossings (like simple under-road culverts) in strategic locations of known activity, or in areas where road-kill is an existing problem, should be a priority. Providing secure travel routes in high-use areas would likely give many other species of wildlife the opportunity to avoid being killed on a roadway. Municipalities could increase signage around concentrated wildlife activity, set speed limits in those areas, provide under or overpasses, and/or small speed bumps to slow cars down in certain places.

New road projects especially, should consider wildlife and their ecological needs in the initial design phases. Areas under consideration in a given locale could be chosen by biologists, based on known sightings of animals, or by locations of frequent road-kills. Town Highway Departments and their personnel should be educated about the value of incorporating the needs of wildlife into their transportation plans and protecting existing wildlife travel paths such as power lines and railroad tracks.

Municipal Education is Key

None of these strategies and laws will be effective unless education is at the core of the mission for eastern coyote management. Pamphlets and brochures, along with scientific documents, need to reach the public along with this book, to encourage support for these goals of protecting our urban wildlife. Organizations need to incorporate their knowledge and use scientists to communicate coyote ecology and behavior and explain its place in all environments, ranging from rural to urban. And ample funding needs to be set aside to accomplish these goals.

Let me share an example of poor public education in a local sector of the population. In May 2004, the town of Hull, Massachusetts declared "A State of Emergency" because coyotes were 'observed on a ball field' at school. Suddenly every major Boston news station was in Hull to announce this state of emergency, yet none of them provided any data or information on the behavior of the coyotes, nor mentioned the fact that no coyote had displayed bold behavior to anyone. They were simply observed 'in the area'. It was obvious that this situation was hyped due to its emotional value, and no one—certainly not the media—was making any effort to provide any real facts regarding the coyotes or their danger, or lack thereof, to humans.

Vying for audience and knowing that any 'animal news' brings the viewers, the news stations continued the coverage unrelentingly. Many of the stations showed pictures of smaller western coyotes. One of the stations repeatedly, but inaccurately, showed the captioned picture of an 8–10 lb gray fox, rather than a coyote.

It seemed apparent that the Boston television stations, having no truth to disseminate, just wanted to embellish a rather mundane issue and perhaps fill-in for a slow news day. And true to form, instead of approaching biologists familiar with canid ecology for information, they sensationalized the situation by interviewing frightened residents who discussed the 'growing coyote epidemic'.

A few days after the original broadcast it became clear that no children were about to be dragged off into the woods, and the issue slowly dissipated. However, as a result of all the hoop-la, someone must have been hired to placate residents upset by the news coverage, because a year or so later a trapper who supposedly killed some of the coyotes in Hull testified at a state hearing that there were now 'just as many coyotes there as before his control activities'. Not surprisingly, this important lesson was ignored by the news stations, probably for lack of melodrama.

One week after the declaration of the 'State of Emergency', our research team captured Maeve on 17 May 2004 in Everett and had two television crews join us for her collaring and release. It was an exciting event because Maeve was a beautiful 32-lb adult female coyote with a full brown coat and noticeable white shoulder stripes. We were interviewed about our research and videoed throughout the handling process.

We were told they took as much video, about one hour, as they ever had for such a short, two-to-three minute, piece. Ironically, it was the same day that gay marriage was legalized in Massachusetts. Needless to say, our story was not the major event of the broadcast, but our piece was still shown early in the newscast. And what segment, among others, did they include on the airing? Maeve biting at the trap just before her release.

Maeve was biting the trap because she was understandably panicked since I had let the photographers stay too close to her in order to get good video just prior to setting her free. A second or two after her biting episode, I kicked the trap to get her to stop. This, of course, was not shown. Even though I immediately released her from the trap after she bit it, I am still angry with myself for putting her in that situation.

Our goal of calling the newscasters when we captured Maeve was to increase public knowledge and appreciation for coyotes in urban landscapes. And it seemed to work. Even with the news station attaching the broadcast catch phrase "A group of researchers capture a coyote in Everett for a different reason than what you might expect; *to release* and study it," our positive spin and educated documentary on coyotes clearly countered some of the claims by unknowledgeable members of the public.

Coyote Maeve and reporters before her release in Everett

However, a week after Maeve's capture and release, a few news stations rebroadcasted the Hull situation because the town was removing all of the brush and woods around the school where the coyotes were simply seen. I was offered a chance, but declined, to go to Hull on that day, realizing that it was a stupid battle to fight and that I could use my time more wisely. After all, coyotes reside throughout the nation and could quite easily be in any other ball field in just about any town.

Establish Secure No-Hunting Areas

Anyone who understands and appreciates natural settings, accepts that there should be certain jurisdictions, such as towns or counties, that are off-limits to hunting. This benefits more than just the wildlife, but all wildlife lovers from animal rights groups, wildlife watchers, and scientists, to kind-hearted hunters who also like to experience these types of settings. Altogether, these constituents greatly outnumber consumptive users. The public should be given incentives to care for the wildlife around them rather than worry every time a coyote is observed in a backyard.

The power of caring for local, place-based components of natural environments such as wildlife has been demonstrated in the literature. Protected areas would allow scientists to study the effects of coyotes in non-disturbed urban areas where cars would be the only human factor endangering animals. This plan would also let people enjoy watching unmolested wildlife in these jurisdictions.

Ideal locations for places like this would be settings that have long-term studies, such as the study areas mentioned throughout this book. In this way, people can watch, enjoy, and study the same animal many times, whereas it can only be killed once. This idea is the same as the goal of the National Park Service where preservation is the number one objective. Hunting is only allowed in a few of the national parks, with the Cape Cod National Seashore being one of those locations.

These non-hunted areas could be termed National (or state or local) Wildlife Watching Areas and the focus of these places would be to allow animals freedom from harassment even in areas where development and building is allowed. This is in contrast to national parks, where preservation of the existing landscape is the first priority. Although, a 2005 Administrative Agenda unfortunately might result in the eventual selling off of some of our parks.

For the first location, I propose the 'Barnstable Wildlife Watching Area', which could include the entire town of Barnstable and sections of the adjacent jurisdictions of Mashpee, Sandwich, and Yarmouth. User fees, such as parking permits, could be required in these public areas and would help to pay for maintenance of this area, as well as scientific research and public education outreach.

Why Would It Work?

Reconnecting to nature has a powerful effect on people. The coyote study has changed my life and has connected me to the land, even in human-dominated areas. It has motivated me to want to share with everyone what I have gained from my exposure to the 'Urban Wild'. There ought to be places in Massachusetts where actual wildlife needs, not human ideas of wildlife needs ("management", etc.), are the primary and dominant forces in the landscape. This will show that humans have some morality and are willing to step back and allow natural processes to be the predominant factors shaping the environment.

People on the East Coast needn't be relegated to following the systems of our western national parks to witness true nature in action. If we are indeed the highest form of intelligent life, shouldn't we be the most adaptable? And therein, shouldn't we reap a blessing out of sharing our space with the wild animals that make our world a better and more sustainable place? Our greatest gift will be to leave an ecological legacy for future generations.

The Uniqueness of Coyotes

My final recommendation is a plea to everyone, to you the reader, to recognize the importance of this magnificent predator in the multitude of ecosystems where the coyote ranges, from southern Central America to the northern reaches of North America. I ask for the coyote to be protected from persecution, at least on federal, state, and other public lands, for a minimum of six months a year in all states and provinces. Included in this time frame would be the time from whelping in March/April through to the fall.

Private lands that are experiencing livestock losses from coyotes would be an exception to this proposed statute. But many people appreciate living with these beautiful carnivores and more needs to be done to recognize their importance. As with a multitude of other projects that suffer from human tampering that lead to poor results, I believe that once we stop "managing" coyotes, their populations will stabilize and no longer need bureaucrats to interfere with their natural ecology.

Land managers also need to take into account the viewpoints of the majority of citizens and that most of them do not hunt. People resent being constantly bombarded with negative media propaganda about their wild neighbors. Most just want to live and let live and appreciate their local wildlife. It is ironic that there are animal cruelty laws for domestic pets where someone can go to jail for abusing them, yet someone can legally kill (or wound and leave behind without penalty) a wild animal for no good reason.

Jurisdictions who have the moral integrity to stand up to special interest groups bent on effectively killing every available coyote (or other wild predator) deserve praise. Those locales should offer them some protection from their current pest status in most states. Massachusetts deserves credit for taking a lead on this important stance of coyote management, but more work needs to be done to better coexist with all our wild neighbors.

States like Massachusetts are at the forefront of urban wildlife management and, taking into account multiple stakeholders, the recommendations in this chapter would further that stance to a more balanced management system. It is absolutely appalling that the three northern New England states of Vermont, New Hampshire, and Maine, among most others in the U.S., allow a year-round coyote hunting season with few limits on cruel and torturous killing methods.

What is most shameful is allowing this unbridled carnage on our public lands. A division of the federal government, U.S. Wildlife Services, whose job is to control predators, is allotted millions of dollars of taxpayers' money (without taxpayers' consent) to kill over 80,000 coyotes annually, mostly in the western United States, yet pennies to study them or achieve more effective non-lethal ways to live with them. This department often spends more money than the dollar amount of losses they are supposedly guarding against, yet the program is being continued despite budget cuts in nearly every other environmental program.

The main reason for this is ignorance of the creatures and their ecology; no one is suggesting any knowledge-based programs to rectify the situation. It's because of the old adage, "We've always done it this way." We obviously need a paradigm shift in the way that our government wildlife agencies operate and that requires new blood, educated in current techniques and willing to work to represent the majority of today's citizens' viewpoints, which are decidedly less brutal than in previous generations.

Just as in the past, today's ranchers are grazing their livestock on our public lands and taxpayers compensate them for their losses by paying for coyote-killing programs. With environmental groups understandably decrying the aerial wolf kills in Alaska where about 250 wolves were gunned down from the air in 2004 by private citizens, the exact same thing has been happening to about 30,000 coyotes per year in the Lower 48 for decades, only this slaughters occurs using public taxpayers' monies.

Don't believe me? Then read *Cull of the Wild* and *Coyotes in Our Midst*. In those books, co-authors Camilla Fox and Chris Papouchis document, in depth, the atrocities which are allowed to occur on our public lands with the government either encouraging it or turning a blind eye. More taxpayers' money is used to kill coyotes than their actual damage to livestock—and this is during a supposed national budget deficit.

It's obvious that killing coyotes has spawned its own industry and supports its own set of employees constantly on the government's payroll. And there appears to be no end in sight. Yet most look the other way and let this happen. Times need to change, starting now.

Protecting coyotes in New England is especially timely considering the potential that wolves, a species not documented to currently exist in the northeastern United States, could reestablish themselves here. The fact that northern New England states claim they support the natural re-colonization of the wolf into some of its former territory yet do nothing to protect the eastern coyote, who looks and sometimes behaves remarkably similar, is bewildering.

It is shocking to go into gift shops in northern New England areas, such as the White Mountains in New Hampshire, and see souvenirs about wolves throughout the stores, ranging from silk-screened T-shirts and sweatshirts to wall hung tapestries and coffee mugs. Even foxes appear in some of the artwork. Why are there no gift items or artwork honoring eastern coyotes, the primary large canid currently inhabiting that region for the past 60–70 years? Do these people and the tourists buying the merchandise actually think wolves live here? Do they realize how those states regard the predators who actually live within their borders?

These products are probably a symbol of the wildness of the area, even if the "elusive and majestic" wolf isn't actually living within the not-so-wild landscape. The coyote could be regarded more positively if public perceptions are changed. Most people would be shocked to find out how little protection many predatory species have. The year-round coyote season may be more of an issue on paper because it is doubtful that many people actively hunt coyotes during the summer, but it does show a particular state's priorities.

Political agendas aside, there should be little reason why Massachusetts and other states cannot accommodate the suggestions in this chapter. These are fair and balanced recommendations that will keep the hunting tradition alive but will also take into account the coyotes' biological needs as a species, and the needs of the greater majority, the non-consumptive wildlife users. Let Massachusetts take the lead. Maybe one day other states will follow the path to a more balanced and equitable management position for these magnificent canids.

Long-Term Goals

It is my hope to track this fascinating predator well into the future. I have had two dreams of mine fulfilled so far:

1) simply starting this wild study; and
2) studying the captive coyotes

These two ambitions are the focus of the book that you are reading. My long-term vision is that I might be fully involved in both the research of urbanized mammals and the implementation of education programs that facilitate sustainable and healthy urban ecosystems.

My dream and ultimate goal is to create an Eastern Coyote Discovery and Research Center where people can learn about, study, and protect our great natural heritage, including coyotes. The idea of the center is to educate people about coyote behavioral ecology in a natural museum and park-like setting and also to make sure that the institute supports the long-term research on and continued monitoring of coyotes in Massachusetts and beyond.

This learning center would be an ideal location for promoting the survival of all species because it would involve education, research, mentoring, creating a long-term vision for science education, and most importantly, creating a database of coyote management information so that decisions for any locale nationwide could be made on accurate and objectively-obtained scientific data.

I receive dozens of e-mails and calls a month from people wanting to know more about coyotes. I have to tell people that I just do not have the resources to allow them to get involved in these studies. But this is where the Discovery Center would be one way to allow interested citizens to be able to gain hands-on experience about the true nature of coyotes.

In order to promote the long-term conservation and management of natural resources, strong emphasis has to be placed on education and research so the information that people obtain is accurate. There need to be sound management plans to gain public support for species that are sometimes controversial. Public funding of research and education projects would allow scientists and educators to provide these services.

Chapter 22

The Future

We're On Our Way

Fall 2080. It is a cool, clear, crisp day, the kind that signals that winter is just around the corner. I am 105 years old and thanks to anti-aging vitamins newly developed within the past few years, I am still able to walk a few miles a day. It is just past dawn and I am out on a stroll around the perimeters of the Eastern Coyote Discovery Center in Marstons Mills, Massachusetts. This facility is now in its 73rd year of operation. The Cape is a much different environment now, with New Orleans style levees surrounding the peninsula which have protected advancing water levels, thanks to global warming.

White-tailed deer are abundant around here since the establishment of the Barnstable Wildlife Watching Area in 2008. And there is too much development for hunters to have any influence on their population numbers. Because of the abundance of prey, coyotes are unusually numerous and live in pack sizes of five to eight animals. There has not been a hunting season on coyotes for 73 years, partially so they can control the deer herds and also to support the research we are conducting on them. In this natural setting, their numbers are naturally controlled simply by habitat factors. Gone are the days of people targeting and shooting collared coyotes.

The coyote packs hunt mainly for deer in the wintertime, but also take a sizable number of rodents and rabbits when the snow is not too deep. The large cranberry industry on the Cape openly caters to them because of their undeniable value in rodent control. People have learned over the years to keep their pets inside, leashed, and behind secure fencing so the amount of human-coyote interactions is minimal, a tribute to the public's understanding of and appreciation for coyotes in our community.

The Discovery Center deserves a lot of credit for this change in public attitude. In addition, it is estimated that coyotes have saved human lives each year as there are fewer deer crossing roads in front of automobiles due to coyote predation (each year in the U.S. many people die from automobile collisions with deer). Engineers visit our study area to design wildlife-protective transportation plans, which we subsequently monitor by collecting data on their effectiveness. It is expected that this work will further protect lives, both human and animal.

The coyote, being a deer's number one enemy, also keeps them wary. This makes them alert to avoid oncoming cars when they move to various parts of their respective home ranges. Nevertheless, deer still live at a very high population density. The advent of Tickgone® in 2010, a formula that kills deer ticks, has greatly reduced Lyme Disease among humans. This lesser risk of disease for humans has made deer more culturally accepted in urbanized areas.

Carrying binoculars in one hand and a small videocam in the other, I scan the woods for life. I have a trained coyote at the center, a large 48-lb female who is a descendant of Casper, 35 generations ago. However, I normally do not take her on walks as this upsets the local coyote pack that lives around the center. This pack, the Marstons Mills group, uses a territory of ten square miles, very similar to what Mole used way back in 2001–2002.

The 46-lb alpha male, Mill, is a descendant of Mole in the Mills, and the 39-lb female, Till (a coyote captured twenty times in the Mills), is related to Sill. Both are collared, as most coyotes in the study area willingly enter our box-traps with nothing to fear, only a belly-full to gain, from getting captured. This meal can be several days worth of food in one quick sitting.

In fact, some coyotes repeatedly enter the traps and become a nuisance, similar to what raccoons used to be before the coyotes started driving away or killing the ones who hung out around the trap sites. However, the coyotes are smart and usually enter the traps just before dawn realizing that one with a new, less than two-year-old, collar will be immediately released as long as it appears healthy.

The mated pair lead a pack of twelve, including a nearly three-year-old offspring, and a couple of two-year-olds. They have seven pups, four of which are Till's, and three are from Till's adult daughter, who mated with an off-territory transient but came back and whelped her pups in a den near her mother. In July the two females combined their litters at the now world famous Coyote Rendezvous Site in Marstons Mills. Tourists from around the world come to view this pack there from a specially designed observatory with sound-proof walls and one-way glass.

In July, already as many as 100 cars line the road to watch the coyotes at this site. Sometimes the traffic makes it difficult for the adults to go hunting. However, speed bumps strategically placed near designated coyote-crossings, as well as our Discovery Center rangers, ensure a very low human-caused mortality and No Parking zones near these locations give the coyotes a safe place to cross.

Gray wolves are uncommon on Cape Cod, first appearing in the late 2070s. They are now the number one source of eastern coyote mortality. These larger canids are descendants of the successful reintroduction to northern New England back in 2008. Wolves now live in all of the more rural parts of New England. Cape Cod is not great gray wolf habitat as there is too much human development and this restricts their well-known long-distance movements. Thus, those on the Cape live in small groups.

In fact, coyotes have been known to kill a much higher percentage of wolves than vice versa in this area, counter to what generally occurs in more pristine ecosystems. However, a lone eastern coyote, which now averages 40–45 lbs, slightly larger than back in 2005, is still no match for a 100-lb wolf. Coyote packs are close-knit and travel together from early fall when the pups can follow the adults, until the next spring when the breeders give birth. They live together mainly to protect themselves from wolves, as well as bears, which naturally recolonized the Cape in the 2050s. Coyotes also form packs to hunt and feed cooperatively.

Our research, similar to other regions, has shown that usually only one or two of the animals does the majority of the killing, but if the pack members were not there they would lose much of their leftovers to scavengers. The Marstons Mills Pack's territory surrounds the Coyote Discovery Center, which at two acres pales in comparison to an average coyote social group's home range. We have collared nine of the twelve coyotes in the group and are still trying to catch and collar the remaining three pups which are now nearly adult size.

Our project made headlines last year when one of the male yearlings from this group dispersed off Cape and paired with a collared female from our north Boston study area, some 70 miles away. This pair and their pack of six resides around the Stone Zoo, the site of the first litter of captive eastern coyotes from our project which was moved to the Eastern Coyote Discovery Center in 2007 to become ambassadors of their kind here.

Before heading outside the compound, I check the signals from the collars of all nine coyotes and they seem to be together roughly a half mile to the east on a public golf course that opened in the early 1990s. Golf course personnel inform me that there was an injured deer, a six-month-old fawn who was apparently hit by a car the previous night. It has a broken rear right leg but is still able to move around, despite obvious pain with each step.

I decide to hike in that direction, but without a radio-telemetry unit in hand. I have a hunch where they are going to be located and I do not need to be carrying the extra weight that would not have even phased me 20 years ago. After five minutes I cross a main road that separates the Discovery Center and the golf course. The 12 mph northeast wind is perfect at masking my scent as I walk east-northeast. I am heading to a hollow in the middle of the golf course that houses an apple orchard, an abundant food supply for the deer. The golf course stocks these trees so the deer feed on them in the woods, or more aptly, off the fairways. I have a feeling that the injured deer hobbled across a green and sought refuge in this patch of woods.

Four minutes later I arrive at a blind on the top of the hill overlooking the hollow. The golf course allows us to keep this small wooden shed (with a front window) here for observations. We bring many of our ecotourists to this spot since it is one of the best places to witness potential predator-prey interactions. Sometimes, usually when the Marstons Mills pack is elsewhere within their range, this involves the group of three resident gray wolves who also visit this site.

I quietly enter the blind without being detected. When I regain my bearings, I wipe the dust off my glasses and notice the entire pack of twelve in the hollow. There are a couple of small herds of deer hanging out on the fairways and I immediately suspect they are avoiding the coyotes. After scanning the fairways to determine that there are a total of 21 deer within view, I focus on the coyotes, dictating my verbal notes into the videocam.

I watch from 50 feet away as the pack is at the southern edge of the woods. The breeders are resting while the pups and yearlings focus on something to the northeast. Last night the pack filled their bellies on voles down in the cranberry bogs two miles to the south so I know they are not terribly hungry. Three minutes later I see what their noses long ago detected, the 22nd deer now in sight. This is the injured fawn who has apparently become separated from its mother. Five of the pups and one of the yearling coyotes hide behind a thick stand of cedar trees and wait for it to approach within 50 feet before making a move toward it.

The deer is completely distracted by its pain and walks directly to the cluster of apple trees in the center of the hollow. It tries to feed. The coyotes wait for the deer to face away from them then rush it. The parents stay back, observing the pups' first large mammal hunt. Two of the pups, both runts, are too frightened to join the other six. Two additional coyotes, the other yearling and the three-year-old watch the action, for they are already accomplished hunters and do not need to prove themselves.

The yearling catches the deer within 56 feet. It grabs the fawn by the throat while the five pups jump at the deer's hamstrings just below its rear end and drag it to the ground. One of the pups joins the yearling and grabs hold of the fawn's throat and closes off its airway. Within less than a minute the deer is dead, even while the four remaining pups rush in to tear open the hunches. Soon the two runts join their brothers and sisters as if helping to finish off the deer.

At that point Mill and Till come over and aggressively claim the deer from their offspring. With winter rapidly approaching they need to make sure that they have first dibs on all carcasses. After all, they are the most important members of the pack, and need to remain healthy and robust. The remaining deer resume grazing, knowing that their health and the coyotes' satiation will render them safe for the time being.

Because they ate many rodents last night, the alpha pair only feed for ten minutes, managing to consume five pounds each. When they relinquish the carcass, the rest of the pack devours the remains. Within 20 minutes the large group leaves the area with little but bones and fur remaining. The pups gorge themselves, needing that solid meal to ensure that they maximize their growth going into the winter. With a pack of twelve coyotes, a 60-lb deer doesn't go a long way.

As the coyotes trot away, I anticipate they are going to the west, to a ridge overlooking the Discovery Center. This is their favorite resting site, and one that allows them to view their captive cousins at the center and the crowds of people who view them. Being a quarter mile away, the public doesn't harass the wild coyotes. In fact, we have built an elevated platform for a viewing area above one of the captive coyote exhibits that has multiple permanent spotting scope stations for use when the wild pack beds down there.

Five minutes later, still in the blind, I watch as Mill and Till lead the pack across the main road dividing the center and the golf course. Five cars stop and take pictures as this impressive pack, with bellies engorged, meanders by in single file. As the pack crosses the road, I see one of the small herds of deer consisting of five bucks and two does, become alarmed. Within a minute I notice why. Three wolves are coming to scavenge on the kill. They appear to emerge from a patch of woods to the south of the hollow where the kill took place, likely to avoid the coyote pack.

The wolves go right to the remains of the small deer carcass and finish the edible scraps in no time, their strong jaws are able to break the skull and femur bones, something even the most voracious coyotes are not capable of doing. As I videotape the wolves I whisper into the camera, "I wonder if wolves will ever become numerous enough to affect the Marstons Mills pack? Nah, I doubt it," I conclude, confident of the closeness of this coyote pack, their relative large size, and the wolves' constant difficulties increasing their numbers due to road-kill mortality.

Wolves in this area have a difficult time surviving since one wolf requires three times more space than a coyote, forcing them to cross many more roads in their hunting forays. Besides the difficulty of surviving road crossings in this urbanized environment, the number one mortality factor for this social group of wolves is the Marstons Mills coyote pack's spring search and destroy mission where the smaller canids strategically set out each spring to kill as many wolf pups as they can in an effort to prevent them from becoming too numerous. If wolf numbers approach a pack size typical of coyotes on the Cape, and comparable to wolves in most of their range (five to eight), then the coyotes may lose their dominance to them, at least in local areas.

Fifteen minutes after their initial appearance at the carcass, the wolves lope off at a rapid pace to the northeast and soon exit the boundaries of the Marstons Mills pack's territory. I depart and head back to the center. The first thing that I say to my wife when I return is, "Wow, what a morning!" After all, I am still especially privileged to be able to witness nature at its wildest, including observing the predator and prey dynamics, right in my suburban backyard.

Epilogue

Well, here we are—not at the end of my story, but at the end of this book. Look for further publications of the episodes of the eastern coyote in New England, as I continue to track and take notes on them so I can inform you all what our wild canid neighbors are up to in new books as time goes on.

As for me, after four months of being a permanent substitute teacher at my high school alma mater in Barnstable, I have secured a full-time job there teaching Ecology and Environmental Science. This job has enabled me to revitalize the wild coyote component of my ongoing research on Cape Cod, as well as some new captures during the past six months. I have even had the fortune (and fun) of involving Barnstable High students in the research process, including the capturing, collaring, and radio-tracking of the coyotes, as well as watching them at their rendezvous sites. On 2 September 2006, and during the first week of school, we collared 19.4-lb Sup, one of Sill's pups, in Marstons Mills. We have since observed him quite often at the Marstons Mills Rendezvous Site.

Several of my students have also experienced a few of the "low-lights" of conducting wildlife research firsthand, like "doing a swan dive into an amphibious environment," which became our code phrase for accidentally driving my truck into a local swamp while tracking the 31.5-lb female coyote Snale. That event then required a team effort to get my vehicle unstuck and out of the marsh. Talk about instructor-student bonding!

In the summer of 2006, I wrote a letter to the town of Barnstable to request that they put an end to coyote hunting within Barnstable, and to make Sandy Neck Beach an official nature preserve. Not surprisingly, though, I was told by the Sandy Neck Governing Board that it is "our unanimous opinion that hunting should continue on Sandy Neck." How many more animals have to die before people in bureaucracy realize that living animals are worth more than dead ones, and are far more valuable for education and scientific research? I sure hope to not have to report more coyotes being pointlessly shot, but I am not so confident that that won't occur. To Snale, I apologize, in advance, what my species might do to your family in the next few months.

Hopefully, future student and parent anger will be channeled to force the town to listen to these reasonable requests. Meanwhile, I will be there to retrieve those collars, and reluctantly hear the hunters' embellished stories on how they heroically 'bagged these pests'.

Regarding the captive coyotes at the zoo, I still have not been authorized to visit them since I was separated from them. To Late and Trans and Cane, Caon, and Lupe: I still miss you dearly and hope to be reunited with you at some point in the near future. There is still so much you have to teach me about your species, although I am not very optimistic about the outcome of this wish, as people higher up seem to be intent on doing nothing to help with our research.

Jon Way, October 2006

Field Adventures with
Way's Eastern Coyote Research

After reading this book, do you want to experience actual field research on eastern coyotes? Well now you can. You can live like a coyote researcher by tracking coyotes and journaling their activities with me, Jon Way, in the suburban wilds of eastern Massachusetts. This is more than just a guided tour of some of the wildest and most beautiful land that Cape Cod has to offer, but provides actual hands-on apprenticeship hours doing authentic research in an ongoing study of over ten years on eastern coyotes in Massachusetts. If you are an Ecology or Biology major, we will work with your college advisor to make school credit available to you through this program.

Depending on the time of year and our current research activities, you may handle and help to collar wild coyotes, view coyote families in the wild at their rendezvous sites during the dog days of summer, track coyote packs in the winter, monitor coyote females and pups at their spring dens, and follow coyotes as they patrol their territories during fall. Night tracking can require physical stamina and include the use of night scopes to monitor animals while it is dark. Sightings can include deer, and all nocturnal animals as well as coyotes.

Best of all, the reasonable fees are what help support our research on coyotes. By simply signing up for these trips, it signifies the interest of average citizens in our beautiful wild lands and animals here in the Bay State. If we can locate a suitable area, we may even be able to renew our study of captive coyotes and you may possibly be able to help in caring for them.

Eventually we will have the tracking schedules listed on our web site, but for now, if you are interested in joining one of our tracking teams, or helping support our eastern coyote research effort, please email easterncoyoteresearch@ yahoo.com for rates and availability dates of legitimate field research opportunities. Tracking dates fill up fast, so do it now. Dates are negotiable, ranging from day trips and single-night tracking forays, to multiple-day and overnight adventures. Get your camping gear and join us for the time of your life![1]

Way's Eastern Coyote Research
Barnstable, MA
Eastern Coyote Homepage: http://www2.bc.edu/~wayjo

[1] All participants will be required to provide a parental permission slip if under age 18. Adults must sign a Waiver of Liability form.

References

The interested reader may obtain PDF copies of all in-print papers by visiting my website (http://www2.bc.edu/~wayjo or http://easterncoyoteresearch. com/). As additional papers related to our work are usually under review, this list will be continually updated on the website.

Way, J. G. In press. A comparison of body mass of coyotes (*Canis latrans*) between eastern and western North America. Northeastern Naturalist.

Way, J. G. In press. Survival of 8-week-old wild eastern coyote pups following the death of their mother. Northeast Wildlife.

Way, J. G., and R. L. Proietto. 2005. Record size female coyote (*Canis latrans*). Canadian Field-Naturalist 119:139–140.

Way, J. G. 2005. Assessing student learning and interest in eastern coyotes. Dissertation, Boston College. 285 pages.

Way, J. G., I. M. Ortega, and E. G. Strauss. 2004. Movement and activity patterns of eastern coyotes in a coastal, suburban environment. Northeastern Naturalist 11(3): 237–254.

Way, J. G., I. M. Ortega, and P. J. Auger. 2002. Eastern coyote home range, territoriality and sociality on urbanized Cape Cod. Northeast Wildlife 57: 1–18.

Way, J. G. 2002. Radio-collared coyote crosses Cape Cod Canal. Northeast Wildlife 57: 63–65

Way, J. G., and J. Horton. 2004. Coyote kills harp seal. Canid News 7.1 [online]. URL: http://www.canids.org/canidnews/7/Coyote_kills_harp_seal.pdf

Way, J. G., and E. G. Strauss. 2004. Old-aged coyote in an urbanised landscape. Canid News 7.2 [online]. URL: http://www.canids.org/canidnews/7/Old_aged_coyote.pdf

Way, J. G, P. J. Auger, I. M. Ortega, and E. G. Strauss. 2001. Eastern coyote denning behavior in an anthropogenic environment. Northeast Wildlife 56: 18–30.

Way, J. G. 2003. Description and possible reasons for an abnormally large group size of adult eastern coyotes observed during summer. Northeastern Naturalist 10(3): 335–342.

Way, J. G., I. M. Ortega, P. J. Auger, and E. G. Strauss. 2002. Box-trapping eastern coyotes in southeastern Massachusetts. Wildlife Society Bulletin 50(3): 695–702.

Way, J. G. 2000. Ecology of Cape Cod coyotes. Master's Thesis. University of Connecticut, Storrs. 107 pages.

Way, J. G. 1996. Baseline data on the interactions of a population of white-tailed deer, eastern coyote and red fox inhabiting a barrier beach ecosystem on Cape Cod, Massachusetts. Honors Thesis, University of Massachusetts, Amherst. 35 pages.

Way, J. G. Hand-rearing a litter of eastern coyotes. Under Review.

Way, J. G., D-L M. Szumylo , E. G. Strauss. An ethogram developed on captive eastern coyotes. Under review.

Way, J. G. Socialization of wild and captive eastern coyotes to a researcher. Under review.

Way, J. G., et al. Activity patterns of a captive group of eastern coyotes. In preparation

Way, J. G., et al. Social behavior of a captive group of eastern coyotes. In preparation.

Way, J. G. and D. Szumylo. Standing over behavior in eastern coyotes. In preparation.

The following list represents additional selected publications.

Way, J. 2005. Life at a Cape Cod coyote rendezvous site. Proceedings of the 10th annual Cape Cod Natural History Conference (abstract).

Way, J. 2004. The Ecology of Eastern Coyotes on Urbanized Cape Cod. Proceedings of Defenders of Wildlife's Carnivore Conference (abstract).

Way, J. 2004. Preliminary results of a captive eastern coyote study. Proceedings of Defenders of Wildlife's Carnivore Conference (abstract of poster).

Way, J. 2003. Eastern coyote ecology on urbanized Cape Cod, Massachusetts. Proceedings of the 59th Northeast Fish and Wildlife Conference (abstract).

Way, J. 2002. Eastern coyote behavior on Cape Cod. Proceedings of the 7th annual Cape Cod Natural History Conference (abstract).

Way, J. G. 2001. The eastern coyote: documenting the habits of one of Cape Cod's newest residents. Conservation Perspectives, the online journal of the New England Chapter of the Society for Conservation Biology. http://www.nescb.org/epublications/spring2001/coyotes.html.

Way, J. 2001. Eastern coyote ecology on Cape Cod. Proceedings of the 6th annual Cape Cod Natural History Conference (abstract).

Way, J. G, and I. M. Ortega. 2000. Ecology of eastern coyotes on suburban Cape Cod, Massachusetts. Proceedings of the 80th annual meeting of the American Society of Mammalogists, University of New Hampshire, Durham (abstract #29).

Way, J. 1998. Coyote research on Cape Cod. Massachusetts Wildlife 4:25–27.

Way, J. 1998. A scientific investigation of Cape coyotes. Barnstable Patriot. 24 September.

Appendix 1

Coyotes We Have Known

The following tables contain a summary of our marked study subjects on Cape Cod and Boston, and the five captive coyotes.[2] Bold font text indicates the origin of a coyote's name.

Coyotes captured more than once are counted on the numbering system for each capture but retain their original identification number for reporting and naming purposes. The following account does not include any of the non-radio-marked coyotes, such as road-kills, whom we also collected data on to obtain body condition, weight, and genetic sampling.

Table 1 Cape Cod Coyotes
(in order of first capture)

Name	ID #	Description
Pon	**9801**	Named for **p**up at c**on**servation area. A 14.7-lb pup captured in Marstons Mills on 8 June 1998 and radio-implanted. Killed by a car on 6 October 1998 on his natal territory and weighed a healthy 35 lb at 6 months old.
Pwo/Poo	**9803**	Named for **p**up number **two** and he smelled bad, like **poo**. A 15.2-lb pup captured 17 June 1998. Also killed by a car, on 13 September 1998. He was a skinny 27 lbs.

[2] Note: We call our study subjects by their names but in most of our scientific papers we use their associated numbers. For wild coyotes, males are given odd numbers and females are given even numbers in the order of their capture, with the 2-digit year as the prefix.

Table 1 Cape Cod Coyotes (continued)
(in order of first capture)

Name	ID #	Description
Snix	9802 (0002)	Named for Sandy Neck patch six (a large conservation area); captured 19 June 1998. A 32-lb female who was never documented to reproduce yet constantly had 1 companion. Located 504 times in the West Barnstable area. Died on 28 January 2000 of kidney failure, probably related to Lyme disease shortly after her second capture (19 January 2000). First coyote I tracked that had a large range (the first 2 were pups). Initially, thought she would use Sandy Neck (a 6 mi. barrier beach) at most, but she nightly traveled 10–12 miles on and off the barrier beach, and sometimes up to 4 mi. off the beach.
Casper	9804 (9904) (9910) (0402)	Large whitish female named for being captured in a cemetery (i.e., a ghost). Many of her offspring had white faces. Captured 4 times as an adult (30 November 1998, 6 March 1999, 26 July 1999, 11 March 2004), weighed 51, 43, and 55.3-lbs respectively. (She was not handled on 6 March 1999). Heaviest female coyote ever documented any where, and the dominant female of the Cummaquid pack. Had at least 6 consecutive litters (assuming she gave birth in 2003 when the batteries on her 26 July 1999 collar were dead). Two of her pups (Cup and Cix) were captured and implanted and her mate Sly tracked. She was located over 1,800 times, providing a tremendous amount of data over 8 years, including when she lost her territory during winter 2004/2005 (probably aggressively evicted, possibly by a daughter). She survived for a year in ~2 square miles on the northeast edge of her original range. In mid-February 2006, at age 10–11, I documented her traveling with Sly in that range. Shortly thereafter she started traveling in all of east Yarmouth, probably to avoid the third coyote (possibly Sly's new mate) sighted with them. She lived precariously on both sides of Route 6, likely staying clear of resident social groups until she vanished from the study area in early July 2006. See Appendix 10 for a fitting tribute to her amazing life.

Table 1 Cape Cod Coyotes (continued)
(in order of first capture)

Name	ID #	Description
Kett	9805 (9905)	Named for the Cotuit **Kett**leers, a summer league baseball team. Dominant adult male captured 16 December 1998 (42.5-lbs) and 5 November 1999 (44-lbs). Had a large 15 sq. mi. range of most of Mashpee. Captured within town of Barnstable both times. His collar died April 2002. May still be alive. He was paired with Gash and we tracked his son Sill (Kett's former helper) for many years as well as his daughter Kash.
Mizz	9902 (9906) (0102)	Named for **M**elody Tent and the 2 ft bli**zz**ard that fell on the day she was captured. A small white female with bizarre brown blotches captured 25 February 1999, 22 April 1999, and 19 May 2001 and weighed 30-lbs, not handled, and 28.5-lbs, respectively. Dominant female in Hyannisport until late-summer 2001, probably displaced by a daughter. Captured her son Hap in 1999. Mizz paired with Glope and had pups in spring 2001. Observed in Centerville with Jog in January 2002 after her collar died (possibly had his pups that summer). Shot and killed in south Yarmouth on a private island in Yarmouth Nov. 2002 along with two associates.
Sly	9901	Named for **S**hootflying Hill Road. Captured 15 May 1999 (39-lbs) as a probable yearling male. Didn't associate with many others but probably used his natal range and was a sloacher until pairing with Casper (an adjacent territory) in December 1999. We confirmed they produced pups for at least 2 years until his collar failed February 2001. Not directly observed (once his collar died we had to confirm he was alive by seeing him) after October 2001, until sighted with Casper in northeast Yarmouth in late-February 2006. He looked very robust at 8–9 yrs old.

Table 1 Cape Cod Coyotes (continued)
(in order of first capture)

Name	ID #	Description
Cup	9908	Named for **C**asper's (and C**u**mmaquid) **p**up. Captured 11 July 1999 and weighed in at 16-lbs; radio-implanted; one of at least 4 siblings. She dispersed the area during January 2000 and is unidentifiable with only an implant. No ear tag. Her whereabouts is presently unknown.
Hap	9903	Named for '**hap**py-to-be-alive' and **Hy**annisport pup. Captured 1 October 1999 (~18-lbs) but mangy. Rehabilitated and released 23 November 1999 (28-lbs). Son of Mizz. Had a tiny range before dispersing westward March 2000; vanished from our radar and has not been observed since.
Glope	0001	Named for Katie-Jo **Glo**ver (student researcher) and a lo**p**ing coyote. Transient captured 14 January 2000 (45-lbs) in Marstons Mills. Settled in Hyannisport and produced 2 litters of pups (1 with Mizz) spring 2001 before being killed by a car during a thunder/lightning storm <200 meters from Barnstable High School, 20 August 2001 (49-lbs).
Sill	0003 (0403)	Silver coyote (Kett's son) in Marstons Mills (Katie-Jo's trap) captured 18 January 2000 (37-lb juvenile). Helped raise pups as a yearling. Dispersed January of his 2nd year. Established a relatively small ~6–7 mi² territory around Newtown Road adjacent to his natal group and produced pups from 2002–2006 (8–9 in 2005). Used part of Mole's range after she died; mostly the cranberry bog rendezvous site. Re-collared 20 May 2004, weighing only 29.3-lbs w/ an injured right hind leg (which healed in fall 2004) and was raising 7 pups with 2–3 others during that year. Still alive in 2006 with 5 adults and up to 7 pups observed in the pack. I have collected well over 2,000 locations on this important coyote.

Table 1 Cape Cod Coyotes (continued)
(in order of first capture)

Name	ID #	Description
Skunks	0104 (0108)	Captured twice in same trap on **Skunk**net Rd within 1.5 weeks; 20 May 2001 (33-lbs) and 30 May 2001 (not handled). Smelled **skunk**y. Yellowish with a white Casper-like face, some mange on rear end. Had 4 pups in a wooded site. Killed by a car 8 June 2001 crossing mid-Cape highway. Her pups were raised by at least 2 other adults (one probably was Jog) and survived until at least September 2001.
Cix	0101	Biggest pup of Casper's litter of six (5.9-lbs) all captured by hand 21 May 2001. Only one radio-implanted. He easily handled the implant and survived at least until April 2002 when he remained on territory and traveled with Casper (Sly was seen near him a few times in 2001 despite Sly's collar having malfunctioned). No ear tag, so there was no way to identify him if he recovered somewhere like after being struck by a car. Only coyote to be captured by hand and radio-tagged. His whereabouts is presently unknown.
Gash	0106	Kett's mate, a magnificent 36-lb **Mash**pee lactating female captured at K-J **G**lover's house on 22 May 2001 (32.8-lb). Located on territory until fall 2003 when her collar's battery was dying. Shot by a hunter in SE Falmouth. Had recently bred and her 9 fetuses died with her. Could not verify that her long-term mate, Kett, was still alive because Kett's collar had died in 2002.
Mole	0110	**M**arstons Mills **ol**d female, lactating. Captured on 8 June 2001 (9 years old, 39-lbs) the day Skunks was killed. Raised pups that and the next summer. Alpha female of a pack of 6 summer 2001; largest documented adult group size on the Cape. Used the Marston Mills rendezvous site that Sill's group eventually took over (his territory bordered Mole's prior to her death). Died in late winter/early spring 2003, apparently of natural causes, at age 11+ after probably whelping 8–9 litters in her lifetime. Possible mother of Pon and Poo from 1998.

Table 1 Cape Cod Coyotes (continued)
(in order of first capture)

Name	ID #	Description
Kash	0112	Female offspring of **Kett** and **Gash**, captured and radio-collared as a 4-mo. old pup 4 August 2001 (16-lbs). Tracked within territory and foraged mostly independently. Killed by a car 27 November 2001 (30.5-lbs).
Jog	0103	Captured at **Jenkins' Bogs** in West Barnstable 22 December 2001 (39.6-lbs). Probable mate of Skunks before her death. Also observed with Mizz (January 2002) in Centerville after Skunks' death. Traveled with Carm, his probable son from the 2001 litter. Killed by a car on mid-Cape highway 3 June 2002 (a skinny 36-lbs).
Sog	0202	Second coyote captured at Jenkins' **Bog** trap (3 January 2002). Large, healthy female (1 3/4 years old, 42-lbs) who dispersed west immediately upon release. Hit by a car off-Cape in Bourne 18 May 2002 (still 42-lbs).
Slot	0201	Second coyote (1st = Snix) captured at Sandy Neck **lot** (Snix's second capture location) 23 February 2002. A red male (10.5 mo. old, 31.6-lbs). Only documented on Sandy Neck once; eventually established territory south of route 6A and Sandy Neck. Shot and left to rot by a duck hunter on or before 2 January 2004 (37.9-lbs).
Carm	0203	Cummaquid male coyote at **farm** captured 23 February 2002 (35 lbs, 10.5 mo. old) off territory and returned to his probable sire and 2 others in West Barnstable. Became dominant male in the northern section of Skunks' and Jog's territory after both were killed. His pack included 6 pups and at least 2 other adults summer 2004. Shot by a hunter (with probable mate) on 28 February 2005.

Table 1 Cape Cod Coyotes (continued)
(in order of first capture)

Name	ID #	Description
Cake	0204 (0602)	Female coyote who came awake while being handled. Captured 6 March 2002 in Cummaquid; (30-lbs ~11 mo. old). Whelped pups in Hyannis/Centerville at the edge of Casper's territory (a possible daughter) but that fall (2002) established a territory south of Carm in the southern part of Jog and Skunk's original range. Gave birth in 2003 and 2004 and traveled with at least 2 other adults through some of the most residential parts of Barnstable (central Centerville). Her collar died in late-fall 2004. Re-collared 7 May 2006 (37-lbs), lactating.
Glif	0205	Glover's fifth coyote capture; caught 8 March 2002. A dispersing male transient (11 mo., 33-lbs). Shot and killed by a policeman on the Chatham/Harwich line on 22 June 2003 (33–34-lbs) while having seizures in a homeowner's backyard. Not autopsied for cause.
Tiny	0207	A tiny 27-lb mangy, adult male (~2 yrs old) captured 8 March 2002 on Sandy Neck. Traveled with others on and off the beach using about two thirds of Snix's range. Last located in late-April 2002. Collar malfunctioned, he dispersed, or was illegally killed and his collar destroyed.
Snour	0301	Named for Sandy Neck 'coyote number four'. Healthy male transient captured in West Barnstable on 23 November 2003 (1.5 yr-old, 40.6-lbs). Seemed to be part of the group west of Sandy Neck (in east Sandwich). Relocated in West Barnstable before dispersing eastward in mid-January 2004. Found intermittently in Barnstable and may have traveled throughout Cape Cod. Shot in mid-February 2005 (assumed legally) on National Park Service lands in north Wellfleet on the Cape Cod National Seashore after having traveled 45 miles in 3 weeks in about 3 feet of snow.

Table 1 Cape Cod Coyotes (continued)
(in order of first capture)

Name	ID #	Description
Cale	0401	Named for Cummaquid male. A very lanky 2 yr old transient, possibly Casper's offspring (skinny 31.8-lbs) captured on 20 January 2004. Notable white face like Casper. Originally thought to be the alpha male of the Cummaquid group. Located intermittently throughout Barnstable and Sandwich. 'Lost' for over a year until located 13 November 2005 in the northwestern part of Mashpee. Died on 23 December from a combination of mange, 8 pellets lodged in his skull, chafing on his neck from the collar, and a severe cold spell. So far the only coyote found to be affected by the collars despite a careful fitting. His poor condition was likely a contributing factor.
Mystic	0601	A very healthy 38-lb 2–3 yr old male, captured 26 March 2006 near Mystic Lake in Marstons Mills. Likely the breeding male of the Marstons Mills Airport pack. Pups (≥4) documented summer 2006.
Squid	0603	A lanky 36.1-lb 2 yr old male captured 25 May 2006, the seventh coyote caught in Cummaquid. Was a transient and quickly left the Yarmouth portion of the study area; has been intermittently located since, usually in Yarmouth.
Snale	0604	5th coyote captured at/on Sandy Neck Beach. A petite but healthy 31.5-lb lactating female captured 27 May 2006. Had 7–8 healthy pups in 2006 with a yellow-brown bodied, white-faced mate.
Raider	0606	A very healthy 37.3-lb 5–6 yr old lactating female captured 15 June 2006 in the woods behind Barnstable High School (mascot = Red Raiders). Is the breeding female of the Hyannis pack; had pups in 2006. Possibly a descendant of Mizz's.

Table 2 North Boston Coyotes

Name	ID #	Description
Maple	BN0202 (BN0204)	**Maple**-colored lactating female captured on **Maple** Street in north Revere on 20 May 2002 (~5 years old, 30-lbs) and 3 June 2002 (not handled). Had ≥3 pups in a conservation area bordering Saugus in urban north Boston. Ranged up to Peabody through Saugus and west Lynn. Killed by a car 9 July 2002 crossing Route 107 in severe lightning storm, the furthest SE we had documented her. Possibly dis oriented.
Bart	BN0301	A bone-skinny, almost bald mangy male captured at **Breakhart** Reservation in Saugus on 6 February 2003 (32-lbs). Used a very, small rendezvous site range (~1 km²) north of the reservation. Apparently starved to death on 9 March 2003 (24-lbs). It was mid-winter when he was captured and released with an injection of ivermectin® for mange mites. We fully expected his survival.
Notch	BN0401	Young male coyote with a **notch** in both ears from frostbite. Had severe mange when captured on 12 March 2004 and brought to a rehabilitation clinic (33.5-lbs). Rapidly gained weight (~40-lbs) and escaped from an outdoor exhibit upon finishing 4 doses of ivermectin on 30 or 31 March 2004. Never radio-collared or returned to his capture site at Pine Banks Park in Malden, and was lost for research purposes to document the success (or failure) of rehabilitation.
Fog	BN0402	First coyote in the **Hog** trap. Transient captured in north Revere on 13 April 2004 (30-lbs). Had a western coyote narrow face, and was moving south through urban north Boston. She traveled under the Zakim Bridge, through north Boston, west through Cambridge and Somerville and disappeared. We re-located her near the Rhode Island border November 2004 in Dartmouth, MA, 60 miles away. She paired and had pups April 2005 with a reddish-blond coy-ote. Died of unknown causes in early June 2005.

Table 2 North Boston Coyotes (continued)

Name	ID #	Description
Maeve	BN0404	A lactating female, possibly one of Maple's 2002 pups (very similar face). Captured in Everett 17 May 2004 (32-lbs). Had 5 pups but only 4 were observed later. Used natural dens and human structures in a very small (~1 mi²) range of mostly cemeteries and woods in urban Malden and Everett. Also captured her mate (Jet) and two pups (Jem and Cour). She, Jet and Cour were poisoned to death in late March/early April 2005 (28-lbs).
Jet	BN0403	Maeve's mate, a reddish male and first net-launching capture on 29 June 2004 (35-lbs) in the Jewish cemetery. Had a small territory (~ 1 mi²) like Maeve. First mated pair collared within 1 year of each other indicating the potential success of using a net-launcher to capture additional coyotes. We tracked his pack until Maeve, Cour and Jet were poisoned late March/early April 2005 (31.5-lbs).
Jem	BN0406	Female pup of Jet and Maeve captured on 26 August 2004 (4.5 mo. old, 22-lbs). Traveled with her family in their small territory before dispersing on 11 December 2004. We lost track of her after her dispersal.
Cour	BN0405	Coyote number four captured 15 September 2004 in the cemeteries of Everett and Malden (5 mo. old, 27-lbs). Remained with his parents Jet and Maeve through the winter 2004–2005. Poisoned and died on 3 April 2005 (37-lbs).

Table 3 Captive Coyotes
Litter obtained 12 April 2002[3]

Name	ID #	Description
Cane	**C1 or A02030**	Named for *Canis latrans*. Dominant female of the group (41–44-lbs). Fought with Caon on 6 February 2005 at the Stone Zoo, which triggered a permanent separation between myself and them since that day (just prior to their third birthday).
Lupe	**C2 or A02028**	Named for *Canis **lupus*** because of his resemblance to a wolf. Most dominant coyote of the captive pack. As an adult he weighed up to 55-lbs. He bonded with me most quickly as a pup. I have not been with or seen him since February 2005 per zoo orders.
Caon	**C3 or A02031**	Named for the subspecies of gray wolf *C. lupus* ly**caon** or the species name for eastern wolf *C. lycaon*. The omega coyote of the group weighing 35–36-lb. Fought with Late, then Cane, causing much turmoil among the litter.
Trans	**C4 or A02029**	Named for *Canis latrans*. The beta male of the pack before his fight with Lupe and the females caused him to be permanently separated from them in November 2003 (37-lbs). Dominant over all of the females before the split, including larger Cane.
Late	**C5 or A02032**	Named for *Canis **latrans*** and **late** developing. A funny-faced, pudgy runt; 26–32-lbs. Caused a lot of mischief and had much fluctuation in her body condition as a result of her high activity levels. Separated from the pack for fighting. Both Late and Trans were transferred from the Stone Zoo to the Franklin Park Zoo in December 2003.

[3] Note: All of the captive coyotes are described more fully in the text.

Appendix 2

Coyotes Studied in Eastern Massachusetts

The following table summarizes the coyotes in both study sites, and tallies their capture and tagging statistics. The Cape Cod component of our study began in May 1998, while the Boston study began May 2002.

Table 4 Capture/Tagging Tally of Study Coyotes

Study Site	Total radio-tagged	# Radio-collared	# Radio-implanted	Box-trap captures[a]	Hand captures[b]	Net-launch captures
Cape Cod	29	25[c]	4	38	17	0
Boston	7	7[c,d]	0	8[a]	0	1

[a] Includes repeat captured coyotes; 29 individuals captured 39 times on Cape Cod and 7 individuals captured 8 times in Boston.

[b] All were pups; only included here are animals who were physically picked up; many others were observed up close but not held; only one, Cix, was radio-implanted.

[c] Includes 2 pups at each site (4 total) in late-summer given expandable collars at both study sites.

[d] One animal not included; it had mange and was rehabilitated at a wildlife facility but escaped before being collared.

Appendix 3

Species Captured in Box-Traps

The following table lists the species of animals captured in box-traps during our ongoing coyote studies.

Table 5 Box Trap Captures

Common name	Cape Cod	North Boston
Raccoon	√	√
American crow	√	√
Opossum	√	√
Striped skunk	√	√
Coyote	√	√
Domestic dog	√	√
Domestic cat	√	√
Red Fox	√	√
Red-tailed hawk	√	√
Muskrat	√	√
Gull	√	
Northern Harrier	√	
Gray fox		√
Turkey vulture		√

Table 5 Box Trap Captures (continued)

Common name	Cape Cod	North Boston
Fisher		√
Gray squirrel		√
Starling		√
Norway rat		√
Finch		√
Chickadee		√

Appendix 4

Coyote Territories on Cape Cod

Map representing different coyote packs monitored over time. This figure is intended to represent an average of our data set as pack home ranges have fluctuated over the years.

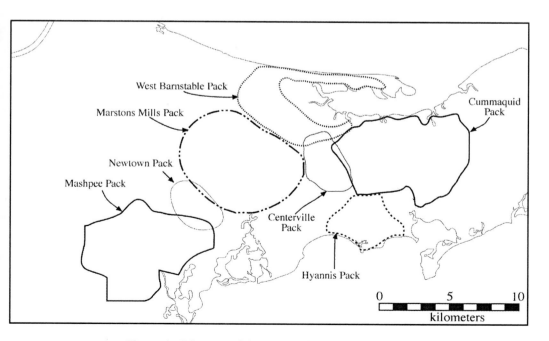

Figure 1   Diagram of Coyote Territories on Cape Cod

Appendix 5

Dispersal of Transient Coyotes in Eastern Massachusetts

Minimum estimate of coyote dispersal in eastern Massachusetts repre-sented by capture location and last find. Coyotes could have travel farther depend-ing on movements on linear Cape Cod (for example, some of the coyotes might have used all of the Cape before being recovered) and their unknown birth loca-tions. All coyotes (except Fog) were recovered dead at their final location. Despite being relatively short dispersal distances, the four coyotes on Cape Cod, when combined their movements are combined, used the entire peninsula.

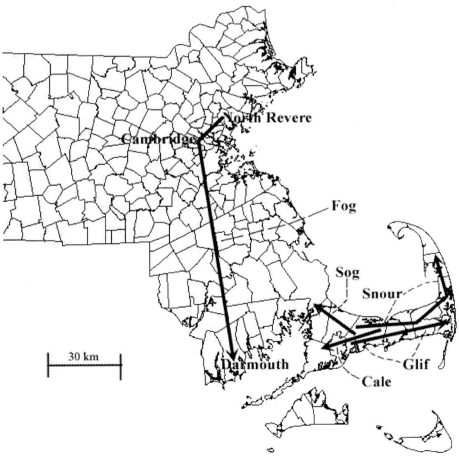

Figure 2 Diagram of Coyote Dispersal in Eastern Massachusetts

Appendix 6

Daily Movements of Two Cape Cod Coyotes

The movements of coyotes 0003 (Sill) and 9901 (Sly) are overlaid on the map to illustrate the daily distances typically traveled for coyotes inhabiting this suburban area. Sill's movement, when he was a helper coyote for his father Kett, actually involved moving through five of the 12 different towns on Cape Cod.

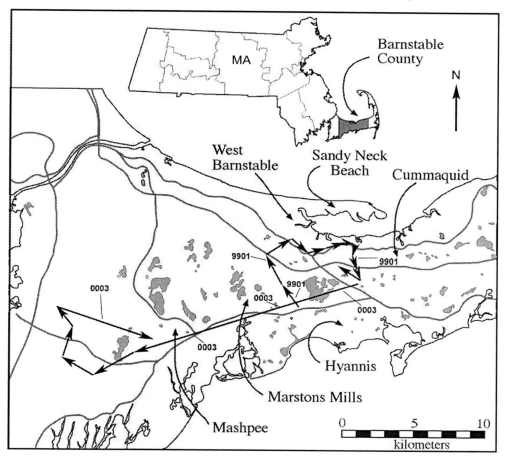

Figure 3 Diagram of Representative Daily Coyote Movements

Appendix 7

Diagram Combining Science and Education

This diagram illustrates a researcher working at the interface between the worlds of science and education. I started with science driving my education questions; now I am examining what education questions will drive the science.

Merging two disciplines: the interface between science and education

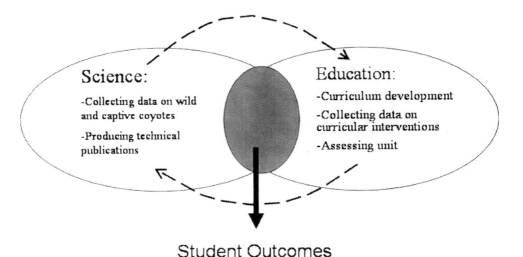

Student Outcomes

Figure 4 Diagram Combining Science and Education

Appendix 8

Peaks and Valleys

Life as a biologist, especially one who studies a persecuted species such as the coyote, can be characterized by many peaks and valleys in attitude and state of mind. The highs and lows associated with field research sometimes come in waves, producing extremes in either range. This diagram tries to depict the fluctuations in my enthusiasm for conducting research during the course of this project.

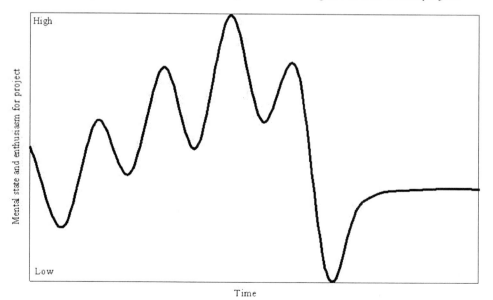

Figure 5 Diagram of Researchers' Mental States
and Enthusiasm for a Study Project Over Time

Appendix 9

Things You Can Do to Help Coyotes

One of the reasons why states increase hunting seasons on certain species is because of the frequency of complaints received, usually by residents, regarding wildlife intrusions. The plan for extending the hunting season on a notorious or problem species is intended to reduce the population, thereby reducing problems. With a territorial species like the coyote, the answer is not that simple, hence my need to write this book.

Recording coyote (or any form of wildlife) complaints is contingent upon a negative feedback system. This system is used by wildlife agencies upon which to base their 'management' decisions. It is also a bureaucratic shortcut in lieu of them doing the right thing, that is, chasing down accurate knowledge-based scientific data or hiring a wildlife biologist to research a problem as to why coyotes or other wildlife are suddenly in our way. The much easier answer is to immediately give someone the right to kill the animal(s) thereby disposing of the problem.

It seems that, as a civilization, we should have evolved past this archaic system of simply killing the 'problem' animal without ever further investigating the roots of the complaints. This simplistic and wrong course of action by the powers-that-be never solves the problem, it just perpetuates it with each new generation of animals and people who move into an area. And the animals always lose, whether they are at fault or not.

We are finally in the midst of a positive paradigm shift where many people no longer agree with the old-style of wildlife management. Since the advent of TV, computers, and video games, most people no longer consider competitive interactions with wild animals as their only form of entertainment. And although our government agencies have a poor reputation for responding to people who want to see old systems change, it is possible for us, the citizens, to encourage them to make changes that can set a precedent for the future; changes that improve a poor system, and that reflect the kinder and more current paradigm of our time.

The way that wildlife management is run hasn't been re-examined for many years or updated based on current research. Those of us who know this, and that now includes all of you who have read this book, have an opportunity to help change things. We need to change the current system where all animals are viewed as a resource to be utilized (i.e., killed) by people. The answer simply isn't to keep killing animals who innocently walk in our yards or graze or hunt in the woods behind our homes.

Maybe you're asking, "What can I do? If an animal is causing a problem, let someone else fix it. And if it's not causing a problem, why make a big deal about it?"

I argue that we should. Animals can't speak for themselves. Wildlife agencies only see one side—the complaints. How often do you think they get calls from wildlife lovers just to comment on how they saw a beautiful deer or coyote in their neighborhood? Next to never. They would probably wonder why that person called, because they expect complaints. People that like coyotes should call, write, and/or email their town and state wildlife branches. You should let them know that you enjoy and value the presence of deer, coyotes, and foxes. Believe me, they rarely hear it—and hear very often from the people who don't like them.

You can also petition your state to make more wildlife friendly laws such as the way Massachusetts offers protection to all animals, including predators. Tell them you care. It makes a difference. If they don't want to listen, try for a public referendum. That is the way a democratic government is supposed to work—to have the public determine such things as coyote management.

For example, voting for a three-month hunting season (as opposed to year-round) and a small bag limit (say two to three coyotes per hunter per year) will ensure that non-consumptive wildlife users have a say in wildlife management. Or, try for extreme measures and vote for no coyote hunting in your state. A similar publicly-voted ban on mountain lion hunting was passed and has been in effect in California for years now.

Let me present a scenario to you, one that might anger you when you think about it. You are an animal lover and live at the very northern part of Massachusetts. The local coyote group around your house dens in an agricultural field just across the border in southern New Hampshire. While you and your neighborhood are wildlife friendly, a hunter from across the border does not like coyotes, just because they are coyotes. That hunter, with a valid New Hampshire hunting license, can legally crawl into that den and kill the pups and any nearby adults year-round.

Out west, coyote dens are commonly found and the occupants gassed, suffocating the young fossorial pups. These barbaric acts even occur on our public lands, and are frequently financed by public tax-dollars in the western United States. And from what you now know about coyotes, you realize that this just motivates existing coyotes to produce more pups. And more coyotes mean more humans inflicting more suffering in this never-ending struggle.

In nature their numbers are mostly self-limiting in localized areas and their mortality rates are relatively high just from living in proximity to humans and automobiles. Contrary to the fear of many, they will not overrun us, and with a little education, we can live together peacefully and enjoy the presence of these beautiful animals. We should give nature a chance to do her own wildlife management. It worked for a long time before man came on the scene, and it's time we learned to get with the program.

Appendix 10

Ode to Casper, the Survivor

Although you don't know it, Casper, it was one of the greatest privileges of my young life to track and get to know you over the past eight years. It was also ironic, considering you actually hated being near me and ran whenever you sensed my presence. But that was part of the instinctive cleverness that preserves you; after all, you are a truly wild coyote.

You were captured four times and wore three different radio-collars beginning in November 1998. You were one of the only coyotes who growled at me each time we caught you! You were one tough lady. I found you nearly 2,000 times and my files on you continue to provide me with boatloads of data. You were by far the heaviest female coyote ever documented anywhere and were even bigger than your several mates, an oddity for female carnivores.

You were the matriarch of the Cummaquid coyote pack for at least six years and I am fortunate to have documented a lot of your life in that roll. I knew where you gave birth behind the Hyannis Airport and how you moved your pups to a rendezvous site across the mid-Cape Highway to the Barnstable County Farm. I was able to radio-tag one of your mates, Sly, and a few of your offspring, including Cup and Cix.

I mourned the decision of the County Farm in 2002 to stop raising chickens because they necessarily disposed of one or two sickly birds per day, specifically for your group to consume. In 2001, I remember watching one of your sons, Cix, wait behind the coup on a nightly basis until his young body was well nourished.

I treasured watching you traverse your 15-square-mile Cummaquid territory and actively displace non-family from your turf as you and your pack scent-marked and howled up a storm. You were cautious when you traveled through the many neighborhoods in your range, carefully avoiding people and cars along the way.

Then I lost track of you for two years as I raised a captive coyote litter and had little time to replace the expired batteries in your collar. But then during that time, I experienced just a little of the responsibilities you shouldered year after year raising similar active families, even as you grew older and less vital. Capturing you for the fourth time in March 2004 was a shock when you weighed in at a robust 55.3-lbs. Before the capture, I wasn't even sure if you were still alive. I should have known better.

I will never forget, after many years of tracking you passed, finding you sleeping under decks and sheds at the southeast edge of your range. This was during that severe winter of January 2005 when it seems you lost your territory to some younger, more aggressive female. I even wonder if it's possible that you voluntarily relinquished your matriarchy as you became too old, and perhaps too wise, to defend it. I wonder how you survived that event, and how you somehow managed to avoid people during those times of sheltering so close to humans, especially with a three-foot deep ground cover of snow—even now it still perplexes me. But you did, because you are a survivor.

I remember worrying about you for an entire month because I could not find you anywhere, until I finally relocated you at the northeast edge of your old territory. You continued to live there following your reign as Queen of Cummaquid. How you managed to live and survive in that small, two-square-mile range was little less than amazing. But you did, and I frequently observed you traveling with another coyote in that new location.

Casper sedated in the author's arms

A highlight of our unacknowledged acquaintance was when I surprisingly documented aging Sly, your former mate, traveling with you, on consecutive days in mid-February 2006, a full five years after his collar malfunctioned and I had no knowledge if he were still alive. What a thrill to see that, considering he was about eight years old and you were at least ten at the time! It was like old times as I observed you loping along 20–50 feet behind him. As usual, I watched you from my car so I could spy on your activities without you being aware of me. But despite my best precautions, you usually somehow still managed to detect me. I'm sorry if my actions ever disturbed you.

You continued to amaze me as you abruptly abandoned your new range in early March 2006, after I saw you and Sly with a very large third coyote at the southeast edge of that area. You then started roaming widely, regularly crossing Route 6 and traveling throughout all of east Yarmouth. I wonder if that third coyote was Sly's new mate who did not take kindly to your renewed acquaintance with him.

I held my breath every time you came near Great Island, fearing that the local residents might recklessly put a bullet into your thick pelage. Despite being alone in your travels, you appeared healthy and still wise enough to keep yourself safe. Then you vanished in late-June 2006. Although I don't know for sure where you went, I suspect you left your old haunts to visit the Lower Cape, where it is more scenic and less people-dominated. Finally, I relocated you in late-summer 2006 and tracked you sporadically as you roamed nomadically in at least the entire mid-Cape area, ranging from Sandwich to Yarmouth. You were very difficult to track as a transient coyote because you used a very large area.

Although you don't know it, Casper, I experienced a personal low in 2005, and tracking you raised my spirits and got me excited about my research again. I think it was partly because you embodied the very definition of survivor as you crossed roads thousands of times, dealt with fluctuations in food sources, mates, temperature and weather extremes, and struggled to maintain social relationships and a home territory. You overcame as many obstacles as a person forced into homelessness, somehow managing to hold yourself together and go on living, especially since you didn't have a territory to call your own in your latter years.

Thank you for all you have taught me—about coyotes—and about being a survivor in every sense of the word. And after all this time, it is so good to still spot you occasionally. You are not only the largest female coyote on record to date, but maybe you will become one of the oldest, and I am beginning to think you may be the wisest, as you wind your way along outside of the pack structure of the young breeders and sometimes even in the company of some of the other oldsters I've followed, like your former mate Sly. As you set your records, old girl, I'll be watching and taking notes, and hoping you end well.

Casper's gazing eyes

Glossary of Terms

Term	Description
Active submission	Submissive behavior shown by canids when one licks the muzzle of a more dominant animal
Affiliative	Positive interactions toward others
Antagonistic (agonistic)	Negative or aggressive interaction toward others
Alpha	Dominant members of a group; in wolves and coyotes, typically the breeding members of a social group
Annuli	Annual rings on teeth used to determine age.
Antenna	Device used to locate or hone in on signals emanating from a transmitter (e.g., a radio-collar).
Anthropogenic	Caused by humans
Anthropomorphize	To ascribe human feelings to an animal
Associate	A helper or beta coyote; typically older offspring from a previous litter who remain in their natal group to help raise the next generation
Authentic science	Activities that enable students to learn to conduct their own research; this could involve direct participation with scientists, or indirect participation such as staged simulations or viewing films of actual research
Aversive	See non-lethal aversive conditioning
Bag limit	Legal limit of the number of animals of any species that can be killed during the hunting season; Massachusetts has no bag limit for coyotes

Bait	Food appetizing to an animal to draw it to a trap or close proximity where it can be observed or photographed (or hunted)
Barnstable	Barnstable County, which encompasses all of Cape Cod; the town of Barnstable (technically it is a city) on Cape Cod where I focused much of my research; and Barnstable village within the town of Barnstable.
Beta	Associate coyote or helper coyote
Biomagnification	An accumulation of toxins in higher tropic levels
Biped, bipedal	To walk on two feet like humans do; animals are quadrupeds or walk on four feet
Bourne	A town located just off of Cape Cod, north of the Bourne Bridge
Box-trap	A large metal cage trap used to humanely catch coyotes and other species of wildlife
Breeder	Alpha coyotes; the dominant males and females who reproduce within a canid group; normally only one male and female breed per group.
Brush wolf	Term for coyotes in the Midwest and some New England regions
Canid	Any animal belonging to the dog (or Canidae) family
Canine	Refers both to animals of the Canid(ae) family (n.) and to the four biting teeth (n.; adj.) used for stabbing prey or fighting by carnivores
Canidae	This is the family that wolves, dogs, coyotes, jackals, foxes and all canines belong to.
Canis latrans	Scientific (Latin) name for coyote, and means '*barking dog*'.
Canis latrans var.	Scientific name for eastern coyote; currently recognized as a variation of coyote
Canis lupus	Scientific name for gray wolf
Canis lycaon	Scientific name for eastern wolf
Canis rufus	Scientific name for red wolf
Carnassials	Teeth adapted for shearing flesh; the carnassial teeth of carnivores are the upper fourth premolars and lower first molars

Carnivore	A meat-eating animal
Cat-ing	A term coined by our research team for a behavior of coyotes that involves zig-zagging in and out of suburban yards as if searching for cats
Centerville	A suburban village in the town of Barnstable
Charismatic species	A species that has proved very popular with the public and can be used to support conservation issues
City	People living in a large densely populated municipality
Colonize	To migrate to and settle in; referring to pioneering individuals of a species first establishing themselves in an area
Conspecifics	Organisms belonging to the same species
Consumptive user	Typically refers to hunting or fishing activities where the goal of a wildlife outing is to harvest or kill some or multiple things.
Copulatory tie	Describes sex for all members of the canid species; after ejaculation, the male's penis swells inside the female's vagina and the two become attached for a period of time (generally 15-20 minutes); thought to be an evolutionary adaptation toward monogamy
Core area	Key areas of wild canid ranges where they spend a disproportionate amount of time such as den and rendezvous sites
Corridor	A strip of habitat connecting otherwise isolated areas of suitable habitat
Crepuscular	Dusk and dawn; active at dawn or dusk
Cummaquid	A village located at the northeastern part of the town of Barnstable
Demographic	Statistics that describe a population
Den	An underground location, usually dug by parent canids, in which they whelp their pups
Den site	The immediate location/vicinity surrounding the actual den where the young are whelped
Depredated	Plundered, marauded; preyed upon.
Disperse	Typically a once-in-a-lifetime event; movement to a new habitat; regarding coyotes, to leave ones area of birth

Dispersing	When a canid leaves the area of birth and moves to a new area; dispersing coyotes are also called nomadic or transient
Diurnal	Active during the day
Domesticate	To train or adapt (an animal or plant) to live in a human environment and be of use to humans
Dominant (behavior)	To exhibit control or rank over other animals of the same species
Dyadic	Paired interactions; comparing two animals
Eastern Canadian wolf	*Canis lycaon*; new name ascribed to wolves in southeastern Canada; believed to be the same species as the red wolf in the southeastern U.S.
Eastern coyote	Large bodied version of coyote living in the northeastern U.S.; current genetic research is underway to determine if this animal is a hybrid of western coyotes and wolves.
Eastern timber wolf	Species of wolf originally present in New England; debate exists if it is *Canis lycaon* or *Canis lupus lycaon*
Ecology	The branch of biology concerned with the relationship between organisms and their environment
Ethogram	A behavior inventory or categorization of a species behavior.
Ethology	The study of animal behavior
Euthanize	Term for 'putting an animal to sleep'; to kill an animal, usually by lethal injection or gunshot
Everett	A city located at the north edge of Boston
Extinct	No longer in existence, usually referring to an entire species; human-caused extinctions are currently happening at thousands of times the natural (or previous) rate
Extirpate	Synonym for exterminate; to make extinct in a local area; for example, humans have extirpated wolves in New England
Fast-feet	Slang expression denoting a form of locomotion in which coyotes travel at an energy-efficient gate similar to a lope but their feet touch the ground in a rapid shuffling gait almost as fast as a sprint, yet maintaining a fairly slow effortless, pace.

Flagship species	See Charismatic species.
FLU (flex-leg urinate)	Typically made by dominant females where they semi-lift a leg to eliminate urine; the female squats and lifts a leg a few inches off the ground; this is unlike RLUs where legs are lifted high and SQUs where legs are not lifted off the ground
Foot-hold trap	See Leg-hold trap.
Fossorial	Adapted for digging or living underground
Furbearing, furbearer	Any species of mammals whose fur is of commercial value, including beavers, skunks, minks, weasels, otters, raccoons, and canids
God's dog	Another name for coyote; often used to reflect the importance of the animal
Habituation	Becoming tame around humans over time so that there is a waning of wild or defensive responses to a repeated, neutral stimulus
Hackles	The erectile hair on an animal's back, neck and shoulders that rises in times of fear or danger; in coyotes, used for displays of aggression and when in physical contact with other coyotes
Helper	See associate coyote
Herbivore	An animal who eats plant matter
Home range	The area that an animal uses
Howl	Vocalizing and long-distance communication used by wolves and coyotes to: 1) advertise territory; 2) call/assemble group members from a distance; 3) rally each other; and 4) possibly for the joy of it
Hunting season	The time of year when it is legal to hunt and kill an animal; in Massachusetts, coyote season is 4 months long; nationwide, it is typically year-round and that applies also to many other predators as well
Hyannis	The most urban village within the town of Barnstable
Hyannis Animal Hospital	Hospital owned by Dr. Larry Venezia who kindly cooperates with us on our Eastern Coyote Project; this is where we bring our coyotes on Cape Cod to have them implanted with radio-transmitters

Hyannisport	A section of Hyannis where the Kennedy family lives.
Identification number	A numbering scheme used to recognize individual coyotes
Implant	See radio-implant
Inter-	Between; a prefix often used to describe canid behavior such as interpack aggression, where two different packs are fighting each other; or interspecific aggression, where two different species are competing for resources.
Intra-	Within; a prefix often used to describe canid behavior such as intralitter aggression, where siblings from the same litter are fighting.
Juvenile	Proper scientific name for pup born of the year
Lactation	The period following birth during which a female produces milk and nurses her young
Leg-hold trap	Trap designed to be hidden underground and capture an animal by the paw when an animal steps on it; artificial lures typically are used to draw the animal near.
Malden	A city on the north edge of Boston
Mammal	Any warm-blooded vertebrates of the class Mammalia having the skin with hair; young are born alive and are nourished with milk
Mange	A persistent and contagious skin condition resulting from mite infestation causing inflammation and itching and resulting in hair loss; affects primarily animals but sometimes people where it is called scabies
Marstons Mills	A village on Cape Cod in the town of Barnstable where the author is from and where much of the research took place
Mashpee	A town adjacent (west of) to the town of Barnstable on Cape Cod
Micro-corridor	A small passageway, such as a hole in a fence, that allows access from one side to the other
Mousing	A hunting technique where a canid jumps up in the air then lands on a rodent
Murphy's Law	"If anything can go wrong, it will"
Natal area	Area of birth

Necropsy	An animal autopsy; an examination and dissection of a dead body to determine cause of death.
Net-gun	A device that fires a net from a gun; typically used from a helicopter to capture large mammals
Net-launcher	A ground-based device placed in a strategic position that shoots a net over an animal
New wolf	Name first given to eastern coyotes to arrive in New England in the 1960s-1970s; name reflected the large body size before further research found it similar to but larger than western coyotes
Nocturnal	Active at night
Nomad, nomadic	See transient coyote
Non-consumptive user	People, such as wildlife watchers and scientists, who may track or observe but do not hunt or kill animals
Non-lethal aversive	Any technique designed to avoid conflicts with wildlife that does not kill the animal; examples include chasing, yelling, throwing things, or putting chemicals in food to negatively condition an offending animal to specific areas or items
Omnivore	An animal that eats both plant and animal matter
Pack	A social group or pack of canids comprising three or more members
Passive submission	When a canid falls on its back, exposing its ventral side (belly) to submit to a more dominant member of its species; opposite of active submission
Pelage	Pelt or fleece; hair or fur covering the body of an animal
Philopatric	To remain in one's natal area or place of birth
Pinpoint	To accurately locate where an animal is; often a loud signal from a radio-collar indicates that the animal was pinpointed, or its location was precise
Piscivore	Fish-eater
Place-based education	Education technique whereby one studies their local environment.
Prairie wolf	Term for coyote in the Great Plains region
Predation	The act of one animal (a predator) killing another (the prey)

Predator	An animal who preys on other animals
Predator call	A simulated call, usually of an injured rabbit or deer, used by human hunters to draw coyotes (and other predators) close enough to be shot
Prey	An animal that is hunted or killed by another animal
Pup	A baby coyote or other canid; scientifically termed a juvenile; at 1 year old, usually in April, it is termed a yearling.
Quadruped	To walk on four feet like dogs and cats, unlike humans who walk on two feet (bipedal)
Qualitative	Observations of quality or kind, made through the senses; in education, often referred to as the lived experiences of people
Quantitative	Observations expressed in quantity like those based on precise or laboratory measurements; this is the backbone of science and data collection
Rabies	A viral disease of the nervous system of warm-blooded animals (usually transmitted by the bite of a rabid animal); is fatal if the virus reaches the brain
Radio-collar	A transmitter that is attached to the animal in the form of a collar; the box on the collar consists of the radio-transmitter.
Radio-implant	A transmitter that is surgically implanted into an animal; typically done on juvenile animals who are still growing where a collar might be ill-advised
Radio-receiver	Device used to detect the signal of the transmitter; tuned to specific frequencies of the transmitters being used
Radio-tag	General term for any radio-transmitter (e.g., collar, implant)
Radio-telemetry	Radio-telemetry enables a study subject - an animal that is wearing a radio-transmitter - to be located; in effect, the animal is a mobile radio-station that the researcher can locate from its broadcast signal.
Radio-transmitter	A collar or implant device that broadcasts a specific frequency signal, affixed to an animal
Receiver	See radio-receiver

Red wolf	*Canis rufus*; a smaller bodied (about 60 pounds) species of wolf previously believed to be native to the southeastern U.S.; now believed to have ranged from the southeast U.S. all the way to southeastern Canada
Rendezvous site	An above ground resting site where coyote packs typically take their young after 2 months of age; characteristics of the site include water, cover, open areas, and hunting grounds; termed 'puppy training centers'
Revere	A city five miles north of downtown Boston where we conducted coyote research
RLU	Raised leg urination; a term referring to alpha canids raising their legs to mark territory; a sign of dominance in wild canids, usually males
Rural	Part of a landscape continuum ranging from rural to urbanized; characteristic of country or farming life; areas that have a low density of people
Salmonella	A bacteria that can cause food poisoning in people; many animals such as rodents, snakes, reptiles and coyotes carry the disease, but coyotes do not get sick from it as they have probably evolved to cope with it
Sandy Neck	A barrier beach on the north side of the town of Barnstable which encompasses a large conservation area
Saugus Animal Hospital	Hospital owned by Dr. Bob Binder who kindly cooperates with us; where we bring our coyotes from north Boston to get radio-collared
Saturated population	An area that has been claimed by sufficient numbers or family units of a species that all available territories are taken; to claim a territory, transient coyotes must either disperse out of the area, wait for a vacancy in a territory, forcefully evict a breeding coyote, or establish a range within the existing matrix.
Scat	Scientific term for animal feces or droppings.
Scent-marking	Behavior by an animal, especially a canid, strategically marking a location with feces, urine, or ground scratching to advertise its presence
Simulation concept	Education concept when something artificial, such as video or an in-class activity, is used to demonstrate a real life situation or behavior

Sink	A low-quality habitat that has poor food resources and/or poor animal survival; humans can potentially make a 'source' (good habitat) a 'sink' through poor environmental maintenance or exploitation
Sloucher	A coyote that remains on its natal range but does little to contribute to the pack such as raising new pups; often a yearling coyote
Snare	A noose-like device used to capture an animal by the leg or neck; neck snares, by design, often strangulate the animal
Social group	A collection of at least 3 animals living together; often referred to as a pack for wolves and coyotes
Socialized	To become familiar with human society; an animal is tamed to react positively to people or companionship with others
Source	A high quality habitat often associated with good food resources and high survival rates
SQU	Squat urination; when a coyote or other canid, typically young or subordinate, squats its lower body but does not lift a rear leg to urinate; usually a show of submissive behavior in the presence of a dominant animal.
Surplus killing	When a predator kills more than it can eat in one sitting; often involves multiple kills such as 2-3 deer killed at once. Carcasses are then revisited and consumed over longer periods of time.
Submissive behavior	An animal willing to submit without resistance to a more dominant animal.
Suburban	In the middle of landscape continuum ranging from rural to urban; residential areas located outside of cities
Tame	Brought from wildness into a tractable state or even friendly relationship with humans; usually refers to wild animals that become comfortable around people but are not fully domesticated such as the captive coyotes I hand-reared.
Territory	The part of a home range that an animal or group of animals defends from others of their species.
Transient	An animal not belonging to a social group; usually a younger animal dispersing to a new location to settle

Transmitter	See radio-transmitter
Triangulate	To obtain a location on an animal from two or more locations; often used in conjunction with radio-telemetry; in education lingo, it refers to using multiple means of qualitative data collection techniques such as notes, interviews, and pre/post surveys
Trickster	Native American name for the coyote; reflects the cleverness and adaptability of coyotes
Tweed wolf	Hybrid canid (ca. 50-lbs) inhabiting southeastern Canada; a probable result of hybridization between eastern coyotes and eastern timber wolves; likely genetically similar to the eastern coyote
Ungulate	Hoofed animals such as the deer family
Urban	Located in or characteristic of a city or city life
Urbanized	Part of a landscape continuum ranging from rural to urban; city environments
Walk-in	When a researcher uses radio-telemetry (or snow tracking) to hone in on a collared animal; usually done to directly observe the animal and its companions.
Weaned	Freed of dependence on something especially (for mammals) mother's milk; having ceased to nurse or suckle
West Barnstable	A village in the town of Barnstable
Whelp	To give birth (canid terminology)
Woof	A warning call given by wolves and coyotes that is akin to a domestic dog bark but with less of the ruff sound of a bark

Index of Names

Index

Note: names in quotations (e.g., "Bart") refer to coyotes studied during this project

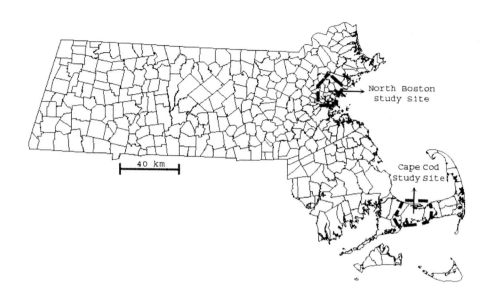

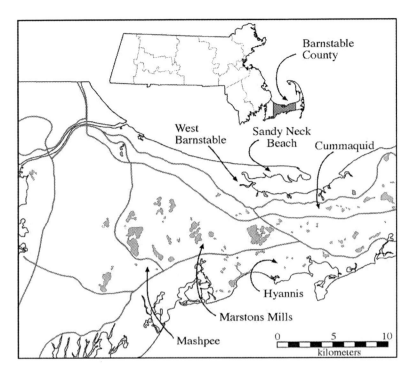

About The Book

This book is about the experiences and findings of a biologist studying coyote ecology and behavior in urbanized eastern Massachusetts. Jon Way is acting out a childhood dream to study wild animals. However, instead of going to far off places such as Africa or the remote stretches of the Rocky Mountains, he began his professional career in high school and college by tracking eastern coyotes in his own hometown on Cape Cod. We hear so much about this unique animal and the conflicts it can create but relatively little is known about the coyotes in the east. The lack of other studies taking place on coyotes in urbanized areas in eastern North America provided Way with the perfect graduate project, and an unending source of information and entertainment.

The coyote is a remarkable animal, being one of the only carnivores to actually increase its range and distribution in the past one hundred years. Coyotes have taken over as top predator in all environments in New England from wilderness parks to city greenbelts. Along its migration to the northeast it has become larger, likely the product of hybridization between western coyotes and eastern wolves, and with that, we see more speculation and theories about what the animal is, how it got here, and why it is here. This book celebrates having these animals living among us and makes a passionate plea for their protection. After all, with the eradication of most of their competition in New England, mainly wolves, a niche for a relatively large carnivore was left vacant for over one hundred years. Coyotes naturally colonized these areas on their own four feet and deserve the respect that any native carnivore should be granted. With their tremendous range expansion in a relatively short amount of time, coyotes proved that it is unnatural not to have a predator in most ecosystems.

In Suburban Howls, Way takes us with him as he navigates dirt roads and wooded paths, travels through cemeteries, around cranberry bogs, in and out of residential areas, down power lines, and even into the city to see where coyotes travel and rest and how they survive, raise pups, prosper as a family, and ultimately die, many before their time. A fascinating account details the author raising a wild-born litter of coyotes, capturing his first coyote in a box trap, tracking a coyote into downtown Boston, documenting an increase in local coyote numbers following the death of resident territorial coyotes, and seeing first-hand how coyotes mourn when separated from their family. The reader will discover that it is perfectly appropriate to have wildlife in developed areas and that people, not wild animals, are the ones that typically have a hard time adjusting to their new neighbors. With a territorial species like a coyote, any land that does not have other coyotes might as well have a "For Rent" sign out.

This book is written for the layman in a humorous, easy-reading style. It highlights the dedication and emotional involvement of working with this needlessly controversial animal, and will offer simple precautions to enable Homo sapiens to coexist with these wild canines that Native Americans called the Trickster. The data Way has gathered over the past ten years will enlighten and educate you with an insight into the behavior and habits of these remarkable wild dogs.

CPSIA information can be obtained at www.ICGtesting.com
Printed in the USA
LVOW010627031111

253324LV00002B/48/A

9 781598 583670